Deciding.

About your belief.

It's all about deciding what you believe.
Consider this book organic gardening for
your mind—an opportunity to change
whatever you desire in your life by
inviting the wealth of nature into the
very core of your being.

Do you want success? More money?
Better relationships? Good health
and happiness? Peace in practice?

All you have to do . . .

is choose.

It's all about the options you select.

The rest will fall into place.

* Silver RavenWolf *

is perhaps best known as one of the most widely published authors of her time, including bestsellers like Solitary Witch and Teen Witch. Artist, photographer, and Internet entrepreneur, she also heads the Black Forest Clan, a Wiccan organization that consists of 58 covens in 29 states and 3 international groups. Wife of 28 years, mother of 4 grown children, and grandmother, Silver has been interviewed by the New York Times, the Wall Street Journal, US News & World Report, and A&E Biography. Visit her at silverravenwolf.com!

Llewellyn Publications, Woodbury, Minnesota

Silver RavenWolf

Hedge Witch

spells, crafts & rituals for natural magick

First Printing, 2008

Book design and editing by Rebecca Zins
Cover design by Kevin R. Brown
Owl photograph on page 113 by John Wells
Papers on opposite page and xiv, 42, 113, 223, 229, 250, and 266 by Debra Glanz, Reminiscence Papers

Library of Congress Cataloging-in-Publication Data
RavenWolf, Silver, 1956-
    HedgeWitch : spells, crafts & rituals for natural magick / Silver RavenWolf.
        p. cm.
    Includes bibliographical references and index.
    ISBN 978-0-7387-1423-3
    1. Wicca. 2. Self-realization—Miscellanea. 3. Magic. 4. Nature—Miscellanea. I. Title.
    BF1566.R32 2008
    133.4'3—dc22

2008022043

Llewellyn Publications
A Division of Llewellyn Worldwide, Ltd.
2143 Wooddale Drive, Dept. 978-07387-1423-3
Woodbury, MN 55125-2989
www.llewellyn.com

Printed in the United States of America
on recycled paper, 15% post-consumer waste

133.43
RAV

Contents

Introduction

The Magickal Garden of Your Mind

Deep in the forest glen of your mind, where the shadows never quite release the world, sits the ancient establishment of the HedgeWitch Academy. A learning center for young and old alike, this edifice of enchanted scholarship welcomes anyone truly magickal at heart who desires to improve the quality of their being. Here, students harmonize with the world of nature, learn powerful potions for self-improvement, and brew within themselves the enigma of the treasures of earth, water, and sky. For years, the outside world saw only a glimpse of these natural empowerment tools—an awareness that has always undulated in the secret world of Witchcraft. Indeed, the workings of the HedgeWitch through various cultures and thousands of years have become legend…and with these easy lessons, formulas, magickal tips, and the inspiring dedication ceremony provided here, you can be one, too!

Relax, take a deep breath, and smile. Success begins with joy!

Nature:
Your Secret Shifter

Nature acts as a secret shifter, gently filling us with the power to change our circumstances whenever we choose. Interacting with Her allows us to switch mental gears in an instant, helping us to overcome boredom, fear, depression, anger, frustration, sadness, and a host of other negative emotions that sap our personal well-being and block our pathway to success. Accessing Nature can immediately place us in the still point of balance—that moment of pure potential that can open our minds to the attractive power of the universe and bring us all that we desire.

To see what I mean, go outside and put your hands in the dirt. Yep! March out there right now and take the first step toward HedgeWitchery! As you place your hands on the ground, feel your deep, primordial connection with the life force of our planet. Close your eyes…dig in your fingers…and open your heart and mind as you inhale the heady aroma of earth's sweet fragrance. Breathe deeply, and welcome the peace. Accept the balance of Mother Nature with joy! Allow the source of all things to course in, around, and through you.

Shift into the connection! Be *One*…there is no other experience like it.

Shift into the connection!
Plug in!
Turn on!
Be One!
There is no other experience like it.

Now, think of the most beautiful garden you have ever seen. Drink in the memory of the lushness, color, peace, and abundant wealth of that sacred space. We're going to change our lives to be like that gorgeous garden, and we are going to do it in just two short weeks. Granted, we'll have to continue to tend our new lives (maintenance is a must), but, by using the HedgeWitchery techniques I've developed, we're going to make marvelous changes in a limited amount of time. How do I know this? Because I did it—and if I can do it, you absolutely can, too!

Using the material in this book, it took me just two short weeks to totally alter many things in my life and bring me peace, harmony, good fortune, healing, and much more. By continuing the practice of working with the abundance of the earth's energy, over the following weeks and months I noticed positive shifts in my personality and my ability to deal with day-to-day stresses. My relationships with my family improved, and interactions with friends and acquaintances that weren't healthy for me or my family dissolved quickly, leaving a wake of calmness and well-being. I found myself in a more serene state on a more frequent basis, at ease with the world around me much of the time. I was able to sit back and enjoy life rather than running full-tilt into walls I'd built myself over the last several years. I began making major renovations to my property. I built an herb garden, a toad house, and a butterfly haven. I literally tore down buildings to make way for continued improvements—lugging, hauling, and sweating with the best of them—and it felt good! As these projects slowly took shape and came to fruition, my life blossomed as well. I shed those wintery pounds, my complexion improved, and I held a more healthy attitude toward my body and my diet. By harvest time, I'd learned a wealth of information on organic gardening, put it into practice, and celebrated the change of season with bounty from the earth as well as enjoying the mental and spiritual fruits of living "in" Nature rather than viewing Her from a distance.

You see, it's all a matter of choice (yours) and belief (your own) that will provide the opportunities you desire. If you expect the worst, that's precisely what you will receive. If, instead, you seek to raise your mental vibrations and incorporate fun physical activities to match happy, life-affirming goals, then you will reap the rewards of positive living and thinking. *You* are the most powerful catalyst in the alteration of your own life—and we're going to prove it with the loving assistance of Mother Nature. I did it. You can, too!

How to Use This Book

Section 1 discusses the mental aspects of this course and provides the basic building blocks of HedgeWitchery thought. Here you will learn how to formulate your thoughts and words to receive the most benefit from your training.

The core of the HedgeWitchery material lies in Sections 2 and 3: the fourteen-day, hands-on guide for transformation and change that culminates with a dedication ceremony performed by you to spiritually affirm your new choices in life. (The dedication ceremony is in Section 3.) Each day you will interact with a different aspect of earth, water, or sky energy that represents the totality of the Earth Mother and your renewed connection to the spiritual source you choose. You can work through the guide in two weeks' time, or you can spend a week on each aspect, or perhaps extra days on a formula that you particularly like. You are not required to rush through the guide, and it will work best for you if you utilize the material at a pace that is comfortable to you. I purposefully designed the material so that it lends itself well to group work—perhaps your circle of personal friends, your magickal family, or a course given through a magickal shop. In my experience, using the two-week process aids in making fast, major changes in your life. Using the fourteen-week process helps you to hold on to those changes and balance out your life for an entire season or more. You can return to the material at any time to reestablish any connection, strengthen your abilities, or enjoy new, creative aspects in your life. You can even make an annual or biannual practice of working through the various patterns offered here, or as a life situation requires. In 2008, I redid the entire fourteen-day process in April as an annual ritual. You can, too!

Sections 4 and 5 of this book contain helpful hints, recipes, tips, and formulas for living the HedgeWitchery life each and every day. From candle making to crafting your own beauty supplies, household cleansers, and magickal ink, to growing and harvesting herbs, there are plenty of ideas to help you master your own version of HedgeWitchery magick! Taking into consideration the fast pace of your life and perhaps limited resources or time, HedgeWitchery celebrates the minimal and encourages you to enhance your day-to-day experience through interaction with Mother Nature. Just being with Her, recognizing Her power, and allowing Her to enter the core of your inner self will help bring the most dynamic, dramatic changes into your life in a very short period of time. Feel free to use the ideas in Sections 4 and 5 as you work through Sections 2 and 3.

I designed the art and science of HedgeWitchery in concert with my own outdoor projects; however, you do not need to plant a large garden, own a plot of land, or invest an extreme amount of money to reap the benefits of the process. You can easily visit Mother Nature every day by simply stepping outside.

Celebrating Your Personal Environment

Live your own wheel of the year as you feel most comfortable and secure. I have been writing spiritual books for many years, and my work is read all over the world, which means your climate and environment may be very different from mine. Although I built the Hedge-Witchery concept here in south central Pennsylvania, you are not confined to my climate, seasons, plant or herbal choices, or spiritual beliefs. In this material, substitutions are expected and encouraged. For example, if a cleansing recipe calls for lemon balm herb and you haven't grown it yourself or can't easily obtain it, choose something similar that has the same type of properties. Let's say you live in a country where lemons are commonly used in your cleansing formulas—then choose lemons instead. For substitutions in any food recipe (like the magickal vinegars), take care that your substitutions are not poisonous. The best way to do this is to check out the herbs at your nearest grocer or open-air market. Remember, magick is all about the mind and your connection to the source; everything else is secondary. View HedgeWitchery as a framework from which to grow your own glorious garden of life.

Take a moment to visualize the massive gates of the HedgeWitch Academy swinging open for you. Breathe deeply, and step inside. The art of HedgeWitchery is only a page turn away!

It always works!

Nature

your connection to the source

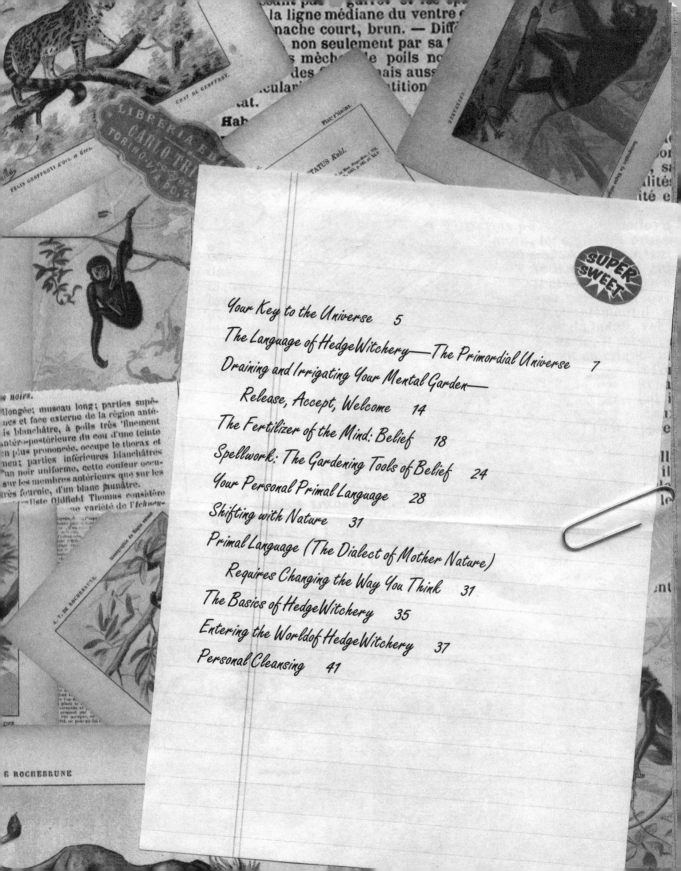

EUREKA

The Frequency of All Good Things

Consider your life as a fertile patch of ground, ready for planting your personal garden of potential. Take a few moments, and think of what you'd like to grow there. Success? Good health? Financial gain? Happiness in relationships? All of what I've just listed and more? Every moment of your life is that fertile piece of ground, capable of producing exactly what you desire. Now let's grow it!

Your Key to the Universe

Whether you are trying to raise a successful business, manifest healing in your life, find a loving partner (or pet), buy a new house, or have a better relationship with a specific person, the starting point of change is always the same: connecting to the source of all things. You need that moment of focused quiet where you acknowledge the pure power of All That Is—and in that connection, anything, I mean *anything*, becomes possible. Getting there is as simple as shifting your weight from one foot to the other. Defining "it"? That truly depends on what you believe. The interesting thing about this engine of the universe is that you don't have to understand what makes it tick to use it, nor is it ego-defined. There's no such thing as a secret pass for the select few. In the practice of HedgeWitchery, the power just "is"—and everyone has access to it. All you have to do is shift your mind from here to the source, and in one breath you can move right into the heart and soul of the power of manifestation. From there, all things are possible. Believing in "it" isn't hard. Getting to "it" isn't difficult. The trick? Remembering to go there in the first place! Once you acknowledge that you *must* connect to your concept of Spirit to succeed, nothing can stop you.

How do you start using the amazing power of All That Is? With a smile.

Many times, we are so busy, frustrated, angry, hurt, depressed, irritated (you name it) we forget that a brief shift *into* the source will allow us the opportunity to fix our unhappiness, solve a problem, or provide just the right creative idea we need at a particular point in time. We let the outside world and our reactive thoughts so thoroughly inundate the situation that getting what we truly desire seems almost impossible. A simple smile functions as a magick key, because although we may be serious, the source isn't. The source is pure joy. Your smile shifts your energy vibrations from impotent to empowered!

Try it! Close your eyes and take a deep breath, exhaling slowly. Give your mind a little time to settle into the source. Now smile! Doesn't that feel great? Oh. You don't feel like smiling? Give it a try, anyway! No, you don't have to be happy to smile. Just do it. You want your smile to be genuine? Okay. Think of something wonderful that has happened to you in the past, something good, something marvelous. Is that a smile I see? Is it? Yes, it is! Now, see how wonderful you can feel when you smile? And when we feel wonderful, we increase our ability to reach our desires, find peace, and maintain happiness.

Hey, not bad for a simple muscle movement.

Time to practice smiling! For the next two weeks, throughout your daily tasks, remember to smile! If you think of a pleasant memory, go ahead and smile. If you see something that amuses you, don't keep a deadpan expression—*smile*! If you hear something funny or are enjoying a good conversation, be sure to pepper the moment and smile, smile, smile! Allowing yourself to smile puts you in a much better emotional place. Too many smiles will never hurt you—they'll only make your life better! To remind yourself to practice smiling, why not carry a special key in your pocket, on your key ring, attached to your purse, or dangle a key charm on your iPod or cell. Spend some time choosing your special key, or just begin collecting keys as a constant reminder that to accomplish anything, we must unlock the door to our connection with the source.

As a HedgeWitch, you're going to learn to smile a heck of a lot! Now that we have our very own magick key (the smile that connects us to the source), we need to learn how to communicate with the source so that we can use this unlimited power to the best of our advantage.

The Language of HedgeWitchery— The Primordial Universe

Have you ever visited a foreign country where you didn't understand the language? Everything seems so strange, doesn't it? Billboards in unintelligible, bright symbols. Whispers, screeches, and varied notes of sound emanating from the lips of strangely dressed people. Books and newspapers that look more like decorative art than a vehicle of direct communication. You seem to float in the world—but, at the same time, you can't quite seem to interact in it. Perhaps you can understand some of what is being said by observing gestures, facial expressions, and mannerisms, but the waiter could be telling you the special today is dog poop with a smile on his face, and how would you know? (Hey, it happened to me.)

Before we dive deeply into HedgeWitchery, we have to acknowledge a vital and important secret about the magickal universe—its language base isn't English, Chinese, Russian, French, German, Spanish, Italian, Cherokee, or Swahili, or any of the others as we understand them. Throw grammar and sentence structure out the window. The universe does not acknowledge big words, flowery prose, or disclaimers. The source operates primordially: noun/verb. It does *not* understand the words no, don't, maybe, possibly, might, not, etc. And the universe is not about creating lack, it is all about attracting abundance...of anything.

For example, let's say you visit your mother every Thursday night, and she always makes chicken. You've politely mentioned that you love her beef stroganoff, and maybe next time she might make that? Chicken, however, always takes the day. You've even tried bringing dinner or suggesting *you'll* make it this time, but somehow or other, Mother *always makes chicken.* Indeed, you've become really focused on how you don't want chicken—and that's the problem. The universe processes only *chicken.* The universe doesn't understand the contraction *don't.* It just hears *I blah-blah-blah want chicken*, which translates to *I want chicken*. Except you don't, do you?

The easiest way to begin using primal language is to say *I want* _____ (and fill in your desire). Examples: I want a new sofa. I want a new mattress. I want a job that pays more. I want to get well. (And no, you are not being selfish in saying *I want*. As children we are told you can't have everything you want and that it is rude to verbalize what you desire by using the word *want*. Wrong. When you are happy, everyone around you is happy. When you get what you want, you can provide others with what they want. Wanting leads to giving. Giving leads to happiness. Happiness leads to harmony...you get the picture.)

Saying what you want aloud speeds up the process. So! Go someplace right now where you will be alone and no one can hear you, and shout out loud *what you want*! Say it three times and really mean it. If you believe you will receive what you desire, you'll get exactly what you stated. A note of caution here: do not *ask for* something. The words *ask for* imply that you need permission from someone or from something somewhere, which becomes a muddy psychological mess. Simply state *I want*, and leave it at that.

Timing

What if what you want doesn't come right away? As soon as you utter what you desire, the universe goes about filling your order. To help the universe do this, you need to:

- Believe (see page 18 for more information)

- Don't confuse the issue by adding more to it or changing your mind (see the haggling appendix for an example of this)

- Remove any blocks by releasing old, negative thoughts or habits (review pages 14–18)

- Accept and welcome your desire (read about this starting on page 14)

If you don't believe, if you don't release, if you don't welcome change—your order to the universe goes in the Cancel bin. Further on in this section we'll talk about belief, release, and acceptance, and how to handle them to make your desires occur faster. Right now, there is only one other block (perhaps) to your success that I'd like to talk about, and that is other people.

Circle of Influence

No HedgeWitch is an island. We have friends, those we love, perhaps children, significant others, parents, partners, co-workers—people that we allow to exert influence over our lives because we like them, because we love them, or because our environments somehow overlap. All of these people are in some way affected by our behavior, and our behavior is somehow affected by them. This influence doesn't automatically disappear just because we want to do magick. Life and magick (for good or ill) are a bit more complicated than that.

In magick, we've always been taught *to know* (belief), *to will* (I want), *to dare* (open the way and accept change), and *to be silent*, because if every Jane, Lisa, and Abby in the world heard about what you want, they might try to block your desires—just by being jealous, they can mess things up for you, especially if your belief is shaky. Yet there is always an exception to any rule; on occasion, you will have to verbally agree with someone in order for the change to happen. By agreeing on any subject, then the stage is set for action. If you disagree, even subconsciously, failure is a possibility.

Let's try an example.

You're reading this book, working through the exercises, and you're feeling really good about the whole thing. You live with someone (significant other, spouse, your child, mother, whatever), you are merrily doing the primal language thing, and you decide you want a new sofa. For brevity's sake, let's say the other party involved here is your husband.

Every day, you say: "I want a new sofa in my living room." Day after day, you repeat these words. You've followed all the other suggestions on manifestation in this book, and so you think you're good to go. Except days progress into weeks, and somewhere along the line you become convinced that primal language doesn't really work, or at least isn't working in this case, because you can't seem to get your mitts on a new sofa. You are stuck with the same old, threadbare, smelly couch—which, by the way, you refuse to sit on.

This actually happened to me until it dawned on me that I wasn't receiving my new sofa because *my husband hadn't let the old one go*! Heck, I'd have burned that blasted couch in a heartbeat, and I'd released the image of it in my mind just fine. But he hadn't: not physically and not in his mind. And, yes, we'd discussed how we needed a new one, but evidently we weren't *really* in agreement. You see, my husband, blessed man, loves that sofa. He takes Sunday naps on it. Cuddles into the cushions. Sips his coffee on it. Wrestles with the dogs, watches the Friday night fights…my husband loves that sofa and hates change to his comfort. (Taurus moon, need I say more?)

Which, of course, resulted in keeping the old sofa just where it was. This was a totally *duh* moment for me. No wonder the universe couldn't fulfill my desire for a new sofa. Only one couch could fit in that living room at a time, and it still sat there—physically and, more importantly, mentally—through my husband's adoration of it. He simply wasn't emotionally ready to part with it.

Okay, I thought, *new line of attack.* Haul out all the good wifely reasons why we need a new sofa, concentrating on, of course, his comfort. Bingo. He mentally released the old sofa, and a brand-new one finally trundled in the door.

My point here is this: those that you love influence you, therefore they will influence your desires if you allow them to. And you usually do…because you love them! (To read more about agreements with others, check out my *MindLight* book, which discusses various facets of human interaction and thought [especially partnerships], and how, simply through conversation, you manifest the circumstances of your own life without even realizing it.)

Dollars and Cents Aren't Always Required

Your response to my sofa story may have been, why didn't you just go out and buy one? Except the kind of sofa I wanted was a large purchase, and that costs money, doesn't it? In a marriage, you usually agree on large purchases, or maybe we just didn't have the money for a new sofa whenever we pleased. At the time, a new sofa was a luxury item, not a necessity (well, I thought it was necessary, but he didn't). The very, very cool thing about using primal language is that you don't worry about the money. Ever. You don't ever think about how much anything costs. Isn't that cool? You just say what you want, and visualize the thing. As long as you believe, one of four things happens…

- You either get what you want for free, or

- You get what you want at a price you can afford, or

- You get the money to get what you want, or

- You get something better than what you originally wanted.

Be Careful How You Wish for Something

Be careful what you simply state and what words precede and follow your statement (which is why I advise setting aside a few moments to place your orders with the universe). For example, my son kept saying "I want a new car." He meant he wanted it when he was ready for it, but he didn't express it that way. Instead, he would say "I want a new car" and then surround that statement with complaints about the car he had. I kept trying to convince him that your life is how you talk it; watch what you say and when you say it.

But I'm a parent, so what do I know, right? He just kept complaining about the car he had and how he really wanted a new one. Indeed, he said some mighty nasty things about his current vehicle—over and over again. I cringed at the frequent torrents of how much he didn't like his car.

Because I knew, you know? I knew *exactly* what was going to happen.

His car didn't disappoint me. Everything seized. It turned itself into junk in less than three minutes: ball joints went bad, transmission went out, engine fried and left him stranded.

Now the way was open for the new car—except he had no money, no trade-in, *nada*. No way to work. No way home. (Uh-huh—*that'll* teach ya not to complain.) Releasing anything with negativity leaves you sitting on an abandoned, winding road. Be careful what you're ordering up to the universe and how you do it. Had I gotten into a big argument with my husband over the sofa, or simply took the old one away and bought a new one, his feelings would have been hurt, and I would have done him a great disservice. Now *that* would have been selfish.

Primal language works for all types of energy manifestation, not just receiving material items. You may wish to have more friends, a happy marriage, good health, great job ... and it all begins with *I want*. Just remember to preface your desire from a positive mindset.

To receive the most benefit out of HedgeWitchery—working with the abundance of the universe—we must choose to alter the way we think and the way we communicate. Thoughts of worry or fear have no place in this type of universe, because if you give these negative thoughts energy, then that is what the universe will bring to you. To neutralize subversive, fear-filled thoughts when they pop up, try these easy transition techniques:

1. Smile.

2. Repeat "Always a blessing" in your mind until you feel the energy shift within yourself.

3. Begin thanking the universe for things you do have. Rattle off anything great you can think of, and don't stop until you feel an energy shift to a lighter mood.

4. End every *I want* statement with the words "It *always* works." Say this several times.

5. Go over what you really *do* believe (see page 21). Many times negative, fear-filled thoughts are a result of old belief patterns. Once we recognize them for what they are, then we can easily release them.

Formulate your thoughts and communications, concentrating on what you do want; your desires will be easily fulfilled! We must live like we believe. If we believe that the universe is an abundant place where all manner of success is possible, then that is precisely what we shall receive. Your choice of belief dictates your future. Rather than living like an outsider in our universe, HedgeWitchery encourages you to fully participate in the process of abundance by acknowledging your own fertile ground and adding the rich compost of basic universal communication. You simply have to learn the language—the fertilizer of how to word your wishes—and your desires will grow! Primal language is a succinct formulation of spoken words describing a single desire that translates into an energy stream. It is this energy stream that the universe understands, not the words themselves.

Primal Language Exercise

Unchecked mind chatter or verbal communication complicates your life by sending mixed signals to the universe. Superfluous words can actually block your desires. Negative words will bring you things you truly didn't want. To get what you want, try the minimalist approach—start thinking only in nouns.

Typically, when we want something, we begin listing and constantly repeating what we *don't* want, thinking the universe understands this elimination process to make way for what we desire. Rather than clearing a nice mental garden path, we are instead throwing a variety of weeds in the way that will bring us a jungle of junk rather than the one thing we truly desire.

In the practice of HedgeWitchery, we use the fewest words possible in communicating our desires to the universe through meditation, ritual, spellwork, and even everyday thoughts. The more precise the verbiage, the greater the possibility of success!

Let's say I want a new lawn mower—something simple that works only on me-power (no gas or electric). The machine needs to fit between the paths of my raised-bed garden, be light enough for me to handle easily, and have blades that stay sharp for longer than one season. Since I'm not sure exactly what I want (the problem that muddles most people), I visit several garden stores to determine what might work best for me. Once I choose the mower (a 16-inch Scotts Elite), I ask for a brochure. At home, I sit down at the dining room table with a piece of paper and the brochure side by side. On my paper, I begin describing this mower in very simple terms. To pinpoint exactly what I want, I'm going to begin with only nouns. As I add each descriptive word, I will also include a visualization of the noun or noun sequence in my mind, so I might close my eyes to better focus. If I do this, however, I need to project the nouns outside of myself *and* see myself interacting with them. For example: with my new mower, I visualize myself smiling and merrily pushing the machine back and forth across my property on a beautiful, sunny day over a rich carpet of green grass. To this, I add the aroma of the cut grass and the sound the mower makes as it *shlip-shlip-shlips* across the green grass (vibrating your thoughts by remembering sounds actually helps you manifest your desires faster—especially if you practice listening and then re-creating these sounds often in your mind). I breathe deeply, thinking how this mower will provide a very good exercise opportunity for me and what a nice tan I'll have as a result of working outside.

Let's try it. We begin with:

Lawn mower

New lawn mower (The universe understands "condition"—new, old, antique—because the universe itself works in cycles.)

New push reel lawn mower (The correct name of this type of lawn mower.)

New Scotts Elite 16-inch push reel lawn mower (Notice I added the brand and the size.)

New, green Scotts Elite 16-inch push reel lawn mower (Introducing color…)

New, green Scotts Elite 16-inch push reel lawn mower or better (Perhaps the universe has something better that can come to me faster, or maybe the store is out of green and they only have red—fine with me!)

Now, I walk outside and look at the beautiful stars (connecting to Spirit by surrounding myself with nature) and slap a big smile on my face. At this moment, I am doing what a HedgeWitch does best: I shift my mind totally into my concept of Spirit through the enjoyment of nature. Being outdoors helps me better connect. I take a deep breath, settle into the moment of the beauty of deep night, and then I say clearly to the universe, "I want a new, green Scotts Elite 16-inch push reel lawn mower or better. It always works. Always a blessing!" I close my eyes one more time, and I visualize all those things I mentioned earlier (sight, smell, sound, etc.), and I smile again. Done!

Although the universe recognizes honor (we'll get to that), it doesn't understand verbal manners, such as "May I please have _____?" This is a question, not a desire. Remembering to say "I want" acknowledges that you really do desire what you are asking for. Don't worry, Spirit won't be insulted.

Time for you to try the primal language formula. Choose something you want to manifest in your life. Begin with the basic noun and then build, being careful to add only enough words to give you a precise description of what you want. Stay away from words like hope, might, maybe, possibly, don't, never, not, perhaps, etc., because they only confuse the translation of your desire. When you have your description finished, go outside and tell the universe what you want (no extra words), and save your description to work on through the next step. Don't forget to smile!

I already know (believe) that the universe will bring me my new mower. My job is to keep the way clear for the mower to come to me *and* accept and welcome the fact that I deserve this mower. Clearing, accepting, and welcoming are actually the hardest parts!

Draining and Irrigating Your Mental Garden— Release, Accept, Welcome

We've talked about how to enrich the soil of our minds by learning the right fertilizer (primal language) to use. The next step, as in any good garden, is to provide an adequate drainage and irrigation system that allows your desires to manifest. If there is no release, there can be no growth! Your desires will drown in old habits, bad feelings, or negative memories. To keep the garden of your mind healthy and productive, we need to find avenues of release *and* we have to allow this discharge to take place! Think of your life as a great big house filled with all sorts of clutter. One day a magickal elf knocks on your door and says, "I heard you wanted a new lawn mower. Too cool! You deserve it, you do! I have it right here. But, since you already have something in the space where you wanted to put it—well, I won't be able to give it to you." See ya, lawn mower!

To get what you do want, you must let go of what you don't want.

Although the premise of release works universally, I've noticed its greatest impact (where we can see the necessity of letting go most clearly) in the arena of personal relationships, particularly when folks say, "I just can't seem to find the right person. Where is the man (or woman) of my dreams?" Many times, these people are holding on to old, dead relationships or memories of hurtful moments in human interaction. If they seriously close the door on old patterns and open doors to new ones, sure enough, the right person comes along! Throw away those "nesting gifts" that remind you of lost love, good love gone bad, or whatever. Change your phone number, block your e-mail, try a new hairstyle, build a spiritual garden, buy some new clothes, apply for a new job, tear down a building on your property, clean out the basement *and* the attic, wear a different scent, move your furniture around so it doesn't remind you of "them." Heck, burn the darned bed and all the sheets if necessary! Even better—move! (That'll keep ya busy and force you to release a lot of junk.) Or, less drastic, find a new hobby: try skydiving, horseback riding, swimming, golf, or bowling; shop at stores you never tried before; take a class at a local college; or get interested in a different cuisine. Work on affirmations, spells, and rituals that are life-affirming and geared toward positive change. Do a thorough house cleansing and a personal ritual cleansing. Pick a new activity where you will meet exciting and vibrant people, and live! *Live! Live! Live!* Let go of the past, because the past isn't really what you thought it was in the first place. (*Star Wars* and the *Scream* trilogy have at least taught us that much!) Even perennial plants don't last forever; they have their proper cycle, too! Just ask my daughter. After a devastating breakup, she did many of the above-listed activities and changes, and in one month—you guessed it—she found the love of her life. She's now married to the man of her dreams, a truly lovely individual that any mother-in-law would be proud of. In essence, my daughter concentrated on what she *did* want in her life (new experiences, people, places, and things), and she was so busy, she let go of what she didn't want—and without the severe, elongated emotional pain one so often experiences after a bad breakup.

Let's go back to my lawn mower example. I need to remove both physical and emotional clutter, clearing the way to receive the machine that I desire. In my shed, I have an old gas-powered lawn mower that is more finicky than a Capricorn maintaining a prize rosebush. This machine works only for my father, who doesn't like the beast because of the amount of time it takes him to get it started and keep it running. Even with the best maintenance (my father is that Capricorn), this mower was the most cantankerous hunk of metal, gears, and gas ever to be built on the face of this planet. It refused to work for anyone else in the household (no kidding—which became a major pain when my father fell seriously ill). So, I wheel this monstrosity out to the curb and slap a sign on it: FREE—RUNS BUT STUBBORN—GOOD FOR PARTS. And away it goes. I've done this before, by the way. Ever tried it? Instead of trashing something, I put it on the curb with some sort of fun sign. I've gotten rid of more junk this way—free, without hurting the environment one little bit, and making someone delightfully happy in the process!

Anyway…I've honestly cleared physical space in the shed (meaning I didn't trick anyone into removing the old mower—bad karma—yet I gave someone who might want it the opportunity to take it; this is good Pagan recycling). Then, I review my mental/emotional standpoint on receiving my new lawn mower. Obviously, I need it (or I'll be fined by the borough for having unruly vegetation—you think I jest!). Second, I deserve having a new lawn mower as much as the next guy or gal; no issue there. Thankfully, neither politics nor religion has entered into the ownership of lawn equipment. Since my feelings tell me whether I'm on track with the receiving end (I feel good about getting a new lawn mower), I'm all set when that imaginary magickal elf (the process of quantum physics in action) comes knocking at my door with my brand-new lawn mower. I *don't* think about *how* I'm going to pay for the machine. I've kept money totally out of my visualization process on purpose, because money, for a lot of people, can have its own emotional baggage, which adds unnecessary complications. We want a cut-and-dry scenario here. Instead, I simply concentrate on the item. The universe will work out how I'm going to get what I want and won't bother me with the finances. (Isn't it a relief to know that there's actually a powerful force on this planet that *doesn't* want your money?)

To be more specific: as I remove the old machine from the shed and push it along its last journey across my property, I concentrate on visualizing my new lawn mower and how wonderful it will feel. I take a deep breath and allow myself to connect with the source (that which runs the universe), and I remember to smile. I imagine I'm pushing not the old lawn mower out to the trash but the new one to make the yard look beautiful. I look at the green grass and enjoy the spicy aroma from my herb garden as I walk past, physically pushing "the stubborn one" out of my life. I simply let myself shift into Mother Nature as I trundle along, visualizing myself delightfully tan, my arms and legs getting stronger, and my over-fifty paunch melting away under the gloriously blue summer sky. I smile broadly at that one. Then I say, "I am grateful for my new, green Scotts Elite 16-inch push reel lawn mower or better; it always works; always a blessing," and I smile again. (Because when you are grateful about something, honestly grateful, you are in a happy mind place.) When I did this, a beautiful butterfly flitted over the old lawn mower—a signal in my mind that my desire was well on its way (I personally use animals, plants, birds, insects, and my physical garden as interpreters of what the universe is trying to tell me about my life). In essence, by the time I pushed the old lawn mower to the curb, I'd mentally and physically released the cranky machine and acknowledged the receipt of my new one. Instead of kicking that nasty, grumpy lawn mower and declaring its foul nature, I said, "I'm grateful for your service," and I meant it. After all, I could have been living without any mower at all, cutting the grass with a pair of kitchen shears. In this way, I honored what it did manage to accomplish and let it go at that (this actually works with nasty people, especially crappy employers or friends of betrayal, too). Then I walked back to the empty spot in the shed, imagined my new mower sitting there, and said, "Welcome, new lawn mower!" (Another big, happy smile!)

Okay, so the lawn mower isn't like the love of your life, and the procedure to obtain it was pretty simple. It's not like I had to legally divorce the old lawn mower, but you get the idea (although you might like to set your husband, wife, or partner on the street corner with a sign that says FREE, STUBBORN, USE FOR PARTS, this isn't legal and is certainly not moral).

The point here: I released (drained) and honored (irrigated positive energy) the old and welcomed the new, shifting into the joy of Mother Nature as I did it. My magickal ritual wasn't performed in the formal way that you've read about before. Here, my ritual was the process of doing—wheeling that old machine out through my yard (which is actually sacred space) and actively meditating (visualizing) what I desired—all done in the arms of Mother Nature.

Whenever I thought about how soon I might get the new mower, I switched mental gears, smiled at the universe, and said, "Thank you for my new lawn mower," then changed my thoughts to something else, because the biggest destroyer of getting what we want is actually our own minds and our myriad secondary thoughts on any situation. In essence, you only need to make your request once; however, your request can be altered by subsequent thoughts. If this mower is what I truly want, and I don't want to change my mind, then I need to keep my thoughts clear of any doubt or worry. In traditional Witchcraft and other magickal disciplines, you'll often see three-, seven-, or nine-day spells. As a rule, the bigger the problem or request, the longer the duration of the working. This type of timing is to assure the mind (yours) that you are actually doing something constructive, and the repetition helps to solidify confidence in yourself and cement your own belief. Likewise, offerings to the gods, another traditional practice, are simply the act of releasing, accepting, and welcoming. You are physically giving something away in order to make room to receive what you want. Honoring the gods by saying thank you is also a release-and-closure function. When you thank someone, you are basically ending the subject with an act of honor. The words *thank you* indicate an automatic closure and affirmation that your desire has come to pass.

Did I get my mower? Yep! Took two weeks. No expense. I named my new lawn mower Elf, put a garden talisman on it, got a great tan, and walked off ten pounds. Sweet!

Your turn: Review your request from the primal language exercise. What do you need to release to receive your desire? What physical steps or actions can you incorporate in your life to clear the way for your success? Remember to honor what has to leave—being grateful for the good is a powerful act of closure! Remove any doubts in your life about what you do and do not deserve. Be sure to clearly accept and welcome, through your words and actions, the changes you are working for. And don't forget—smile, smile, smile!

The Fertilizer of the Mind: Belief

I'm sure you've read many spiritual articles over the past several years that have in one way or another discussed the universal connection of all beings and how we are all an integrated part of the whole. Writers teach about how to access what you most desire by using techniques and ideas that have worked for them. From motivational speakers to magickal practitioners, you'll find a plethora of information just waiting to be downloaded into your eager brain.

Sometimes these tips serve the reader well, and sometimes, depending upon the reader's belief structure, they don't work at all.

Belief, truly, is the key.

Our beliefs are structured on what we think to be true. Some of us delve into the scientific to give us a firm base of belief, others go the more mystical, spiritual route, and then there are those who don't believe anything unless it works first (which is rather a conundrum). Finally, everyone's beliefs are somehow shaped by the boogie-bird in the closet, commonly known as childhood misconceptions, which we either dreamed up ourselves or were exposed to by parents, caregivers, siblings, extended family members, teachers, spiritual advisors, neighbors, organization leaders, etc., as they peddled through their own lives doing (to be fair) the best they could. Which leaves us a bit on shaky ground when it comes to creating our own reality, which is nothing more than manipulating the world through quantum means. What I'm trying to say is: if you believe it is possible consciously *and* subconsciously, then it is. Period.

Each individual functions within the parameters of two types of belief: that which you consciously say to be true, and that which your subconscious has already accepted to be true. Which means you have two very different animal crackers in your head when it comes to what you believe in, and why you can say you believe in something and receive just the opposite. Both conscious *and* subconscious beliefs have to be in alignment in order for any desire to manifest.

Your conscious belief can be represented by the above-ground part of a plant, and your subconscious belief can equate to the root system; as you know, if your root system is lousy, you can baby the top of the plant all you want and still it will either die or grow poorly. Conversely, the root system can be great—but if pests or blight attack the above-ground portion of the plant, you can only go so long until the plant weakens beyond saving and dies. Just as the root system and the above-ground portion of a plant must be in alignment to create a beautiful, healthy plant, so your conscious and subconscious beliefs must also match to make a beautiful, healthy you.

Which brings us to why humans have created a compendium of religions. The various designs have occurred in an effort to create a system that appeals both to the conscious and subconscious minds of a particular culture. Did you ever wonder why you can't force someone to believe like you do (well, people try), and why the belief in angels may work for some but not for others, and why the Holy Spirit performs like gangbusters for your sister but not for your father? Ogoun helps your best friend dance on the head of a pin, pulling in super sales, and your brother-in-law may swear by snake charming to get those eBay deals, and then there's your uncle, who claims nothing works like a nice dead relative to provide assistance from the other side when the chips are down. Many cultures, many beliefs…who is right?

The one you believe in, of course.

Belief, quite frankly, isn't as easy as it sounds. Let's say everyone around you fervently believes that a Great Rabbit runs the universe. You have always been told, and therefore it must be true, that he sits up there, munches on carrots, wants you to be a good boy or girl, has an instruction manual for you to follow, and demands sole fealty. Everyone in town believes in the Great Rabbit (or so they say). They pray to the Great Rabbit and have holidays in his honor. You, however, sane person that you are, have always been a little iffy on that puffy-tailed furball-in-the-sky scenario. Perhaps you've outwardly questioned the validity, and you have certainly inwardly gone over it a million times—nothing with teeth that long can be good. You are told the Great Rabbit is also a wrathful rabbit because, if he isn't pleased, he can cause hurricanes, drought, fires—you know, the normal Mother Nature stuff, which is now bad stuff and not normal because you, you infidel, did not believe deep down inside. So much for the concept of universal love in deity form. Indeed, the worst type of believer is the secret nonbeliever. Do you see where I'm going with this? I'm not poking fun at any specific belief—what I'm saying is if you *make believe* you believe, it ain't gonna work for ya, no matter how hard you try. What is worse, we can *say* we believe, but lo and behold, our subconscious (for whatever reason) doesn't.

Then again, we can tell everyone what they believe in isn't quite right and that they should change their beliefs, or at least tweak them so that we can all really believe now, because if everyone thinks the way we do, then we have created a believable comfort zone.

Therefore, what we all believe must be true—because we all believe it.

Except we know we told everyone what to believe without empirical evidence. So, therefore, in our subconscious, we know what they believe in is not true, and therefore, we don't really believe it either.

And if you don't believe, you can't make *nothin'* happen.

Let's, for the moment, move this topic away from religion and our All-Powerful Bunny. The same premise works for other things in your life as well: health, income, politics, perceived status, love, friends, working environment (flap hand, yada yada)—religion, really, is just one facet of the totality of your beliefs. Just one. So, even if you work diligently on your spirituality and let the rest go (or ignore them or deny their importance), then all you've done is focus the conscious mind in one direction while your subconscious mind is having a banquet—at your expense.

You'll not find a truer bait-and-switch scam than what occurs in your own brain each and every day. Money problems? Don't check what's in your wallet—check what's in your brain.

How do you know that your subconscious beliefs aren't in alignment with your conscious mind? That's easy. What part of your life has just gone down the toilet? Or, what in your life could be better? Or, maybe things have been holding steady, but you are bored, bored, bored. Or, where have you been placing your primary focus of thought and activity because you had to? Let's take a look at what beliefs might be attached to that issue. We'll keep it simple, one issue at a time. Pretty soon, you'll see how troubles that seem separate can actually be the result of a single negative thought.

What's Growing in Your Belief Garden?

In a physical garden, you need to test the soil to ensure the chemical balance is right for what you wish to produce. Indeed, you can buy all manner of kits and products to determine the integrity of what you've got in that physical garden of yours. Your mental garden also requires specific elements for harmonious balance; the problem is you can't buy them (although we often try)—you gotta make this mix yourself. Just as in a real garden, where you have to dig nice and deep to see what kind of soil you've got down there, so, too, will you have to be willing to test your mental soil, which consists of the totality of your beliefs. Only when you understand the fullness (or lack thereof) of your own beliefs can you plant anything and expect it to grow. Only by testing the contents of what's hidden in your brain can you determine what fertilizer you'll need for a bumper crop of a full and harmonious lifestyle.

Before we begin, I'm going to tell you straight up: this isn't easy. We have so many thoughts zooming around in our heads at any given time it can be hard to follow a single thread, especially if your subconscious mind wishes to pull that fast bait-and-switch. I think this thought about my past—whoops! I'm having tuna tonight. Wait. Where did that come from? Your subconscious mind will volley the strange and bizarre to center court just to keep you off-guard and away from ferreting out the boogie-bird that resides in the recesses of your deepest troubles. Then, too, it might be that rabbit...therefore, a concerted effort on your part is required if you truly want to accomplish the good riddance of your woes and create better days ahead.

Let's take a few general examples to help you on your way. First, meet Marissa: age twenty-seven; career okay; health general; attractive (she's got great eyes and knockout legs)—and she has a history of broken romances that would prove enough fodder for at least two full-time romance writers (without the happy endings). She goes to the gym and buys expensive makeup. Yet the love fairy has completely forgotten Marissa exists. For the purposes of this example, the main question we are always going to ask is: what did your parents say to you about love, relationships, and marriage when you were growing up? Or what did your primary caregiver say to you about these things, and what comments *did they always make* when the subject arose? Here is Marissa's reply:

"My father died when I was ten. My mother constantly talked about how he abandoned us. She would say, 'Good men never live long,' or 'There aren't any good men around like your dad.' Even her offhand comments were negative when discussing any male (family or friends) in almost any situation, from politics to spirituality, let alone a serious relationship. To her, the day my dad passed away, all good men abandoned the planet and ascended into heaven—the biblical rapture, only for males. I've said repeatedly to myself that her beliefs are her own, but now, thinking about it, I realize that I absorbed those very same beliefs subconsciously and have been sabotaging my own relationships. You know, this is my life, not hers! My mother was not a bad parent—she treated me extremely well and loved me very much—but I realize now that I've been living her fears."

Let's move on to Harvey, fifty years old, general health with a few nasty bouts of this or that over the years, particularly during a financial crisis, a product of the Great Depression babies. "I grew up listening to how my grandfather and grandmother lost everything except their home during the Depression; about how my father was ignored and treated badly by his siblings; about how rotten the government is and how they (politicians) hurt and cheat people. How our family name screams that we'll always be lower middle class—that there was no bright and glorious future for people like us. You know, come to think of it, I never heard anything nice—nothing about love, or caring, or sticking up for each other. Just the same old crap. In fact, my father is eighty-nine, and I'm *still* listening to the same garbage. He doesn't tell a single story (and he has a ton) that doesn't end on a depressive note. A Yank with a broken pickup, a dead dog, and a deceased wife. You know, I was doing really well for a while, and then I let my father move in with us. I just realized that the moment that happened, his beliefs brought our whole family down and kept us trapped for twenty-five years because we subconsciously believed his repeated negative comments about life and personal finances. As a parent, we treated him with respect and didn't argue. Don't get me wrong, the man had golden credit and still does to this day, yet I allowed his acid thoughts to almost completely destroy my career. I expected what he predicted about how I would be treated, and that's exactly what I got. They aren't my beliefs anymore!"

Julia, age thirty, has repeated health problems. Married, one child. Both she and her husband are overweight. Both have a terrific sense of humor. "My grandmother raised me. She was all about God smiting the sinner, especially when it came to health problems of congregational members—always said God made you sick to teach you a lesson, even for the most minor infraction. We used to make jokes about God doing overtime in our parish, and how with Him around, who needed the devil to blame your troubles on? Growing up, I truly thought she was just being loony. She was skinny as a rail and always this side of sickly, trying every wacky cure by a compendium of snake oil salesmen; but, you know, now I'm wondering how much of her insecurity, terror, and fear I absorbed as a kid, because she repeatedly told me that I was lazy, and that God made lazy people fat as they grew older as a punishment for not doing a hard day's work. I'm a writer by trade, working at a desk for a newspaper, and even though I work long hours, my job isn't physically exhausting. Like, I'm not out in the fields or anything, and I'm not up at dawn canning, baking bread, or washing laundry by hand. I suddenly realized I've been living her terror and fear. Not anymore!"

In these three examples, we followed the issue to the source, and it wasn't easy for Marissa, Harvey, or Julia to go back there. They had to sit and think about the question for a while, and in one case (Harvey) it took him several days to work through all the negative programming he heard as a child. Every time he thought of another comment his father used to make (and evidently still does), his mind would flip to something else—from what time he needed to pick up his son to trouble with a new insurance company dropping the insurance on his house. The light finally dawned on Harvey when he drove his father to a doctor's appointment and once again sat through the same string of worldly complaints. Finally, light bulb: Harvey deftly switched the subject and from then on endeavored to keep changing the subject every time his father began to work through the same verbal scenario and depressive soap-opera yarns. Harvey also discovered that some of his father's newer negative ideas were actually coming from a klatch of seniors that had lunch at the same establishment as Harvey's father (all Depression-era babies). Then Harvey started looking at the unsolicited mail his father was receiving, shocked to discover that many of the advertisements were targeting Depression-era mentality seniors, focusing on their fear to solicit money and sell products. Harvey made the comment, "What you create in your mind, you bring into your life. Sadly, my father is living proof."

Granted, going back in time and dragging original fears out into the light of day isn't going to solve all your problems. However, now that you know where the negative programming may have come from, you can adjust how you think and in what you choose to believe, as well as reprogram what you are saying to (and around) your own kids (should you have any). With your conscious and subconscious minds now in agreement, there is nothing you can't accomplish. Take this exercise further and pay close attention to what you are listening to on the news, what you are reading, even the conversations you hear at work. Weed out what you don't believe and let the boogie-birds stay where they belong. With a fresh look at the universe, all you have to do is…

Believe!

Spellwork: The Gardening Tools of Belief

In a recent *A&E Biography* interview, I was asked what constitutes a "spell." I wasn't surprised at the question, because those who have never cast a spell find the process alluring but (thanks to the negative programming of some religious sects) frightening. Personally, I find spells fascinating, and I've been working them for over twenty years! Spells are nothing more than tools to focus the mind and support your beliefs in a positive way, to bring your desires to fruition through the means of quantum physics (energy manipulation). Spellwork focuses the mind on a specific subject in a specific way, many times using an activity (such as burning a candle) to bring the two parts of your belief (conscious and subconscious) into alignment. Words and tools are used together to poise your mind at its most capable point of manifestation. When you cast a spell, you are throwing out your energy net through words and actions to bring something to you, whether that something is a new car or inner harmony. Choosing your words and your tools carefully and succinctly becomes very important, because it is not the universe you have to convince that you deserve whatever it is you want, it is yourself. Therefore, the tools and words of a spell are mental garden stepping stones that should:

(a) pull in divine energy through positive, uplifting thought and behavior, and

(b) align your conscious and subconscious beliefs.

If the spell does not do both of these things for you, your desire will not manifest.

The Universal Telephone Line

Remember Harvey? And do you recall how he said that his house insurance was cancelled? Here is the creative way in which he handled it:

"I got this darned letter in the mail that said 'your house insurance is cancelled because your windows have peeling paint.' I'd just finished arranging for a new loan on the house to fix the place up, and here I get this letter. I was furious, because the insurer knew about the loan that cleared not thirty days before and that I was planning to use the money to repair the house. Frustrated, I decided to fix this problem … promptly!

"The day before, I'd purchased an old-fashioned phone at the mall, thinking it would add a special touch that the wife would like. I marched to the bedroom and took the phone out of the package, repeating a mantra: 'Always a blessing.' I placed the phone on our bedroom dresser. I didn't hook the phone up to the house line. In fact, I didn't hook it up at all. In my mind, if a cell phone could call my kid, my magick phone could call the universe! What's the difference?

"On a notecard, I wrote: 'I want this house insurance mess fixed immediately, to my benefit.' I stuck the card under the phone, picked up the receiver, and dialed 911. I said, 'Hello, Universe? Harvey speaking. I want this house insurance mess fixed immediately, to my benefit. Thank you for helping me,' and I hung up. In less than one hour, I had the phone number of a new agent. In less than twenty-four hours, I'd made arrangements with that new agent to come view the house. In forty-eight hours, I had a new policy that was cheaper than the old one, and it covered the exact same thing. And seventy-two hours after that phone call, the old agent phoned, wanting to fix things, where before when I originally called them they had all but ignored me.

"I didn't stop there. My son has a new job as a salesman, and he was lamenting he needed at least two sales his first week to show his employer he would be good at the job. So, I went to the phone in my bedroom, dialed 411, and said, 'Hello. This is Harvey. I want my son to land at least two sales today. Thank you,' and hung up. Sure enough, my son called me that night. He made his two sales, and by the time the week was out, he'd made a total of four. You can bet I'm going to keep using my magick phone!"

Harvey's example shows us that a simple spell can work miracles. Now, let's check Harvey's beliefs so we are all on the same page. Harvey believes that something runs the universe that is good, caring, and all-loving. He isn't sure what that something is, but when he is addressing the universe, he believes that he is somehow aligning himself with divinity. Secondly, Harvey has always believed that a solution to every problem exists; you just have to find it sometimes. Therefore, solving this problem was well within both his conscious and subconscious minds, and calling on a solution was not out of bounds in either type of thought.

To help his mind believe that he could contact the source of all things, he used a vehicle familiar to all of us: the telephone. Like Harvey said, if he could call his son on a cell, he could call the source on his magick phone. The act of dialing familiar numbers—911, in most areas of the United States, is the three-digit Emergency number, and 411 is Information. Harvey later explained that he used 411 because he wanted the universe to find two people who needed what his son was selling. In both cases, remember, the phone was dead—he never hooked it up, so he didn't really call 911 or 411. He just went through the motions. Also, in the desire for his son to land the sales, Harvey had the greatest confidence in his son's ability—he'd seen him perform before, and knew his son could do it—meaning he believed his son was capable

of landing the sale. As his son's desire and Harvey's desire for him matched, the sales were made in less than twenty-four hours. When two or more people are joined together in a single thought in which they both believe (both consciously and subconsciously), then that desire will manifest quickly. Finally, Harvey had this to say: "I didn't for one moment allow myself to doubt. I just forged ahead, knowing that I would get what I wanted. I used a HedgeWitch technique whenever I felt doubt coming on. I said, repeatedly, 'It ALWAYS works!'"

And it did!

Linking your mind to a physical object to support your belief or matching your words to something you know to be true is not new. Magickal practitioners have been doing this for centuries. The trick is that you must believe in what you know to be true. Sounds funny, doesn't it? We find an excellent example in mental fluidity when studying Pow-Wow spells (Pow-Wow is a German-American magickal system). In Christianized Pow-Wow, the practitioner often adds a rider, such as:

"As surely as Mary gave forth Jesus Christ, so will Suzanne experience the fullness of healing in His name."

For a Christian, this works perfectly, but that isn't the original text. Indeed, the original version states rivers and territories that no longer hold the same names, so to update a bit, we might say:

"As surely as the Mosel River flows through France, Luxembourg, and Germany, so too will Suzanne experience the gentle flow of healing energy until she is completely well."

Both versions work—again, it is what you believe that counts.

Conscious and Subconscious Mind: Your Personal Filter

There is a really good reason why your subconscious and conscious minds don't readily believe the same thing, and at this point, you may wish you didn't have a subconscious at all, because it manages to be a major pain on certain issues and definitely can stand in the way of what you want. Both your conscious and your subconscious minds act as police, trying to filter thoughts and silly statements so that you don't manifest a shark on your dining room floor, a monster in the closet, or blow up the world. Both definitely have a unique function—gatekeepers to your running mouth and rambling brain. This way, you can think all you want, but it's what you *believe* that is the key.

Your Personal Primal Language

Discussing the law of attraction and release based on your thoughts, words, and deeds and supported by your belief isn't new (it has been done for centuries through different venues, especially in magickal circles). What's different here is really this section of the book: you have to personalize your primal language for it to work for you continuously. As I mentioned in my book *MindLight*, many seekers try a technique for a month or two, have great success, and then something seems to go wrong. Success is overshadowed by failure, and we find ourselves once again back at square one, debating on whether a particular technique really works for us and perhaps jousting once again with a nasty mental monster we just can't seem to shake. After contemplating this problem for several years, I realized that just as in everything else, no one human is like another, and therefore, no one human processes thoughts exactly like another. Yes, we all have certain human capabilities in common (like breathing), but it is those nuances that make us so unique that also make our approach to the law of attraction exclusive unto ourselves. If this is so, then how can everyone enjoy the laws of attraction and release equally? By determining what specific words, thoughts, and actions have meaning to our personal way of thinking. If we use our own favorite words, we can create the emotional certainty ensuring that what we want, we will recieve. If we can keep that emotional certainty at full power for sixty-five seconds, what we want has already begun to manifest. Once we have found those words and actions, using props and triggers—a motion of the hand, the scent of an herb, or the feel of a rock or crystal—helps to elongate a single thought, holding that heightened emotional certainty in place, giving us the necessary time for our desire to take root. These props or triggers can tie the unseen to the seen, the ephemeral to the physical, giving us an even flow of energy. As above, so below.

I know a woman who can always get a broken car started, no matter where she is. We'll be standing in a parking lot or on the street and hear the familiar grind of someone desperately trying to start their car. She'll wink, turn her back on the car, flip her hand, and three tries later (if they have kept at it), the car will start! When I asked her how she does this, she said, "I close my eyes, and I think of power filling the engine of the vehicle. At the same time, I clearly hear the sound of a perfectly running motor in my head. I flip my hand as if to turn on the car. I add to this my certainty that this always works and let the thought go." Voilà!

I have a friend who runs his own business, and he's also a fringe Voudon practitioner. Whenever sales are low, he simply surrounds a white candle with a mixture of white sugar and coconut, lights the candle, and within twenty-four hours he always has a sale. "I call on Ayizan," he says, "goddess of the marketplace. Her offerings can include white sugar and coconut. I believe that she will answer me, and she always does. When I set out the candle and other things, I'm completely concentrating on how happy I am that money is coming in. The offerings I give are my act of releasing—giving something away to make room for the sale coming in. I've never been disappointed. It always works."

A student of mine decorates her home for abundance with every Wiccan high holy day. "To receive abundance," she says, "I need to welcome it, so I clear out all old decorations and either pack them away or throw them out, clean the house from top to bottom, and then spend a few days before the holiday decorating my home. I especially don't like the dark days of winter, so I take extra care to brighten up the place any way I can think of. This allows me to be creative, busy, and think about new, fresh, exciting events and people surrounded by positive energy entering my life."

Does this work? She says, "I've been happily married for over twenty-five years, and all my grown children are doing well. I have a job I love, and I haven't had any serious medical problems. Yeah, it works for me. It always works."

When my friend Jane wants money, she buys makeup. "It all started when I was super desperate for money," she says. "I was doing the grocery shopping on a shoestring and decided to go next door to the pharmacy. As I walked through the pharmacy, I thought that even though I felt bad that I was in a poor financial state, I wanted to look good (if that makes any sense). I'd seen an advertisement on television for a new lipstick, and I really wanted to try it, but hadn't found it at the grocers or anywhere else. I looked up and there were the lipstick and companion products right in front of my nose. I bought the lipstick and one or two other items. I tried the new products that night, and I liked them, so I threw away my old, yucky makeup. The very next day, I received a large check in the mail I hadn't been expecting. From that day on, I associated drawing money to me with buying new makeup. I know that sounds silly, but it works for me. I don't go overboard. I only buy what I need. I even understand that it works because I made the initial association. If things get tight for me at the end of the month, I look through my bathroom cabinet and determine what beauty products I'm low on or have run out of. That's how I keep the spending under control. Then, when I go shopping, I try something new in that line. I've been doing this for about nine months, and I've yet to run out of money. It always works. The mind is an incredible thing!"

In some of my other books, I've written about the road fairy and the parking lot fairy—here, I take a mythical creature (or, if you believe in the Sidhe, a real one) and petition for what I need. I always merge safely on a major highway, and I always find the parking spot I want. I simply say aloud, "Okay, road fairy, give me a nice, long, clear space of road so that I can merge onto this highway safely," or, "Hey, parking lot fairy, I want a good space by the cart return." In this book, we'll be using many aspects of nature as triggers for your future success.

Conversely, triggers can also spell failure. If you say, "I know that mint is a magickal correspondence for money, but when I use the plant as a trigger, it never works for me," of course it won't—because you believe, right at the onset, that it doesn't.

For you to do: You already have loads of successful triggers stored in your mind—actions, thoughts, affirmations, sounds, colors, habits, etc. Think about actions, thoughts, or symbols you've used lately when experiencing success. Write them down on a piece of paper. Try using these triggers again on future endeavors! In the future, when you experience great joy or super success, think about the triggers you naturally used to obtain what you desired.

Shifting with Nature

Nature isn't the only shift mechanism every human being has in his or her attraction arsenal—there are others, such as music, memory recall of happy events or feelings, art, dance, even race car driving (no kidding, my son-in-law does it)—anything that mentally and emotionally makes you feel super good! When I first learned how to do magic, I used music as my primary shifter in ritual and spellwork. As I grew to understand the vast scope of Witchcraft, revisiting its building blocks time and again, studying Hoodoo, herbal magick, and spiritism under Houngan Ray Malbrough, learning hypnosis and Reiki, delving into classical astrology, learning tai chi, etc., I realized that Mother Nature has an incredible power that moves through all my (and your) interests—and She is more than willing to share! Her power can change your life in a heartbeat, and it's right here, under your nose, all the time, day or night, rain or shine, no batteries necessary, wand included. All you have to do is state what you want and follow through. Mother Nature *is* the universe. She *is* quantum physics!

Primal Language (The Dialect of Mother Nature) Requires Changing the Way You Think

So far, I've explained that the basic idea of manifesting anything you want is to say exactly what you want, visualize it, feel good about it, and as soon as you open your eyes, think of something (anything) that makes you very happy. Then let the thought go and make the effort to release ideas, thoughts, and physical objects that may be blocking your desire. If you have been working magick for a long time, you'll be sitting there saying, "This is spellcasting 101. So what?"

In spellcasting, the primary focus is on the preparation, the focus of the spell itself, and the closure, often done in sacred space or a magick circle (which defines the field for your focus). The HedgeWitch material you will be working with uses both sacred space and the magick circle, and this is explained as you work through Sections 2 and 3 of this book. I mention this here because we tend to forget that those thoughts and conversations we have with ourselves and with others before and after any working also communicate to the universe, which can result in a mixed message as to what we really desire.

My son's situation with his car in the earlier example shows us that what you think, say, and do affects your life *all the time*. It shows us that we waste an inordinate amount of energy sending mixed messages to the universe. By complaining and being angry, he was transmitting a load of garbage that finally manifested into a broken car. To really make primal language work for you (remember, primal language is a succinct formulation of words that mirror a thought—that thought being your desire), you have to pay attention to what you are saying and doing *outside* that sacred space or magick circle.

Therefore, we must stop saying what we don't want. We must stop complaining. We must stop transmitting garbled information, which means we have to make a concerted effort to change the way we think, the way we speak to ourselves, and the way we converse with others if we truly wish to manifest what we desire on a continual basis. Magick doesn't just occur in circle. Magick and manifestation occur each day, every day, 24/7.

The old teachers asked us: where is the center of any circle? And our answer was to be: where the Witch is. That is the center of manifestation, inside or outside of the circle: where you are. Manifestation naturally happens all the time. How does it happen? That is entirely up to you. In the magick circle, we know to be observant and how to direct the energy with honor. But what about outside the magick circle? When you are outside of the sacred area, are you directing your thoughts in the same way as you do within sacred space? What is within is without. What is inside is outside. As above, so below.

Why use a magick circle at all? Because it succinctly defines a specific field wherein we can work in harmony with the universe. (Note: As you work through the HedgeWitch material, if you have more questions about how a magick circle works and why we use it, please refer to my book *Solitary Witch*, which provides a broad compendium of information about basic Witchcraft techniques.)

Those of us who have been working magick for a long time have learned that what we say or do within a magick circle is important, because we have defined a field of manifestation by using the circle as a boundary. When we speak to ourselves or others, this translates into symbols (or an energy stream) that the universe tries to interpret and, in turn, responds in kind to our desires. If our thoughts or conversations are muddy and unclear, how the heck is the universe supposed to know what we are saying?

We tend to believe that outside of the circle, or when we have taken the circle down, the power we wield becomes limited. This is not the case. The universe hears what we say inside or outside that circle. It is how we think that is different. The universe is as it is. It is what we believe that makes the difference to us.

The universe, remember, does not understand disclaimers, codicils, or addendums—the universe only understands nouns and verbs; that's it. If you say, "I don't want to be responsible for handling this project at work," you are most likely going to get the darned project. The universe drops the word *don't* in the translation. Why? Because we tend to think in pictures and symbols, even though we don't realize we do. In this primal language, there isn't a symbol for the word *don't*. If I say, "I don't want to be responsible for this project at work," what symbols am I transmitting to the universe? That's right. I have formulated the project and my work environment in my mind. The *want* word generates strong emotional content (good or bad), which magnifies the thought and often works as an attraction device, not a repelling device. So, in all your thoughts, you need to train yourself to say what you *do* want—nothing more. All of us who have worked through this material have agreed that training your mind to *not* say "I don't want" was the biggest challenge. Why is the concept of primal language confusing to some? Because we are trying to translate the spoken word (no matter our language—English, Spanish, Chinese, French, German, Russian, Japanese) into the universal one—that of feelings and thought symbols and energy streams. And as we all know with translation devices, miscommunication often occurs!

The universe does not speak English or French or Chinese. It speaks "universe." The universe does not hear your words—the universe vibrates to your thoughts and feelings. That's how it communicates.

Your thoughts (not words) are vibrational symbols translated into a stream of energy. Your emotions dictate the strength of that transmission (for good or ill). Your belief determines the clarity of your transmission.

By using the primal language I recommend (nouns and verbs), you are training your mind to speak to the universe in a way it understands. When you speak a word out loud, your mind has already formulated a vibrational symbol, or stream of energy. It is that symbol or energy stream, not the word itself, that communicates to the universe. It is your emotion when saying the word, not the word itself, that quantifies the intensity of that communication to the universe. It is your clarity of belief, not the words themselves, that speaks to the universe. Words aren't for the universe, they are for us. The fewer words spoken, the stronger the message.

Which is why you can be deaf, dumb, and blind and *still* be able to communicate with the universe. There are no handicaps in the world that prevent you from this communication. You are never alone. And you have always known how to manifest anything you desire, you just didn't realize it. The reason why we often don't get what we want is because we don't really know what we want—we are confused, ourselves, as to what we really desire. By using primal language, factoring down the number of words we use and how we use them, we are helping ourselves determine precisely what it is we truly desire. Once we have honed our words to a precision thought, the world is ours!

Prove It to Yourself

Just because I wrote the above doesn't mean you have to believe it—right? So I'd like you to do an experiment for yourself. I'd like you to take one thing you complain about all the time, and I'd like you to totally rearrange your thinking on the subject. Remove words like don't, not, hate, dislike, bugs me, crappy, irritate, etc. Change your thinking to what you *do* want that involves this subject. Translate this into as few words as possible that still gets your point across. Every day, communicate that positive statement to the universe. And every time you think about the subject or talk about it with others, do it in a positive way—no more complaining. If you open your mouth to complain, snap it shut and say to yourself, "Always a blessing," and change the subject. Keep doing this until the change occurs, no matter how long it takes. Don't give up, and don't give in! You'll be amazed at the consequences.

Putting It All Together

The HedgeWitch material combines the natural magick you already have within yourself (your ability to communicate your desires to the universe) and the techniques of Witchcraft (a natural platform on which to focus the mind) to create a super life-changing experience. Below, I've listed the basics of HedgeWitchery.

The Basics of HedgeWitchery

In this section, you are learning the basic building blocks of the mental aspects of Hedge-Witch magick. Here's a "remember" list with a few additional tips:

1. Always connect to Spirit first. By Spirit I mean that which you believe runs the universe. Some call it the source, others God or Goddess, or both, or neither, or whatever, or lots of names with particular influences from different pantheons. The details don't matter —what matters is that you believe in a greater power. As everyone's needs for and in spiritual connection are different, there isn't any *one* right belief. What you believe is right for you as long as it doesn't purposefully hurt anyone. Power "over" in anything will bring you a whole lot of hurting in the end. Power "within" is the ultimate vehicle of success. (The universe does not take kindly to negative beliefs, thoughts, or actions.) Warning: Be careful that the beliefs of others don't inhibit you; conversely, don't shove your beliefs on others (it lessens your own personal power). Believe that you will receive, and it will be so.

2. Start and end everything, and I mean *everything*, with a smile! Smiling raises your personal vibrational level, moving you toward the essence of the universe, which is pure joy. The magick key of the universe that opens the door to every opportunity is a simple, sincere smile.

3. Learn to speak the true language of the universe! The source of all things has its own language: basically, nouns and verbs that focus on the attraction of any given thing. The All doesn't acknowledge the rules of grammar as humans have made them. Instead, we must learn to think and speak in a simple, fundamental syntax when focusing on our desires. Stick with nouns and verbs to begin. For example: "I want cookies." The words "I" and "cookies" are nouns. "Want" is the verb. Then, embellish carefully. "I want chocolate chip cookies." More? "I want delicious, freshly baked chocolate chip cookies." Remember, by using primal language, we condense our desire into a translation that the universe will understand.

4. Visualize yourself absolutely delighted with what you want, which should produce a smile, which raises your personal vibrational level, which brings the thing faster. If you need something right away, be happy!

5. You must ensure that your conscious and subconscious beliefs about the issue are in agreement. If they do not agree, then your transmission to the universe will either be changed in a way you didn't desire or will not manifest at all.

6. Nothing can grow if there isn't space. You can't receive if you've blocked the door and bolted the gate. For every specific thing that you want, whether it is healing, money, a new job, or a great relationship, let go of anything that inhibits the flow of what you desire. If you start listing a bunch of excuses, you've just lost *big time*. No magick elf presents for you! Allow change.

7. While you are waiting for what you desire, focus your attention on positive aspects in your life. Allow new and different energies to keep you occupied, rather than worrying or fretting about what you don't have. Instead, learn to honor what you do have (or had), and go from there. When we are legitimately grateful, we bring closure to any situation and allow fresh, new experiences to energize our lives. And always remember to say thank you!

Entering the World of HedgeWitchery

Most traditional spellwork and ritual form a mental vehicle to help you communicate your desires to the universe. Such practices keep the mind busy and centered in a positive place, freeing you to fully accept that which you desire. Spells and rites of worship encourage you to connect with the source of the universe smoothly, without interruption. They require a time and place for you to specifically plug in and turn on, raising your vibratory level for your ultimate success. Adding physical objects to a spell or ritual (flowers, candles, gems, stones, shells, ribbons, food offerings, herbs, etc.) provides vibrational benefits designed to keep you focused on your intent. Incorporating sound (music) and aroma (incense or magickal oils) heightens the physical and mental experience, helping you to shift easily into the primordial language of the universe. These things can assist you to form a more open dialog with Spirit, simply because they make you feel good. And when you feel good, miracles can happen!

Totem Representations

You may also wish to collect images of the HedgeWitch totem representations for your personal altar. If these totems don't suit you, simply change them to what you feel best matches your needs and personality.

The Praying Mantis of Wisdom—*South*

The Butterflies of Communication—*East*

The Toads of Luck and Prosperity—*West*

The Bats of Earth's Center—*North*

The Serpent of Wisdom—*Sacred Center*

These totem representations were chosen in direct association with organic gardening. Each brings vibrational benefits as well as prevents pests from destroying your work.

Other garden friends include: Ladybug, Bee, Wasp, Owl, Fox, and Turtle

Traditional Colors

I've chosen a set of traditional colors for the practice of HedgeWitchery; however, if this doesn't interest you, that's just fine. If you feel the recommended colors are too dark for your taste, you may wish to employ floral colors and patterns in your HedgeWitchery work. Traditional colors are usually used in candleburning magick, in ritual garments, on altar cloths, etc.

Black—for the earth and the birth of all things

Green—for the lifeblood of the vegetation we employ and the growth we accomplish

Gold—for the light of Spirit, the sunlight that nurtures our craft, and to remind us to look up to the stars with our hopes and dreams rather than focusing on what we do not have

White—for the energy of the nourishing waters of Spirit and of the liquid that sustains us and the herbs of our study

You may also desire to fashion a robe or other ritual garment in the HedgeWitch color scheme. Those who have gone through the training here wore a green garment with gold and black trim or a gold and black sash, or a white garment with green, gold, and black trim or a green, gold, and black sash. You may wish to embroider the Sacred Serpent of Wisdom (shaped like a figure eight) or perhaps your personal signature herb or flower on one item of your ritual wear. (Note: You will choose your HedgeWitch signature herb the first night and work with this plant throughout your fourteen-day experience.) In HedgeWitchery, your creativity is encouraged and deemed highly important. Wear what you desire. Your HedgeWitch experience can be as formal or eclectic as you like!

Simple Formula for HedgeWitch Spellwork, Prayer, and Meditation

1. Go to the still point. This means relax, close your eyes, take several deep breaths, and let nothing fill your mind. Be at peace. In your mind, surround yourself with white light.

2. Next, be grateful for something—anything. Say out loud what you are thankful for. These things do not have to be in line with your intent. By being thankful, you will lift your spirits.

3. Align yourself with Spirit. Shift into nature, and it is easy to touch that-which-runs-the-universe. Be grateful for this moment of peace and inner pleasure.

4. Say: "There is one power, which is within and without" (and mean it). This statement means that you acknowledge your magnificent connection with Spirit, and that together you are one.

5. State, in language as simple as possible, precisely what you want. Say the same exact statement three times, slowly and with meaning.

6. Say: "It always works! Always a blessing!" This means that you believe, consciously and subconsciously, that you will receive what you desire.

7. In your mind, see yourself having what you want, and smile.

8. Say thank you, and smile again.

This simple format can be used within a longer ritual or alone for spellworking or as a simple rite, meditation, or prayer format. It works both for group and solitary use.

Personal Cleansing

Before any rite or ritual of dedication or initiation, the seeker is normally required to undergo a body cleansing—a bath or shower to remove all negativity, both physical and spiritual. It is suggested that before you undertake each phase of this dedication, you practice the time-honored tradition of cleansing to reap the most benefits on your spiritual journey. Sections 4 and 5 of this book contain several formulas for soaps, cleansers, salts, etc., that can be used in your personal and environmental cleansing activities.

Remember, you can choose to work through the HedgeWitchery guide in fourteen days or take your time and elongate the process to fourteen weeks—it's your decision.

Are you ready?

Then let's go!

*remember to
smile!!!

The Five I's of Manifestation

I thank you... (puts you in direct alignment
    with Spirit)

I want... (be clear and use primal language)

I believe... (both consciously and subconsciously)

I release... (any negative patterns, behaviors,
    or thoughts)

I receive... (be ready to receive what you
    wanted!)

section 2

Thirteen Rites

guide for personal transformation

The HedgeWitch Guide to Personal Empowerment

The HedgeWitch guide is separated into fourteen segments, each segment entitled a "night" because that is the time normally scheduled for the rite. Begin in the morning by reading the affirmation and the focus for the day. For example, the first night segment concentrates on wind, associating this energy with that of Spirit. Close your eyes, quiet your mind, smile, and allow Spirit to fully enter your body. Then repeat the word *wind* softly, conjuring your vision of wind in your mind. Open your eyes, and repeat the affirmation at least three times. Remember to smile as you finish! Throughout the day, repeat the affirmation as many times as you like. Begin and end with a smile. Write down in a small notebook anything unusual about this day and events, people, or places that carry a strong wind association for you.

In this way, you will be prepared to perform the first night ritual. Continue this process for the remaining segments.

Each segment also contains a "to do today" requirement. For example, the first night segment suggests that you choose a signature plant that you will continue to work with for the entire HedgeWitch experience. You will need to have a physical representation of this plant for the fourteenth segment (the dedication ceremony).

Each day requires that you release something negative, old, or worn from your life to make room for positive growth. You can't keep filling your life with new things without learning closure and releasing things that are no longer serviceable to you. For example, on the first day you will air out your house. Of course, what you get rid of is entirely up to you—what I have written is merely a suggestion. I realize that you are very busy, so if you miss a suggestion to release on a particular day or evening, try your best to fulfill this release sometime during the successive days (and definitely before the final ceremony).

Each "night" focuses on a set of herbs that, through correspondence, match the rite's energy intent. If you cannot find these herbs, substitutions are recommended. To find these substitutions, surf the Net (there is a compendium of information there on magickal herbal correspondences) or use *Cunningham's Encyclopedia of Magical Herbs*.

Your magick key: Each sequence encourages you to draw a personal sigil, or symbol, that represents the focus of that day. This is done during the ritual sequence and relies on your observations throughout the day. You can make the symbol as simple or elaborate as you desire. Once you have completed the HedgeWitch sequence, you will have fourteen powerful "keys," or gateways, that you can use in any type of working. Because you have designed the symbol yourself, it will have great meaning to you. In the future, you can use this symbol in candle magick, on petitions, to embroider on clothing, to place in conjuring bags, etc. Only you will know what this symbol stands for, thereby making the significance that much greater. When all the symbols are completed, you can begin mixing them together like bind runes, experimenting with how they will work best for you.

A recommendation: Keep a HedgeWitch journal as you progress through these rites. It doesn't have to be fancy. When I teach the HedgeWitch course, my students use a simple composition book that they decorate with colorful papers, stamp art, glitter, dried herbs—whatever suits their fancy. Your journal will contain your dreams over the next fourteen days, any unusual experiences you may have, the HedgeWitch sigils you create, thoughts, insights, and so on. Writing a great deal is not necessary—jotted notes will do, as this record is only for you.

Can I reorder the rites? Yes, you can reorder the first eleven rites as they might suit you; however, please be aware that some of the rites use materials presented in rites preceding it. If you plan to reorder your ceremonies, be sure to take this into consideration and jot down necessary adjustments. For example, if you experience a wonderful rainstorm or thunderstorm early in the sequence of days, you may wish to take advantage of the weather and work the Rite of Rain or the Rite of Thunder.

Ready? Let's begin!

First Night

I am always connected to Spirit. Spirit fulfills my every need and my every desire. I know that Spirit lives within me.

Your affirmation for today: (see above)

Your symbol for today: the wind

Begin your day: Begin in the morning by reading the affirmation for the day. Today's segment concentrates on wind, associating this energy with that of Spirit. Close your eyes, quiet your mind, smile, and allow Spirit to fully enter your body. Then repeat the word *wind* softly, conjuring your vision of wind in your mind. Open your eyes, and repeat the affirmation at least three times. Remember to smile as you finish! Throughout the day, repeat the affirmation as many times as you like. Begin and end with a smile. Write down in a small notebook (or your HedgeWitch journal) anything unusual about this day and events, people, or places that carry a strong wind association for you. In this way, you will be prepared to perform the first night Rite of Wind.

To do today: Choose your signature plant/herb/flower. It may be your favorite, or it could be a particular plant with a special meaning to you. You may wish to spend a little time surfing the Net, or visit a bookstore or library to read all about the plant you have chosen. Remember that you will need a physical representation of your choice. If you already have it growing in your garden, that's great! If not, you might visit a local nursery, the grocery store, or shop on the Net. If you are already familiar with the plant's wild location out-of-doors, a short trip to collect it might be in order. The physical plant can be dried, but you may wish to obtain a living one to forge a better connection.

Today I will release . . . all unpleasant odors in my home! I will open windows and air out stuffy areas and stagnant air. I will burn scented candles or use air fresheners to keep my home smelling pleasant and fragrant. If I own a vehicle, I will clean it out, removing all trash and junk that has collected there. If I have time, I will take it to be washed. If not, I will reserve this task to be completed before I have finished this fourteen-day HedgeWitch guide.

Weekly planner: If you are spending a week on this rite, look through Sections 4 and 5 of this book and choose one or more projects, techniques, or formulas that you feel relates to spiritual cleansing, and make those items. In this way, you will begin to build your HedgeWitch magickal cabinet of supplies.

Herbs for today: lavender, rosemary, chamomile, lemon verbena, lemongrass

Supplies for tonight: your magick key, incense, small bowl of spring water, a white candle, a representation of your signature herb (just the word or a picture will do for this evening), cleansing herbal mix (see recipe, page 52), cotton conjuring bag or small net bag to hold herbal mix, mortar and pestle to grind herbs if you are not using fresh herbs, paper (on which to draw your wind sigil), pen, pin to inscribe the white candle

Rite of Wind

Light incense. Pass over working area. Place the representation of your magick key (see Section 1) near your other supplies for this night. Smile. Close your eyes, and envision yourself surrounded by white light. Take thirteen slow, even breaths, inhaling through the nose and exhaling through the mouth. When you feel relaxed, open your eyes, smile, and repeat today's affirmation three times. Smile again.

Cleansing Herbal Mix

Combine equal amounts of:

Lavender

Rosemary

Chamomile

Lemon Verbena

Lemongrass

—If using fresh ingredients, no need to grind.

Loosely grind a small amount (about ½ teaspoon) of cleansing herbal mix with mortar and pestle. The ingredients for this mix are lavender, rosemary, chamomile, lemon verbena, and lemongrass. If you are using fresh herbs, you won't need to grind them. Place herbal mixture in a cotton conjuring bag or white piece of cloth tied with white string. Hold your hands over the bag, smile, and breathe deeply. Now, repeat the following conjuration:

> *Sunlight to activate*
> *Moonlight to blend*
> *Spirit to bring the power to cleanse*
> *Touch of wind!*

Hold your hands over a bowl of spring water, smile, close your eyes, and breathe deeply, remembering to allow yourself to become one with Spirit. Say: "Joy, peace, and perfection. Peace with the gods, peace with nature, peace within." Smile.

Dip the bag of herbs in the water and sprinkle the water over your magick key (do not let the bag touch the key). Say: "Joy, peace, and perfection. Peace with the gods, peace with nature, peace within." Smile.

Dip the bag back in the water and begin sprinkling on yourself (if the bag touches you, that's okay). Envision that all negativity you may be carrying around is lifted from you with gentle breaths of fresh air. Allow the winds of peace, healing, and harmony to circle about your mind and body. You may experience a tingling, a rush of energy, or simply pleasant and well-deserved peace. If you are having trouble releasing any unhappiness or fear, repeat the same conjuration you initially used to empower the water. You can sprinkle as much or as little of the water as you think you need. Throw the bag out when completed.

Note: If you are doing this activity with more than one person, each individual should use water empowered only for them and a personal herb bag.

Say: "Thank you!" and smile.

On the white candle, inscribe the word *wind* with a pin, nail, or clay-inscribing tool. Place the candle in safe holder, and light. Intone the following charm:

Herbal magick, speak to me

Of wind and language in the trees

Of cleansing breath and harmony

Of balance, knowledge, destiny

Spirit power lies in me!

Face east, and hold the candle out in front of you. Slowly, so that you can fully experience the impact of your own words, say:

I seek the source

I breathe in the source

I connect completely with the source of all things

Peace with the gods

Peace with nature

Peace within.

Face south, continuing to hold the candle out in front of you, and repeat: "I seek the source…" Face west, slowly intoning the same conjuration, followed by the north. Stand still, close your eyes, and raise the candle out and above your head, and repeat the conjuration ("I seek the source, I breathe in the source…") one last time. Lift your thoughts as you say this, and join the sea of peace flowing throughout the universe. You should feel refreshed and experience a glorious connection with the source of all things.

At this moment, clearly state your signature herb aloud and say why you have chosen this plant.

Note: You need not begin with the east if this feels uncomfortable to you. Perhaps you've had previous training that places north as the source of all things. Or you could incorporate a bit of Spiritism, beginning with the west, moving across to the east, then down to the south, and up to the north. I would recommend against moving backwards, though, as this is a universal symbol of undoing, unless you really desire that type of energy in your life (which I wouldn't recommend for HedgeWitch work).

Quietly meditate for a few minutes on the meaning of wind in the life of a spiritual person and the necessity of connecting with the source at all times, even when we are tense, angry, sick, or unhappy (when this connection is most needed, but we often let our emotions overshadow this wonderful connection). You can close your eyes during this meditation, or you can simply sit outside and enjoy nature and take a walk in a field, by the beach, or in the woods. If you are having trouble with a jumble of thoughts, simply repeat any of the conjurations given so far or use the affirmation of this day. When you are finished, draw your personal sigil of the wind on the paper. Repeat the word *wind* as you lay your hand over the finished drawing. Smile. Say: "Thank you! It always works. This rite is finished. Always a blessing!" Remember to smile!

Allow the candle to burn completely, if you can. In your journal, dedicate at least one page to FIRST NIGHT WIND. Record any experiences that occurred today which you feel are relevant. Write about the rite and your feelings. Leave space to record your dreams from this night and a large-enough area to add more notes about the wind, your connection to Source/Spirit, or your new purpose in general that might unfold tomorrow. Redraw or place your wind sigil in your journal, and be sure to record your signature herb. Carry your magick key with you. Dispose of water, cold candle end, used incense, and wet herbal bag in a way that is comfortable to you.

Before you drift off to sleep, close this evening by saying:

> *Peace with the gods*
> *Peace with nature*
> *Peace within.*
> *It always works.*
> *Always a blessing.*

Remember to smile!

Second Night

I carry the fire of profound creativity within me. I have access to the creative power of Spirit whenever I need it!

Your affirmation for today: (see above)

Your symbol for today: fire

Begin your day: If at all possible, begin this day by watching the sun rise. Using primordial language, as explained in Section 1, make a wish. Keep this wish to yourself; tell no one. Read the affirmation for the day. Today's segment concentrates on fire, associating this energy with that of creativity. Close your eyes, quiet your mind, smile, and allow Spirit to fully enter your body. Then repeat the word *fire* softly, conjuring your vision of sacred fire in your mind. Open your eyes, and repeat the affirmation at least three times. Remember to smile as you finish! Throughout the day, repeat the affirmation as many times as you like. Begin and end with a smile. Write down in a small notebook (or your HedgeWitch journal) anything unusual about this day and events, people, or places that carry a strong fire association for you. In this way, you will be prepared to perform the second night Rite of Fire.

To do today: Choose one small, creative project that you have always wanted to try but just never seemed to get around to doing. Use the primordial language of the universe to state what you want to do. Today, look for opportunities that might help you begin this little project. Find a small red box. Decorate it if you like, or leave it as is. This will become your HedgeWitch project box.

Today I will release...all old photographs and memorabilia that remind me of negative events, people, and bad behavior. I will, if I can, burn all these items and repeat aloud my intention to remove these memories from my life. If I can't burn them, I will...(you choose how you will dispose of them off your property).

Weekly planner: If you are spending a week on this rite, look through Sections 4 and 5 of this book and choose one or more projects, techniques, or formulas that you feel relates to fire magick, passion, or inspiration, and make those items. One suggestion might be learning to make HedgeWitch candles (see Section 5).

Herbs for today: dried (whole or powdered) cinnamon, hot peppers, galangal, cloves

Supplies for tonight: above-listed herbs, one red candle, one red piece of felt (or a red envelope), red string, a lock of your hair, incense and holder, your red HedgeWitch project box, your HedgeWitch journal, pen, small piece of paper

Rite of Fire

Light incense. Pass over working area. Place the representation of your magick key (see page 48) near your other supplies for this night. Smile. Close your eyes, and envision yourself surrounded by white light. Take thirteen slow, even breaths, inhaling through the nose and exhaling through the mouth. When you feel relaxed, open your eyes, smile, and repeat today's affirmation three times. Smile again.

Pick up the red candle and hold it with both hands. Smile. Close your eyes. Imagine the candle is filled with radiating light. Say: "Peace with the gods, peace with nature, peace within." Smile. Open your eyes.

On the red candle, inscribe the word *fire* with a pin, nail, or clay-inscribing tool. Place the candle in the appropriate holder. Mix the cinnamon, hot peppers (just a tad), galangal, and cloves together. Sprinkle the herbs around the base of the candle. Put your magick key beside the candle and herbs. Light the candle, and hold your hands toward the candle and herbs. Intone the following charm:

> *Herbal magick, speak to me*
> *Of fire! Passion! Creativity!*
> *Of Spirit's gift of steady flow*
> *And herbs of flame that make things go.*
> *Thank you!*

Meditate for a few minutes on the meaning of fire in the life of a spiritual person. Smile, and repeat today's affirmation as much as necessary, followed by the word *fire*. To conclude, chant the word *fire* several times, smile, and then open your eyes. Draw your personal fire sigil in your journal and on a small piece of paper. On the back of the small paper, write the project that you wish to begin. Place the paper on top of the felt square. Sprinkle the paper with some of the herbs from around the candle. Add a lock of your hair. Fold the felt toward you and then roll it toward you. Tie it with the red string. Place the rolled felt in your red HedgeWitch project box. Close the box. Tap the lid three times, and say:

> *Easy! Easy! Easy! It always works. Always a blessing.*
> *This rite is ended. Thank you!*

Remember to smile!

Place the box where you can see it but where no one else will disturb it. Allow the candle to burn completely. Offer remaining herbs outside to Spirit, saying: "Thank you!" Dispose of cold candle end and incense. Remember to record any feelings or experiences about fire energy in your journal. Don't forget to write about any dreams you may have this night!

When you have successfully finished your project, burn the red felt packet, remembering to thank the source of all things, and sprinkle the ashes to the wind. Cleanse the inside of the project box by sprinkling a bit of fresh HedgeWitch formula cleansing water (like you made for the first night's rite) in the box. Allow the box to completely dry before closing. Your project box will then be ready to use again anytime you desire!

Before you drift off to sleep, close this evening by saying:

Peace with the gods
Peace with nature
Peace within.
It always works.
Always a blessing.

Remember to smile!

Third Night

I accept the richness and abundance of the universe. The pathway is always open for me to receive the gifts of earth. I deserve and accept the gifts of an abundant universe.

Your affirmation for today: (see above)

Your symbol for today: earth

Begin your day: Begin in the morning by reading the affirmation for the day outside, with both hands placed firmly on the ground. Today's segment concentrates on earth, associating this energy with that of the richness of the universe and the abundance of spiritual energy. Close your eyes, quiet your mind, smile, and allow Spirit to fully enter your body.

Then repeat the word *earth* softly, conjuring your vision of earth's riches in your mind. Open your eyes, and repeat the affirmation at least three times. Remember to smile as you finish! Bring inside at least a half cup of the earth you put your hands on, and store it in a small jar. Throughout the day, repeat the affirmation as many times as you like. Begin and end with a smile. Write down in a small notebook (or your HedgeWitch journal) anything unusual about this day and events, people, or places that carry a strong earth association for you. In this way, you will be prepared to perform the third night Rite of Earth.

To do today: Find one large, flat stone, at least twelve-by-twelve inches and at least a half-inch thick. This stone will become your HedgeWitch altar stone—representing a small, sacred area where you can pray, burn candles, work with your herbs, etc. We are choosing stone because it is easy to clean and fire-retardant. If you cannot go looking outdoors, visit your local nursery. Most carry all types of stones for the garden. Many have decorated stepping stones that will fulfill our purpose. If you are feeling very crafty, you can make your own stone, using a stepping-stone mold and cement for that purpose. You could decorate this stone with mosaic tiles. However, should you choose to make your stone, note that this type of project takes a few days to dry. You may also wish to select one living plant from the nursery or a favorite garden shop. Lucky bamboo would work well for this rite and is easy to maintain. If you can, before your ritual, take a bath and use a cleansing sea salt mixture added to lavender, chamomile, and rosemary in a tub tea envelope or bag.

Today I will release... any sick or dead houseplants. I will remove all dead flowers and replace them today, if I can, or replace them at a future date. If today is nice outside, I will walk my property and determine what I need to remove or change in the coming months. I can bring fresh flowers into the house, but I must remember that as soon as they wilt, the dead stalks and leaves can attract negative energy.

Weekly planner: If you are spending a week on this rite, go shopping at your local nursery and choose items to make an indoor kitchen herb garden, or choose a variety of houseplants suitable to the lighting available in your home. As you care for these plants over the successive weeks and months, remember that as your garden grows without, so you grow within.

Herbs for today: lemon verbena (if you can't find lemon verbena, substitute with the juice of one squeezed lemon), rosemary, frankincense and myrrh resins (powdered or chips), a half-cup dried marigold petals

Supplies for tonight: above-listed herbs (fresh is preferable) and resins, your new altar stone, a small bowl, one cup of spring water, the earth you gathered today, salt, incense, incense holder, brown candle, brown sugar, one tablespoon of honey, the words *treasures of earth belong to me* written on a small piece of paper, essential lavender oil, essential chamomile oil, essential patchouli oil

Rite of Earth

Light incense. Pass over working area. Place the representation of your magick key (see page 48) near your other supplies for this night. Smile. Close your eyes, and envision yourself surrounded by white light. Take thirteen slow, even breaths, inhaling through the nose and exhaling through the mouth. When you feel relaxed, open your eyes, smile, and repeat today's affirmation three times. Smile again.

Begin by preparing tonight's holy water. To one cup of spring water, add lemon verbena and rosemary sprigs (the number is up to you). Drop in a few small nuggets of frankincense and myrrh. Add three drops each of lavender and chamomile essential oils. Stir with your finger or a copper rod. Connect with Spirit. Smile. Hold your hands over the water, and say:

> *Molecules of liquid light*
> *Digitize to make things right.*
> *Moon above and earth below*
> *Center point, I make it so!*
> *Holy oils and sacred herbs*
> *Frankincense and blending myrrh*
> *Joy and peace will come to me*
> *As I will, so mote it be. Thank you!*

Remember to close with a smile. Hold your hands over the salt. Take a deep breath, and exhale slowly. Smile, and say:

Gifts of earth, cleansed you'll be
Speak of treasure and divinity.
Change my life in happy ways
Guard my work both night and day. Thank you!

Smile.

Sprinkle the salt generously over your new altar stone. Follow by sprinkling the surface with the holy water mixture. Hold your hands over the stone and repeat today's affirmation three times, remembering to connect with Spirit, smile, and close with a thank you.

Dot the four corners and the center of the stone with essential patchouli oil, repeating the affirmation once again.

Brush off the altar stone. On the back of the paper that says *treasures of earth belong to me*, draw your personal earth sigil. Place your key and the paper on the stone. Put the bowl of brown sugar on top of the paper. Dot the brown candle with honey (not too much). Place the candle sturdily in the bowl (if you think a plate will work better, that's just fine). In Hedge-Witchery, a brown candle signifies the gifts of the earth and miracles. The brown sugar and honey are used as an attraction correspondence. Sprinkle the earth you collected this morning on top of the brown sugar. Light the brown candle.

Meditate for a few minutes on the meaning of earth and the willingness to open the way and accept the abundance of earth's treasures. Remind yourself that everyone deserves to be rich, happy, and healthy, leading a life of pure joy. When you are ready, say: "This rite is finished. Thank you!" Smile. Allow the candle to burn completely, and dispose of it when it's cold. Place the brown sugar, earth, and honey mix back in the jar. Add your *earth's treasures* paper. If you have some of your signature herb, add that too. Cap. Bury it on your property. Sprinkle holy water on your new altar to clear the stone of residual energy. If you have holy water left over, you can refrigerate it—it has a shelf life of about two weeks as long as the mixture is kept cold. Place your lucky bamboo plant in the center of your altar and leave it there until tomorrow morning, where you can move it to an appropriate indirectly lit area of your home.

Tonight, take a few minutes to go over your journal, adding notes and entries you may have missed. Copy your earth sigil, along with any impressions you may have on the power and strength of the earth. Remember to observe all that takes place the following day in relation to the work you have begun. Remark on any dreams you may have this night. Keep your work secret.

Before you drift off to sleep, close this evening by saying:

> *Peace with the gods*
> *Peace with nature*
> *Peace within.*
> *It always works.*
> *Always a blessing.*

Remember to smile!

From earth
we move to sky.
As above, so below.

Fourth Night

My world is filled with unlimited opportunity. Opportunities that are right for me come easily. I always choose that which will be best for me and my family.

Your affirmation for today: (see above)

Your symbol for today: stars or starry sky

Begin your day: Begin in the morning by going outside (if you can) or sitting by a large window so that you can look at the sky while you are repeating today's affirmation. Today's segment concentrates on our starry sky, associating this energy with that of limitless potential and opportunity. Close your eyes, quiet your mind, smile, and allow Spirit to fully enter your body. Then open your eyes and repeat the words *starry sky* softly several times. Repeat today's affirmation at least three times. Remember to smile as you finish! Throughout the day, repeat the affirmation as many times as you like. Begin and end with a smile. Write down in a small notebook (or your HedgeWitch journal) anything unusual about this day and events, people, or places that carry a strong starry sky association. In this way, you will be prepared to perform the fourth night Rite of Starry Sky.

To do today: View the sky as often as possible. Pay particular attention to the horizon, color, how you feel when looking out into the distance, clouds, birds and insects you may see as you look up, etc. Teach yourself the mysticism of numbers by observing how many of any given item attracts your attention. Although you may wish to form your own keywords in number associations, here is a brief poetic guide:

> *The power of one*
> *The unity of two*
> *The trinity of three*
> *The stability of four*
> *The change of five*
> *Six—center, earth to sky*
> *The success of seven*
> *The mastery of eight*
> *The wish of nine*
> *Ten—the infinite blend*
> *Spirit here will never end.*

Before tonight's rite, review your list of observations today. Was one number particularly significant? If so, write that number down. We will use the number in tonight's ceremony. Also use your other senses, particularly sound, to receive messages from Spirit.

Our deep connection with nature can bring us a compendium of information if we only take the time to be silent and view the world around us. For example, one of anything can represent pure focus. Perhaps you see an unusual butterfly today, and right before that, you were contemplating the solution to a problem. Here, Spirit might be telling you that your answer can be found through a unique avenue that combines several of your resources into one powerful vehicle. Over time, you may fine-tune the messages you receive by reviewing your thoughts at the moment of a particular observation. Write this association down, and when it happens again and again, you will learn Spirit's way of repetitious communication designed especially for you. For example, a butterfly can mean gifts of good fortune, a good message in the mail, or an exciting experience ahead. Although there are traditional meanings to animal and insect associations, you'll find nature speaks more clearly to you if you build your own private dictionary of signs and symbols.

Today I will release...all old paperwork that no longer serves me. If I hold negative legal paperwork, I will box it and place it in a security deposit box. I know I must keep all financial records for seven years, so I will find a plastic tub or fireproof safe to store this information. I will shred all other documents that no longer pertain to my life. If I have questions on what I should keep, I will consult an attorney or tax representative.

Weekly planner: If you are spending a week on this rite, try your hand at the hand-dipped taper candles, as explained in Section 5. Use the chant given in today's "to do" section.

Herbs for today: Use fresh white or blue flowers (or a combination of both), your choice.

Supplies for tonight: a bag of pebbles, one light blue candle, candle holder, special bag to hold the number of pebbles you will choose in the ceremony, clear spring water (blessed, herbal additives okay), bell, tuning fork or chime, Florida water (see recipe in appendix if you would like to make this yourself), a bouquet of white/blue flowers

Rite of Starry Sky

Tonight we are not using incense but enjoying the aroma of the Florida water and the fresh flowers. Sprinkle yourself with the Florida water. Go outside (or look out a window), and count the number of stars you see in the heavens for one minute. Write down this number. If it is over ten, reduce the number by adding the double digits. For example, if the number you counted is 15, then you would add 1 + 5 = 6. Six, then, is your lucky number in HedgeWitchery. If you could not count a single star, then your lucky number is 8. If the night is pleasant, you may wish to continue this rite outdoors. If you need to work inside, arrange your lucky number pebbles in a circle (if you have several) or place the smaller number near the light blue candle on the altar stone you blessed last night. Sprinkle the pebbles with Florida water. Arrange flowers on your altar.

On the light blue candle, inscribe the words *starry sky* with a pin, nail, or clay-inscribing tool. Place the candle in a safe holder, and light. Place your magick key beside the candle. Intone the following charm:

> *Herbal magick melody*
> *Signs and symbols meant for me*
> *Wisdom, knowledge, peace of mind*
> *Speak to me through heaven's chime. Thank you!*

Smile. Ring your bell or chime to correspond with your lucky number. From now on, this sound is your personal call to Spirit—and after repeating the practice a number of times, this sound should help you focus and become one with Spirit. Some individuals call this practice a magickal trigger individually designed as an audio gateway to peace, balance, and power. If you are hearing impaired (or just want to be quiet), you may wish to use a tuning fork, touching the vibration of the sound rather than hearing it.

Meditate for fifteen minutes on the meaning of sky in the life of a spiritual person. Draw your personal sky sigil, and record it in your journal. Also record any observations or insights you may have received during tonight's ceremony. Allow the candle to burn completely. If you can, leave the pebbles on your altar. If you can't, place them in their own special bag. Offer the flowers to Spirit outside. Speak not of what you are doing; silence, as of a perfect, peaceful night, will serve you best.

Before you drift off to sleep, close this evening by saying:

> *Peace with the gods*
> *Peace with nature*
> *Peace within.*
> *It always works.*
> *Always a blessing.*

Remember to smile!

Fifth Night

I welcome healing energy into my life. Every day and in every way, my body enjoys the healing perfection of the universe. Thank you for my healing. Rain cleanses, regenerates, and blesses all it touches. I welcome the healing of rain.

Your affirmation for today: (see above)

Your symbol for today: rain

Begin your day: Before doing your affirmation today, ring your bell or chime the number of times that matches your lucky number. Take your time; let each note drift and fall silent before you begin the next. Now, begin in the morning by reading the affirmation for the day. Today's segment concentrates on rain, associating this energy with that of the healing power of Spirit. Close your eyes, quiet your mind, smile, and allow Spirit to fully enter your body. Then repeat the word *rain* softly, conjuring your vision of rain in your mind. Open your eyes, and repeat the affirmation at least three times. Remember to smile as you finish! Throughout the day, repeat the affirmation as many times as you like. Begin and end with a smile. Write down in a small notebook (or your HedgeWitch journal) anything unusual about this day and events, people, or places that carry a strong rain association. In this way, you will be prepared to perform the fifth night Rite of Rain. Don't be surprised if it actually rains today!

To do today: Find a unique and interesting bottle to hold the water used for tonight's rite. You may wish to select a bottle that has a large-enough opening to insert herbs and a good cap with an easy-pour function. A fancy oil/vinegar bottle might suit your needs. From now on, this will be your healing bottle, used in various cleansing and healing ceremonies. Sterilize the bottle before tonight's ceremony.

Today I will release... anything in my life that refers to sickness. I will replace these things with bright colors, affirmations of healing, etc. Rather than worry, I'm going to do activities that keep my mind off my fears of sickness. Instead of saying: "I feel sick," I am going to say: "I feel good. Thank you for my healing," and then I will smile. I will wash all my curtains, throw rugs, pillows, etc.

Weekly planner: If you are spending a week on this rite, look through Sections 4 and 5 of this book and choose one or more projects, techniques, or formulas that you feel relate to healing, and make those items. In this way, you will continue to build your HedgeWitch magickal cabinet of supplies.

Herbs for today: Yarrow, one vanilla bean, birch or willow leaves, rose petals, spearmint; place a small amount of this mixture in the sterilized bottle. For incense: a ground mixture of dried allspice, peppermint leaves, pine needles, and pulverized lime peels (or two drops of lime essential oil).

Supplies for tonight: small fire-safe cauldron, above-listed herbs, one bottle of rain water (best) or spring water (if rain water is unavailable; you will need enough to place in your special bottle and the cauldron), one aqua candle, a candle holder that can fit in the cauldron, incense mixture, incense holder, charcoal tab made specifically for incense, a light blue or light green (or this color combination) piece of cloth with the type of healing you desire in your life written on it (size of cloth varies to suit your needs—use one square yard for asperging a large area with sacred smoke, or you can choose an eight-by-eight-inch or six-by-six-inch cloth)

Rite of Rain

Place your magick key and the special glass bottle filled with the listed herbs beside your pebbles on your altar. Fill bottle with blessed water. Swirl the bottle nine times, intoning the following charm:

> *Gifts of rain and flowing grace*
> *Create for me a sacred space*
> *Where peace and healing now abide*
> *And Spirit travels by my side.*

Sprinkle the pebbles with a bit of the holy water from the special bottle. On the aqua candle, inscribe the word *rain* with a pin, nail, or clay-inscribing tool. Place the candle in a safe holder. Put the holder in the cauldron. Fill the cauldron with blessed water, covering the candle holder with water. The bottom of the candle should be immersed one inch in the water. Light the candle. Add seven drops of the herbal holy water to the water in the cauldron, repeating today's affirmation three times. Step back, smile, relax, and connect to Spirit. Ring your bell or chime the number of times that matches your personal magick number. Intone the following charm at least nine times, until it begins to sound like a sweet mantra:

> *Herbal magick's secret seal*
> *Of rain, of hope, and how to heal*
> *Spiral power in my palms*
> *I activate the healer's song.*

Light the charcoal incense tab and sprinkle the herbal mixture on the tab. Waft the smoke over and around your body with the healing cloth you prepared, pushing the smoke (negativity) down and into the ground. Repeat this action until you feel cleansed and peaceful.

Meditate for fifteen minutes on the meaning of rain and healing in the life of a spiritual person. Draw your special rain sigil in your journal. Allow the candle to burn completely until it is extinguished by the water in the cauldron. Bury the candle end off your property. You can either burn your healing cloth or carry it with you, filled with healing herbs, until you are fully healed, and then burn it. You can also cut the cloth into small pieces to burn in a small cauldron. If you absolutely cannot burn it, shred the cloth and distribute it off the property in various trash bins. Now that you have experienced using cloth and sacred smoke as a cleansing vehicle in ritual, you may wish to embroider a special cloth that can be washed and hung out to dry after each use. You can also refrigerate the remaining water in your special bottle (shelf life is about two weeks). This water can be used to asperge sacred space, in healing work, dotting on petitions, etc. Dispose of the water that was in the cauldron off your property, preferably at a crossroads. Do not drink.

Contemplate, in your journal, how you are continuing to build your spell of personal transformation. Speak not of what you are doing. Silence, as in a garden of perfection, will whisper great power in your ear.

Before you drift off to sleep, close this evening by saying:

> *Peace with the gods*
> *Peace with nature*
> *Peace within.*
> *It always works.*
> *Always a blessing.*

Remember to smile!

Sixth Night

My personal journey is a worthwhile contribution to the world within and around me. I always find riches and treasures wherever I travel. The stability I desire is already a part of me. I see the truth of joy in all things.

Your affirmation for today: (see above)

Your symbol for today: mountain

Begin your day: The mountain represents journeys that are worthwhile; of treasure hidden beneath the surface, teaching us to look deeper into any situation; of learning not to take people, situations, or things at face value; of burying good habits deep inside of us for activation at will; and of protective, long-lasting life and stability. If you live near a mountain, begin in the morning by reading the affirmation for the day while viewing the mountain. If you don't live near such a land form, you may wish to find a picture of a beautiful mountain on which to gaze, or you can look to the horizon for the highest point. Even if you live in a city and can't see a mountain, you will most likely see a structure built of stone. Speak to the mountain as if it is an honored ancestor, teacher, or friend. Today's segment concentrates on mountain energy, associating this energy with the stability and gifts of Spirit. Close your eyes, quiet your mind, smile, and allow Spirit to fully enter your body. Then repeat the word *mountain* softly, conjuring your vision of the mountain in your mind. Open your eyes, and repeat the affirmation at least three times. Remember to smile as you finish! Throughout the day, repeat the affirmation as many times as you like. Begin and end with a smile. Write down in a small notebook (or your HedgeWitch journal) anything unusual about this day and events, people, or places that carry a strong mountain association. In this way, you will be prepared to perform the sixth night Rite of the Mountain. If you can enjoy a sunset over a mountain today, please do so. Be sure to whisper a special request to mountain energy as the sun slips under the horizon and the shadows come out to play.

To do today: You will need to collect at least fifteen to twenty stones the size of your palm, and two cups of either potting soil, dirt from a mountain, or one pound of ground coffee. Contemplate the path you are on and what changes you may wish to make. Remember to think and write in the universal primordial language, as you learned in the beginning of this book. Clean out at least one closet or dresser drawer, or a whole room if you can!

Today I will release... anything broken and unstable in my house. I will call the junk man if I have to, or bag up this stuff for the next trash day, or make an effort to find someone who may need it for parts. I will make sure these items leave my house today, even if I have to set them outside until the scheduled pickup. I will replace these with quality items at my convenience if I need to.

Weekly planner: If you are spending a week on this rite, why not use your talents to create an object that a loved one will treasure? From knitting a scarf to building a cabinet, the choice is up to you! At the end of the week, cleanse and bless the item, and give it to the intended. In giving our talents, we receive fulfillment.

Herbs for today: dried sage, frankincense, sandalwood (chips or powder, preferably white), or plants collected by yourself from a local mountain where you have permission to do so (a few leaves will do)

Supplies for tonight: above-listed herbs, one purple candle, candle holder, water from the special bottle empowered in last night's rite, one nine-inch-long, thin dowel rod, two small pieces of white parchment (on one piece of parchment, write something good that you would like to bury within yourself), pen, tape, fifteen to twenty palm-sized stones, a half-cup of ground coffee, sandalwood incense (or burn some of the sandalwood powder or chips on an incense charcoal tab), one conjuring bag (white cotton or color of your choice)

Rite of the Mountain

Light incense. On a purple candle, inscribe the word *mountain* with a pin, nail, or clay-inscribing tool. Place the candle in safe holder, and light. Intone the following mountain charm:

> *Herbal magick, speak to me*
> *Of mountain's sacred journey*
> *Of strength and will along the way*
> *Of choosing carefully what I say.*
> *Treasures lie inside myself*
> *Tonight I grasp my own true wealth*
> *And give to earth that magick seed*
> *To grow and thrive deep in me. Thank you!*

Mix coffee, sage, frankincense, and sandalwood, and "charm" it by using the following incantation:

> *Sacred Spirit, light the way*
> *Bless my work with herbs this day!*
> *Air bestowing…*
> *Sunlight glowing…*
> *Droplets flowing…*

Earth for sowing…

Moonlight nourish garden growing

Hand of joy and heart of knowing

Leafy vines and sweetened fruit

Cast this pattern of pursuit!

HedgeWitch power I invoke

Heaven's prayers like sacred smoke

Clear the way to manifest

That desire which I think best!

Empty the herbal mix in the cotton bag. Insert the paper with the quality you wish to nurture and grow within yourself in the bag, along with a lock of your hair. Tie the bag shut. Place it on the north edge of your altar. Cover the bag by stacking the stones over it. As you place each stone, either repeat the above mountain charm (the first incantation you spoke this evening) or repeat today's affirmations, whichever applies best to you. Then say: "As surely as I have placed these rocks, so will my desire manifest. Thank you! It always works. Always a blessing." Smile.

Sprinkle the stones with a bit of the water you prepared yesterday. Pass the incense smoke over the stones. Meditate for fifteen minutes on the meaning of a mountain in the life of a spiritual person. Draw your mountain sigil on the other piece of paper, and put it underneath the top stone of the pile. Copy the sigil in your journal. Allow the candle to burn completely. The following day, you may be filled with a new sense of purpose. On the night of your final ceremony, you will uncover what you wish to grow inside of yourself.

Before you drift off to sleep, close this evening by saying:

Peace with the gods

Peace with nature

Peace within.

It always works.

Always a blessing.

Remember to smile!

Seventh Night

I walk in perfect balance. I have the power within to accomplish anything! I can have anything I desire!

Your affirmation for today: (see above)

Your symbol for today: lightning

Lightning results when the negatively charged bottom of a cloud reacts to the build-up of positive charges on the earth. When the negative charge is within 150 feet of the positive charge, a stepping-stone phenomenon occurs with the two charges meeting each other, which results in lightning. The energy of one bolt can power a light bulb for three months. Lightning strikes the earth 100 times per second every day. It teaches us the amazing power in perfect balance. There are three kinds of lightning—ball, cloud, and spider. Research these for a little (pause) *enlightenment* on energy.

Begin your day: Begin in the morning by reading the affirmation and the focus for the day. Today's segment concentrates on lightning, associating this energy with that of the perfect balance required to produce a surge of energy that can power your magickal work. Close your eyes, quiet your mind, smile, and allow Spirit to fully enter your body. Then repeat the word *lightning* softly, conjuring your vision of lightning in your mind. Open your eyes, and repeat the affirmation at least three times. Remember to smile as you finish! Throughout the day, repeat the affirmation as many times as you like. Begin and end with a smile. Write down in a small notebook (or your HedgeWitch journal) anything unusual about this day and events, people, or places that carry a strong lightning association. In this way, you will be prepared to perform the seventh night Rite of Lightning.

To do today: Research the different forms of lightning, and contemplate how each could be used metaphorically in your life. Jot notes in your journal on how you might use the power of lightning in your future. Be sure to entitle this entry AS ABOVE, SO BELOW.

Today I will release . . . all my old clothing that is torn, no longer fits me, or doesn't suit the style I have envisioned for myself. At the same time, I would consider, if my budget was unlimited, what my dream wardrobe would be.

Weekly planner: If you are spending a week on this rite, consider creating and decorating your HedgeWitch magickal robe or garments chosen specifically to work HedgeWitchery. If a robe is too much, think of decorating an apron, magickal carry bag, etc. (Read about magickal stitchery in Section 4 for further information.)

Herbs for today: Lightning is often associated with fire, because it can create a burst of flame when it hits an object. Ash and walnut trees are believed to attract lightning. If you can obtain the bark, leaves, nuts, or a branch of such a tree, add this to your ritual this evening. Walnuts can be purchased at your local grocery store, or you can take a trip into the woods to find either tree, should you live in an area where they are bountiful. Better to take a limb off the ground; however, you can take from the tree as long as you do it with honor and permission and leave a gift in return. For this rite, you need only a very small piece that will fit in the center of a plate.

Supplies for tonight: one white candle, above-listed herbs, a picture of lightning that you can write on, pen, one white plate, one black plate, today's affirmation written on a notecard, along with your initials and a lock of your hair

Rite of Lightning

On the white candle, inscribe the word *lightning* or draw a lightning bolt with a pin, nail, or clay-inscribing tool. Place the candle in a safe holder. Put your magick key beside the candle. Put your representation of ash or walnut in the center of the black plate. On the back of your affirmation card, indicate an area of your life where you would like to be empowered. For example: "I want to empower my creative abilities to the best of my advantage," "I want happiness," "I want to work in a peaceful atmosphere that inspires me," "I want good health every day in every way," or "I want the body weight that is perfect for me and my good health." Put this card on top of your herbs along with a lock of your hair. Cover the black plate with the white one. Place the candle holder on top of the plate. Light the candle. Intone the following charm:

> *Positive and negative*
> *Unite to make the flame*
> *Perfect charge between them*
> *Manifests the change*
> *Sparks of power lie within*
> *Just waiting for the lead*
> *Knowledge is the thunder*
> *Of planting any seed. Thank you!*
> *It always works. Always a blessing.*

Smile. Meditate for fifteen minutes on the meaning of lightning in the life of a spiritual person. Again consider the different types of lightning and how they are scientifically manifested (from your research). Draw your personal representation of lightning in your journal.

Allow the candle to burn completely. Leave the plates with their contents untouched on your altar, as you will be using this symbolism in tomorrow night's rite.

You are now over halfway through your dedication process. Take a few moments to review what you have learned in the past several days. Write down anything you feel is important to this journey. Tomorrow, we invoke the thunder of change!

Before you drift off to sleep, close this evening by saying:

> *Peace with the gods*
> *Peace with nature*
> *Peace within.*
> *It always works.*
> *Always a blessing.*

Remember to smile!

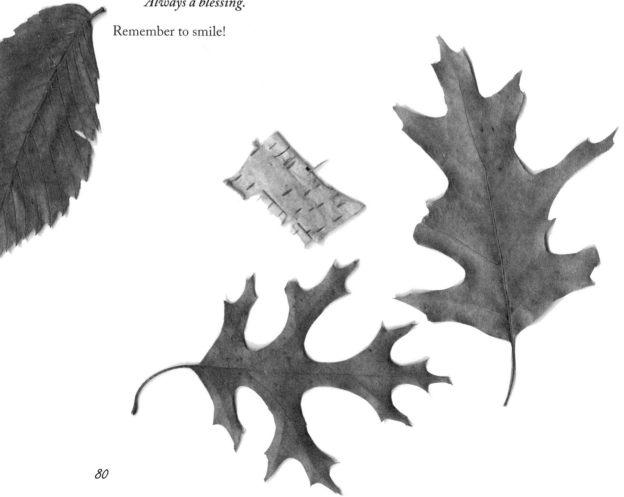

Eighth Night

Through my thoughts and actions, I am in complete control of my destiny. I am the lightning and thunder of my own being.

Your affirmation for today: (see above)

Your symbol for today: thunder (visualizing a thundercloud may be helpful, or the number eight, as explained on the next page)

Begin your day: Begin in the morning by reading the affirmation and the focus for the day. Today's segment concentrates on thunder, associating this energy with that of Spirit. Close your eyes, quiet your mind, smile, and allow Spirit to fully enter your body. Then repeat the word *thunder* softly, conjuring your vision of the partnership of lightning and thunder in your mind. Open your eyes and repeat the affirmation at least three times. Remember to smile as you finish! Throughout the day, repeat the affirmation as many times as you like. Begin and end with a smile. Write down in a small notebook (or your HedgeWitch journal) anything unusual about this day and events, people, or places that carry a strong thunder (or the partnership of lightning and thunder) association. In this way, you will be prepared to perform the eighth night Rite of Thunder.

The rapid expansion of heated air causes the amazing sound of thunder. Thunder results at the same time as lightning; however, because sound travels slower, you don't always hear it right away when lightning strikes, depending on your position in relation to the lightning. Lightning and thunder are indicative of all actions in life. We don't necessarily see the results (thunder) of what we have done (lightning) immediately, depending upon our position (personal vibration). Metaphorically, all of our actions include the duel phenomenon of this incredible partnership of light and sound. Nature shows us, too, that our thoughts are exactly like lightning and thunder. What we think, we subsequently create. The delay of the thunder allows us to adjust our thinking so that our thoughts serve us in the healthiest way possible. The more focused our thoughts, the more powerful our "lightning" and the louder and faster the resulting *boom*!

In the HedgeWitch material, we associate the number eight as a representation of the partnership between lightning and thunder—the totality of manifestation in balance. Eight is the first master number (eleven and twenty-one are subsequent master numbers). Eight represents the mastery of the material world and your place within it—the body in life. Eleven reflects the mastery of self—the personality and how it presents itself both internally and externally—the perfect mind. Twenty-one signifies one's mastery of mind, body, and spirit, creating a perfectly balanced human being—the integration of self with Spirit.

To do today: Find a tape, CD, or sound recording of thunder. You may find a visual DVD helpful. You can even pull the sound of thunder off the Internet from free files if you cannot afford to visit a music store or simply don't have the time to do so.

Today I will release... all old movies or music that I no longer listen to and have no desire to hear or see again. I can take them to a second-hand shop, give them away, or simply dispose of them in the trash.

Weekly planner: If you are spending a week on this rite, compose your own ritual music by lining up specific selections to play during your HedgeWitch dedication. With today's advanced electronics, you may have the skill to seamlessly create several recordings. Take the time to learn HedgeWitch tea-leaf reading, and try it out on a friend (see Section 5). Remember, learning to listen is the key!

Herbs for today: Choose one herb/plant that has a strong and pleasant aroma. Research the magickal associations of this herb/plant before beginning tonight's rite. Have a plentiful supply that you can crush in your hands to release this aroma.

Supplies for tonight: chosen herb, one white candle, last night's combination of black and white plates that has remained undisturbed, one blank three-by-five-inch card, pen, one battery-operated light (this can be a flashlight, a stick-up closet light, etc.—I frequently use one of those small, round closet lights in my own work), your magick bell or chimes

Rite of Thunder

Arrange the white candle, the bowl of aromatic herbs, and your magick key on your altar near the black and white plate project from last night. This particular rite is mostly mental, so relax and take several deep breaths before beginning. Prepare the thunder sound effects you will use shortly. Check the closet light to be sure the batteries are working properly. We will start with the light turned off.

Begin playing this recording. On the white candle, inscribe the word *thunder* with a pin, nail, or clay-inscribing tool, or draw the figure eight symbol. Ring your magick bell in accordance with your magickal number, then ring the bell again, slowly, eight more times.

Light the candle, and intone the following charm eight times:

> *The boom of roiling thunder reminds me of the sound*
> *Of power at my fingertips to bring the energy down!*
> *Drums beat out the chant of magick in the air*
> *Thunder tells of cause/effect—that what I do is there! Thank you!*
> *It always works. Always a blessing!*

Smile. On the notecard, write down eight qualities you would like in your life, or eight items, or a mix of both, or use what you wrote on the back of your affirmation card last night—your choice, because the changes we are making in your life are tailored specifically for you. And, once we produce the lightning of the thought, then the thunder of manifestation will follow. For example, you might write as your eight choices:

Happiness

Good health

Rewarding job

New, black Ford F-150 pickup truck or better

Needlepoint computer software program, professional version or better

Good reputation or better

Healthy body weight that is perfect for me

A fun, safe, and exciting vacation at a tropical island this year or better

As you can see, I mixed up qualities and items—the order doesn't matter. Place the closet light where you can easily reach it. Settle back and close your eyes, keeping your list close by for reference if you need it. Listen to the sound of the thunder. Visualize that each rolling rumble represents the manifestation of one of the items on your list. Smile. See yourself happy with this desire. Repeat the words (for example, "happiness" to match the sound of the thunder). Let this thought go. Immediately reach forward and turn on the light, saying: "Done! Thank you!" Squeeze the herbs in the bowl to release a pleasant aroma. Smile again. Take a deep breath. Turn off the light, and go to the next item on your list. Do this same procedure for all your desires written on the notecard. Ring your magick bell eight times, slowly, allowing each note to fluidly extinguish.

When you are through, leave the light burning for the next twenty-four hours. Allow the candle to burn completely, if you can. Bury the cold candle end and the used herbs on your property. Copy your sigil for thunder in your HedgeWitch notebook. Remove the ash/walnuts from between the plates. Put the leaves/walnuts, the notecard, and the lock of your hair in a small bag. You can carry this with you, or you may wish to burn it outside. Be sure to say thank you. You might wish to wash the plates to use them again. Finally, before you go to bed, draw an imaginary figure eight in the air over your altar to seal your work. Softly say thank you, and smile.

Before you drift off to sleep, close this evening by saying:

> *Peace with the gods*
> *Peace with nature*
> *Peace within.*
> *It always works.*
> *Always a blessing.*

Remember to smile!

Ninth Night

I am connected to Spirit every day in every way. In every day and in every way, I move in harmony with Spirit. I easily integrate Spirit in my life.

Your affirmation for today: (see above)

Your symbol for today: a piece of jewelry

Begin your day: Begin in the morning by reading the affirmation for the day. Today's segment concentrates on metal, focusing on the flow between yourself and Spirit. Close your eyes, quiet your mind, smile, and allow Spirit to fully enter your body. Then repeat the word *metal* softly, conjuring your vision of metal in your mind. Open your eyes and repeat the affirmation at least three times. Remember to smile as you finish! Throughout the day, repeat the affirmation as many times as you like. Begin and end with a smile. Write down in a small notebook (or your HedgeWitch journal) anything unusual about this day and events, people, or places that carry a strong metal association. In this way, you will be prepared to perform the ninth night Rite of Metal.

Metal represents the solidification of any project and in many cases is a conduit and booster in working with flowing energy. On this night you will dedicate a favorite piece of jewelry that represents your study of the HedgeWitch craft. Your choice is entirely up to you—a ring, bracelet, necklace, pin, or even key ring if you often carry your keys on your person. The only requirement is that it must be made of metal; the type of metal chosen is entirely up to you—gold for success and good fortune; silver for intuitive ability; sterling silver (which is made of copper and silver) for flow as well as intuitiveness; etc. The cost of the piece is immaterial.

To do today: Choose your piece of jewelry that most suits your needs.

Today I will release...all old and tarnished jewelry that is of no value. If I have jewelry that I wish to keep, I will clean them myself or make arrangements to have them cleaned. I will also remove any and all broken tools or bent, broken, or tarnished silverware and cutlery that is of no value.

Weekly planner: If you are spending a week on this rite, spend six days collecting photos that represent the essence of Spirit to you. Design a collage that can be hung on your wall or used as a divider in a magickal notebook. This collage will become a marvelous meditation vehicle for you in the future, as well as a signature of what you are thinking right here, right now. In a year or six months, design a new Spirit collage. Contemplate how you have grown!

Herbs for today: lavender, rose, eyebright, frankincense resin

Supplies for tonight: above-listed herbs, spring water, incense of your choice, your chosen jewelry, one white candle, a favored magickal oil, mortar and pestle, container to hold water, two white candles, cleansed pieces of copper (pieces of solid copper are best, but pennies will do)

Section 2

Rite of Metal

Once upon a time, magickal symbolism in jewelry, such as the pentacle, the Star of David, or even the Helm of Awe could render the wearer a death sentence. Although we no longer live in the Dark Ages, the tradition of empowering gemstone jewelry rather than magickal symbols has persisted. The empowerment process given here is appropriate for magickal symbol jewelry as well as those gemstone treasures from the Earth Mother.

Note: If jewelry is second-hand, add lemon juice to the holy water. Rub your chosen piece with a bit of the herbal cleansing mix you created on the first night, and place the jewelry item beside your "metal" candle representation.

You will need this recipe for tonight's rite:

Holy Water & Herb Potpourri
for Charming Jewelry

⅛ teaspoon lavender herb

⅛ teaspoon rose petals

⅛ teaspoon eyebright herb

Small amount of frankincense resin, ground

Hold your hands over all items. Take several deep, cleansing breaths. Say the following conjuration, in your mind seeing all items aglow with white light:

One heart, one mind, one magick

One truth, one body, one energy

In perfect joy and perfect peace

In perfect love and perfect trust

I open the gateway of transformation

And call forth the power of Spirit

Bringing the serenity of divine order

To these gifts of the earth

As above, so below.

Done. Thank you!

With mortar and pestle, grind herbs together to a powder (or leave whole). Mix with ground frankincense (you don't need much). Place the bowl on the altar or sacred area along with the candle, incense, magickal oil, your chime or bell, magickal key, and the jewelry to be empowered. Dot the candle lightly with magickal oil (not too much) or "dress" in the enchanted manner you are most comfortable with. Add a bit of the herbal mix to the holy water bottle, along with three drops of your favorite magickal oil.

Light the incense. Pass incense over the herbs, holy water, candle, and jewelry. Say:

Sacred smoke, I do invoke one heart, one mind, one magick.

I cleanse and consecrate thee,

Filling thee with the universal power of _____

(you choose—harmony, love, passion, etc.)

Light the candle. Pass the flame over the incense, holy water, jewelry, and herbs. Say:

Sacred flame in holy name

One heart, one mind, one magick.

I cleanse and consecrate thee,

Filling thee with the universal power of _____

(you choose—harmony, love, passion, etc.)

Sprinkle jewelry with a bit of the holy water, saying:

> *Liquid light, sacred sight*
>
> *One heart, one mind, one magick*
>
> *I cleanse and consecrate thee,*
>
> *Filling thee with the universal power of* _____
>
> **(you choose—harmony, love, passion, etc.)**

Sprinkle jewelry with a bit of the magickal herb mixture, saying:

> *Enchanted flower, lend your power*
>
> *One heart, one mind, one magick*
>
> *I cleanse and consecrate thee,*
>
> *Filling thee with the universal essence of* _____
>
> **(you choose—harmony, love, passion, etc.)**

Take several deep, cleansing breaths, and relax. Hold your hands over the jewelry, and speak the following incantation nine times:

> *The power of one*
>
> *The unity of two*
>
> *The trinity of three*
>
> *The stability of four*
>
> *The change of five*
>
> *Six—center, earth to sky*
>
> *The success of seven*
>
> *The mastery of eight*
>
> *The wish of nine*
>
> *Ten—the infinite blend*
>
> *Spirit here will never end.*

As you chant, see the purpose going into the piece as if that energy is living light permeating and undulating around the jewelry. Dot the piece with your magickal oil to seal your working, then lay your hands directly on the piece, close your eyes, and say: "Done! Thank you!" Smile. Ring your magickal bell matching your magickal number. Draw a figure eight in the air over the jewelry. Snuff the candle, and remove this candle from the altar. The jewelry is now ready for tonight's rite.

On a fresh white candle, inscribe the word *metal* with a pin, nail, or clay-inscribing tool. Scatter cleansed pieces of copper around this candle to increase the power of the working. Place the candle in a safe holder, and light. Intone the following charm, holding your hands over the jewelry:

> *Gifts of metal, speak to me*
> *Of flowing grace in energy*
> *Of bringing thoughts to vibrant form*
> *Of symbols cast that can adorn*
> *Yet carry secrets in their mist*
> *Of how to move and make the shift.*
> *It always works. Always a blessing!*

Remember to smile! This charm is a riddle, and the word *mist* is spelled correctly. It may take awhile until the secret is revealed to you. Be patient. The answer will come.

Meditate for fifteen minutes on the meaning of metal in the life of a spiritual person. Allow the candle to burn completely. Draw your own symbol that represents metal in your Hedge-Witch journal. Wear your chosen jewelry until the complete dedication is over. At that time, you may wish to re-cleanse it or continue to wear the piece and re-empower every thirty days for maximum benefits. When not in use, place the jewelry in a black bag to protect it from harmful energies. Give the remainder of the herbs and holy water to the spirits out-of-doors, or create a conjuring bag of the herbs along with other ingredients, such as a lock of your hair and a petition to carry with you, that match the purpose of the original empowerment.

Before you drift off to sleep, close this evening by saying:

> *Peace with the gods*
> *Peace with nature*
> *Peace within.*
> *It always works.*
> *Always a blessing.*

Remember to smile!

Tenth Night

*In gratitude I find accomplishment.
In accomplishment I find gratitude.*

Your affirmation for today: (see above)

Your symbol for today: stone

Begin your day: Begin in the morning by reading the affirmation and the focus for the day. Today's segment concentrates on stone, associating the energy of accomplishment with that of Spirit. Close your eyes, quiet your mind, smile, and allow Spirit to fully enter your body. Then repeat the word *stone* softly, conjuring your vision of stone in your mind.

Open your eyes, and repeat the affirmation at least three times. Remember to smile as you finish! Throughout the day, repeat the affirmation as many times as you like. Begin and end with a smile. Write down in a small notebook (or your HedgeWitch journal) anything unusual about this day and events, people, or places that carry a strong stone association. In this way, you will be prepared to perform the tenth night Rite of Stone.

To do today: Choose thirteen gemstones or small pebbles from your property or a local stream. If you have a garden, you may wish to arrange thirteen stepping stones in a prominent area to represent your HedgeWitch journey.

Today I will release . . . anything that reminds me of a failure I am holding on to. As I clear out my living space, I will keep repeating: "I am making room for success!" I will get rid of broken or unappealing statues, knickknacks, trinkets, and baubles that are cluttering up my personal space. I will make arrangements to fix cracks in walls.

Weekly planner: If you are spending a week on this rite, build or create something out of stone for sacred work. This could be pouring and decorating a stepping stone for your garden, making an outdoor stone altar, working with mosaics that also incorporate gemstones, or even stringing gemstone jewelry. You may wish to make a set of HedgeWitch prayer beads (see Section 5).

Herbs for today: lavender, rose, eyebright, myrrh resin

Supplies for tonight: incense, white candle, the candle you have chosen for your final dedication ritual, thirteen gems or small pebbles, the above-listed herbs, freshly prepared in the same way you blended the herbs for the ninth night rite

Stone represents your steps (stepping stones) and your accomplishments along the way in your personal journey of transformation, and your ability to be grateful for what you have accomplished and received. Gemstones carry their own inherent beauty and power and can heighten our herbal magickal abilities. Also, stones—whether gems or the stones in your garden—come in many shapes and sizes. The shape of an item also has significance in the practice of HedgeWitchery, as all shapes carry a mathematical vibration (their volume, shape, and size) as well as a correspondence associated with the type of stone (granite, quartz, lapis lazuli, etc.). We can also create shapes and patterns by arranging small stones on the altar top. Here is an easy-to-follow magickal list to use in tonight's rite as well as in future practices.

Note: The list is a combination of Eastern and Western cultural beliefs.

Square—Earth Element (Roots/Stability)

Colors: Tan, beige, caramel, toffee, orange, gold

Directions: Northeast and southwest

Purposes: Education, learning, luck, romance, love, mother's luck, stability, foundation

Circle—Metal Element

Colors: White, silver, gold

Directions: West and northwest

Purposes: Family luck, father's luck, guides and mentors, assistance, protection

Triangle/Chevron—Fire Element

Colors: Red, purple

Direction: South

Purposes: Success and recognition, action and movement, target, passion, the spark of creativity

Rectangle—Earth Element (Growth/Flowering)

Colors: Green, brown, sienna, red ochre, bronze

Directions: East and southeast

Purposes: Good health, growth, prosperity (primary ruler of paper magick)

Wave—Water Element

Colors: Blue, lavender, black

Direction: North

Purposes: Career advancement, life work, emotions, movement
through flow (secondary ruler of paper magick)

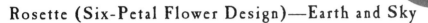

Rosette (Six-Petal Flower Design)—Earth and Sky

Colors: Green, blue, gold (plants, sky, sun)

Direction: Center

Purposes: Balance, harmony of heaven and earth, spiritual
growth

Stars—Fire and Ice

Colors: Gold, white

Direction: Heaven

Purposes: Protection, good luck, good fortune (the number of
points make the stars more significant)

Hearts—Spirit Element

Colors: Red, pink

Direction: None (as love infuses everything)

Purposes: Love, compassion, humility, healing

Crescent/Archway—Combination
of Spirit, Metal, and Water

Colors: White, silver, gold, blue

Directions: West or north and northwest

Purposes: Moon magick, timing, protection, women, children,
creativity, luck from heaven

Rite of Stone

Arrange your thirteen chosen gemstones around your dedication candle. You will not light your dedication candle tonight; instead, we are preparing your altar for the final ceremony. Put your magick key beside your dedication candle. Light the incense and pass it over all the items on your altar.

On a white candle (not the dedication candle), inscribe the word *stone* with a pin, nail, or clay-inscribing tool. Place the candle in safe holder, and light. Sprinkle your herb mixture around the base of the candle. Intone the following charm, holding your hands over the stones:

> *Herbal magick, speak to me*
> *Of gems' and stones' ability*
> *In dark of night or sun's bright day*
> *To help me in my witching way!*

Pick up one stone and say aloud three times something that you are grateful for. Then say, "Thank you, it works, always a blessing," and smile. Do this with the remaining twelve stones, indicating something different you are grateful for with each successive stone. Meditate for fifteen minutes on the meaning of stone in the life of a spiritual person. Using the stones or gems, create a shape that signifies accomplishment to you. This will be your magickal stone shape. Be sure to draw this image in your HedgeWitch journal. Allow the candle to burn completely. Leave your gemstones in the shape you chose near your dedication candle until your final ceremony night. Take an extra fifteen minutes this night to contemplate the changes you have experienced and what you truly desire in the transformation of the self. And most of all, never forget to be grateful!

Before you drift off to sleep, close this evening by saying:

> *Peace with the gods*
> *Peace with nature*
> *Peace within.*
> *It always works.*
> *Always a blessing.*

Remember to smile!

Eleventh Night

Just like the sun and the moon, I bring light to the world. I shine in everything I say and do. Just like the power of the sun, I attract all good things into my world and share this light of good fortune with others.

Your affirmation for today: (see above)

Your symbols for today: sun and moon

Begin your day: Begin in the morning by reading the affirmation for the day. Today's segment concentrates on heavenly energies, specifically that of the sun and moon, but all planets and stars can be a part of your contemplation, especially if you currently study astrology. If you can catch both the sunrise and the sunset today, all the better!

Close your eyes, quiet your mind, smile, and allow the peace of Spirit to fully enter your body. Then repeat the words *sun and moon* softly, conjuring your vision of these glowing orbs in your mind. Open your eyes, and repeat the affirmations for today at least three times. Remember to smile as you finish! Throughout the day, repeat the affirmations as many times as you like. Begin and end with a smile. Write down in a small notebook (or your HedgeWitch journal) anything unusual about this day and events, people, or places that carry a strong sun and moon association. In this way, you will be prepared to perform the eleventh night Rite of Celestial Power.

In HedgeWitchery, the sun, or Greater Light, stands for your will, and the moon, or Lesser Light, equates to the second sight of Spirit. In primordial speech, the sun translates to "I want," and the moon is your connection to Spirit, which is communicated through your emotions. If you feel good, then you are in harmony with Spirit. If you are unhappy, angry, or sad, this is your signal that communication is blocked, and the manifestations you desire in your life will either take a very long time or not occur at all.

Sun/moon is an example of partnership as well as duality. There is always a "have" and a "have not" to any situation. Be sure today you are not concentrating on the "have not" while you are trying to think of the "have." Go over primal language again, and double-check your thoughts and visualizations today. Be sure you are not concentrating on "lack" in your life. Instead, fill this void with the light of promise by your thoughts and actions focused on the attractive power of the universe.

To do today: The number eleven stands for the empowerment of the mind. It is through the perfection of our thoughts and our connection to Spirit that any change or manifestation can take place. Today you are to find a calendar that marks the new and full moons for the next thirteen months. You can find this information in the wide selection of Llewellyn calendars and datebooks, on the Net by visiting the Farmers' Almanac website, or by picking up an almanac at your favorite bookstore. Garden shops often carry calendars and almanacs as well. Write the dates and times of the new and full moons in your HedgeWitch journal. Beside each moon, write what astrological sign the moon is in on that day. Next, using primal language, write a goal beside each new and full moon. Use the information below to help you determine what type of goal fits each type of moon. I've also provided the quarter information, as you may find this helpful in the future as well.

New Moon and First Quarter: Beginnings

Second Quarter: Building, growth

Full Moon: Harvest and additional power

Third Quarter: Adding finishing touches, closing

Fourth Quarter: Complete endings, review (strongest the day before new)

If you understand astrology, you may wish to match your intended goal to the energy of the astrological sign. Remember not to focus on "lack"—only on attraction. Next, research the lunar and solar eclipses for the coming year. Write down where the moon and the sun will be (in terms of astrological sign) on those days. Write a goal for each that matches the astrological sign energies present at those times.

Today I will release… trapped energy. Clear out and illuminate a dark corner in your house. Go through your kitchen cabinets, and throw out old cans, boxes, bottles, and jars of food. Wipe down the refrigerator, microwave, and other electrical appliances.

Weekly planner: If you are spending a week on this rite, learn to make the magickal berry ink and quill pen in Section 5. Use this ink in your magickal petitions and to write your goals for the coming year.

Herbs for today: Choose any seven herbs or resins from the list provided below. Combine your choices to make your own herbal power mix; a blend that can be used in a variety of future workings. This will become your signature blend. You can also substitute scents rather than the herb. For example, you might choose a combination of sandalwood, myrrh, cedar, clove, copal, and orange rind mixed with a few drops of gardenia or jasmine essential oil or fragrance. This particular blend is suited to use as a potpourri or burned loose on an incense charcoal tab. Both lists were chosen for what you may readily be able to obtain from the grocer, florist, your own garden or property, or from your favorite magickal store. There are many more herbs with sun and moon correspondences. For a fuller selection of what you might choose, see *Cunningham's Encyclopedia of Magical Herbs*.

Sun herbs: allspice, ash, basil, bay, carnation, cedar, celandine, chili pepper, cinnamon, clove, copal, dill, dragon's blood, fennel, ginger, hyssop, juniper, lime, marigold, nutmeg, orange, pepper, peppermint, pine, rosemary, rue, sunflower, walnut, woodruff

Moon herbs: coconut, eucalyptus, gardenia, jasmine, lemon balm, mallow, myrrh, poppy, sandalwood, willow

Supplies for tonight: your signature herbal blend, one gold and one silver candle, the calendar with your goals, your magickal bell or chimes, incense of your choice

Rite of Celestial Power

Place your calendar on the center of the altar, along with your magickal key. Ring your bell or chimes eleven times. If you can, go outside and light your favorite incense. If you are confined inside, try to position yourself near a window with a good view of the heavens. Stand looking up at the heavens, and say:

> *Celestial magick, speak to me*
> *Of sun and moon and heaven's sea*
> *Of signs and lights of starry sky*
> *That shine within the HedgeWitch eye*
> *That flow around the HedgeWitch heart*
> *To focus into HedgeWitch art.*
> *Thank you!*

You may wish to bless your herbal mixture with the following charm:

Sacred Spirit, light the way

Bless my work with herbs this day!

Air bestowing…

Sunlight glowing…

Droplets flowing…

Field of sowing…

Moonlight nourish garden growing!

Hand of joy and heart of knowing…

Leafy vines and sweetened fruit…

Cast the pattern of pursuit!

HedgeWitch power I invoke

Heaven's prayers like sacred smoke

Clear the way to manifest

That desire which I think best. Thank you!

Place the herbs on top of the calendar. Write the word *sun* on the gold candle. Write the word *moon* on the silver candle. Ring your magick bell to match your personal power number. This is to help you focus. Light the sun candle, and say:

I focus my will.

Light the moon candle, and say:

I empower my will with my emotions.

Ring the bell eleven times to match the mind-mastery significance of the number eleven.

Sit quietly and stare at the dual burning candles. When you are ready, intone the Hedge-Witch incantation of power, focusing your mind on those thirteen goals you wrote in the calendar. Once you have focused on the goals in this ceremony, you will let them go. You won't look at this calendar for a full year, until the anniversary of this night.

Incantation of Power

Power of the east, winds of sacred birth

Gather all your forces and bring desire to earth.

Power of the south, winds of hot creation

Separate the earth by fire, refine this incantation.

Power of the west, winds of down below

Bubble up to meet the sky and make the pattern so!

Power of the north, winds of sacred treasure

Solidify my own desire and formulate the measure!

Power of the spirit, winds of dusk and dawn

Align the planets in their places, words convey the song!

Power of myself, the winds of my demand

Emotions seek to formulate and bring about my plan!

Power of the still point, from which I manifest

I have the key to make it be, and Spirit does the rest!

Ring the bell eleven times, and then say: "Thank you! That was easy! It always works. Always a blessing!"

Meditate for five minutes on the meaning of the sun and moon in your magickal life and how your thoughts and actions bring light to the world. How have you changed in the past eleven days? How do you wish to continue to shine your light into the world? In your own life? In the lives of your family members and friends? Draw your secret symbol for the celestial power of the sun and moon in your HedgeWitch journal. Allow the sun and moon candles to burn completely if you can. Wrap the calendar and herbs together in a brown paper bag. Seal securely with tape and write TO BE OPENED ON: and next year's date. Put in a safe place.

Before you drift off to sleep, close this evening by saying:

Peace with the gods

Peace with nature

Peace within.

It always works. Always a blessing.

Remember to smile!

Twelfth Night

Through personal education, I open the door to knowledge. Every day I will seek to learn something new and beneficial to my well-being.

Your affirmation for today: (see above)

Your symbol for today: a tree or grove of trees

Begin your day: Begin in the morning by reading the affirmation for the day. Today's segment concentrates on wood, associating this energy with that of the longevity of Spirit and the protection it offers to plants and animals. Close your eyes, quiet your mind, smile, and allow Spirit to fully enter your body. Then repeat the word *wood* softly, conjuring your vision of wood in your mind. Open your eyes and repeat the affirmation at least three times. Remember to smile as you finish! Throughout the day, repeat the affirmation as many times as you like. Begin and end with a smile. Write down in a small notebook (or your HedgeWitch journal) anything unusual about this day and events, people, or places that carry a strong wood association. In this way, you will be prepared to perform the twelfth night Rite of the Enchanted Woods.

To do today: If you could learn anything, without regard to budget, what would it be? Whether it is learning to fly a plane or knit, there are several things you've always said you'd like to learn but just don't seem to have the time. Rather than making excuses, why not make time right now? Even if you can't start today, you can look into avenues to bring you the education you desire. By the end of the day, you should have chosen at least one thing to learn and have taken the first steps to pursue that knowledge. Various cultures over the centuries have associated good fortune and personal luck with animal symbology. Today, you will look for your personal HedgeWitch lucky animal symbol. Here you will find a quick, cross-cultural list of lucky animals and their traditional colors that may help you in your search.

Bats: red—good fortune and prosperity; black—occult learning

Butterflies: purple and blue—freedom, beauty, creativity, healing; red, yellow, and orange—prosperity and opportunity

Bears: good health, long life

Birds, Flying: good luck and opportunity; red—action; blue—healing; black—information

Black Tortoise: support, longevity, protection

Green Tortoise: prosperity and spirit

Cat: independence and magick; physics

Cranes: white—longevity

Crimson Phoenix: good fortune, hearth and home; rebirth

Crows/Ravens: thought, memory, and messages

Deer: longevity, the male aspect of God (no traditional color)

Dog: loyalty, family, heightened senses (no traditional color)

Dragon: general good fortune, harnessing the world (In the Asian cultures, different colors relate to various magickal properties.)

Dragonfly: green—fast cash; blue—visions and dreams

Ducks: matrimonial bliss (always seen in pairs; no traditional color)

Elephant: silver—good fortune, good health, and career luck

Fish: gold—career luck, especially if depicted in pairs

Frogs: green—good luck and prosperity

Geese: long, happy marriage (especially in pairs); good fortune and the spirit of adventure (no color)

Hippopotamus: silver—protection for women and children

Horse: gold—running or war horse, courage, speed, and success; white—great wealth

Hummingbird: green or gold—fast cash, attraction

Lions: gold or red—protection against robbery or theft

Lizard: green—laughter and joy

Monkey: gold—promotion

Dogs
have no traditional color!!!

* find out what this <u>means</u>

Ox, Bull, Cow: gold or red—wealth and wishes

Snake: gold—wisdom

Toad: red—supreme good fortune, especially if the toad has only three legs

Wolf: silver—family luck and harmony, education

✶ ✶ ✶

Today I will release . . . any and all fears I have about my future.

Weekly planner: If you are spending a week on this rite, spend your time making potpourri or magickal sachets, using barks, leaves, flowers, and essential oils, or decorate a wreath that matches the magickal correspondences of what you desire to bring into your life. Hang this wreath on your front door as a welcome signal to those energies. Remember: accepting your desire is just as important as formulating it!

Herbs for today: any magickal wood or bark

Supplies for tonight: none

Rite of the Enchanted Woods

There are two ways in which you can perform this rite. You can visit the physical woods (with a friend) in a safe area sometime throughout the day or afternoon, or you can use the magickal wood chosen under the "herbs for today" category and creatively visualize, in quiet surroundings, a trip to the woods while holding that representation. Your goal is to reach a magickal clearing and find a gift that is just for you. This gift will be a quality, such as patience, good humor, etc. Standing in the clearing (either physically or in your mind), you will ask your ancestors to help you pull this shining quality into yourself.

Begin with the general HedgeWitch conjuration, which you can use for all types of magickal work in the future:

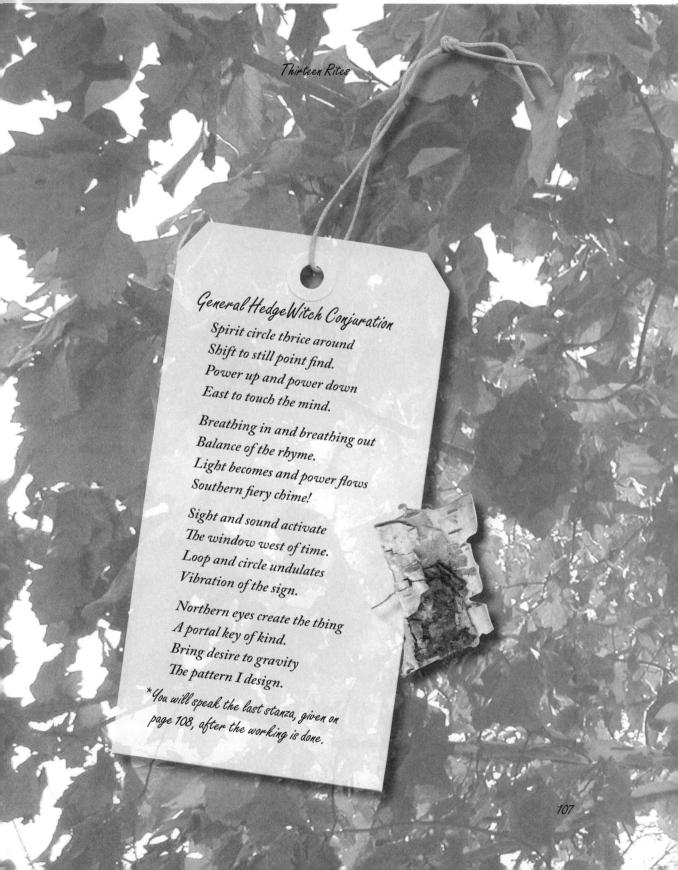

General HedgeWitch Conjuration

Spirit circle thrice around
Shift to still point find.
Power up and power down
East to touch the mind.

Breathing in and breathing out
Balance of the rhyme.
Light becomes and power flows
Southern fiery chime!

Sight and sound activate
The window west of time.
Loop and circle undulates
Vibration of the sign.

Northern eyes create the thing
A portal key of kind.
Bring desire to gravity
The pattern I design.

*You will speak the last stanza, given on page 108, after the working is done.

To bring your ancestors to you, with your eyes closed, turn around slowly with your left hand raised. Where you feel pressure on the palm of your raised left hand is the gateway to your ancestors that, from this time forth, will be known only to you. Stop. Take a deep breath, ask for their assistance, and then visualize the quality you desire. Pull this quality into yourself, breathing deeply and smiling. In no way should you experience any negative feelings. If you do, then you haven't asked for what you really need or you really do not desire this change. Choose a different quality and try again. When you are finished, be sure to thank your ancestors and the universe for the gifts you have received. Don't forget to smile!

Repeat the last stanza of the general HedgeWitch conjuration:

> *As above and so below*
> *This working now is sealed*
> *O spell, be secret, safe, and sound*
> *Fruition in its field!*
> *It always works. Always a blessing.*

Remember to smile! In your HedgeWitch journal, inscribe your secret sigil for wood, or learning new things. Add to this your choice of a personal good luck animal. On a separate page, draw all the symbols you have created for the past twelve days. We will be adding two more—the sigil for the thirteenth night and the sigil for your own personal change, which will be designed the night of your dedication ceremony. This evening, review what each of the previously drawn sigils now means to you.

Here is an example:

> *First Night—Wind—My connection to Spirit*
> *Second Night—Fire—My personal creativity*
> *Third Night—Earth—Richness and abundance of the universe*
> *Fourth Night—Sky—My unlimited opportunity*
> *Fifth Night—Rain—My good health and healing*
> *Sixth Night—Mountain—My stability and treasures within the self*
> *Seventh Night—Lightning—My personal power, confidence, and balance*

Thirteen Rites

Eighth Night—Thunder—My power of thought and action

Ninth Night—Metal—My flow and harmony within Spirit

Tenth Night—Stone—My gratitude

Eleventh Night—Celestial Power—My light within

Twelfth Night—Wood—Knowledge, wisdom, and education

This way, you will have a quick reference to your symbols. Feel free to change the meanings of the symbols to more perfectly match your meditations the past twelve days.

Before you drift off to sleep, close this evening by saying:

Peace with the gods

Peace with nature

Peace within.

It always works.

Always a blessing.

Remember to smile!

Thirteenth Night

By observing in silence, I shape my life. I seek to listen and hear people, art, music, and events that bring peace, happiness, and tranquility into my life.

Your affirmation for today: (see above)

Your symbol for today: Choose a symbol that signifies personal transformation and the combined power of all your sigils to you.

Begin your day: Begin in the morning by reading the affirmation for the day. Today's segment concentrates on silence, associating perfect quiet with the intuitive power of Spirit. Close your eyes, quiet your mind, smile, and allow Spirit to fully enter your body. Then repeat the word *silence* softly, conjuring your vision of perfect peace (the still point) in your mind. Open your eyes, and repeat the affirmation at least three times. Remember to smile as you finish! Throughout the day, repeat the affirmation as many times as you like. Begin and end with a smile. Write down in a small notebook (or your HedgeWitch journal) anything unusual about this day and events, people, or places that carry a strong silence association. In this way, you will be prepared to perform the thirteenth night's Rite of Silence.

To do today: Today I will endeavor to listen rather than speak without thinking. I will make special note of what I am observing. I will find a representation of my personal good luck animal that I chose last night. I will either wear this symbol or carry a picture of it with me.

Today I will release . . . dirt and grime from my living space. If necessary, I will wash the floors, vacuum, and clean windows, especially in the room where I spend the most time and in my ritual area. I will throw out all old bedding and linens that are of no value, torn, or stained. I will throw out all old projects that I know I will never finish. If they are of value, I will give them away or sell them. I will go through all my bathroom cabinets and drawers that hold personal-care items and remove all old or unused products.

Weekly planner: If you are spending a week on this rite, design something permanent to display in your home that speaks of the culmination of your hard work in HedgeWitchery study and transformation. This could be something you have manifested using the five Is; something you have made by hand, such as an altar cloth; something you have refinished, like a stool or altar table, etc. The choice is entirely yours.

Herbs for today: Any cleansing herb or scent: pine, lemon, cedar, mint, orange, lemon verbena, lemon balm, green tea, or a combination that is pleasing to you. During the day, place a mixture of these herbs or scents on top of a picture of yourself positioned in the center of your altar. You can empower these herbs by using the herbal conjuration you used last night, or choose your own words.

Supplies for tonight: Any item you choose to pamper yourself. If we do not feel good about ourselves, then we emotionally inhibit the changes we desire to make in our lives.

Section 2

Rite of Silence

Tonight's ritual is dedicated to pampering yourself, which means you won't be working at your altar. You may visit a gym or a spa, or take a long, luxurious bath followed by a personal hygiene regime. You might decide to have your hair styled in a new way, shave off a beard, or color your hair in a new shade. Visit a nail salon or have fun shopping for new makeup or personal-care products. Choose a daring scent in a perfume or aftershave—something that encourages the new you to blossom!

When you are finished, review your day and make notes in your HedgeWitch journal. Draw a symbol that represents the still point of peace and tranquility in today's entry, as well as on the separate page you started last evening.

Before you drift off to sleep, close this evening by saying:

Peace with the gods

Peace with nature

Peace within.

It always works.

Always a blessing.

Remember to smile!

Rite of Passage

the fourteenth ceremony

The HedgeWitch Dedication Ritual

Ceremony Night

You've worked extremely hard these past thirteen days and nights (or weeks) to make the changes within yourself that you desire. This ceremony is an acknowledgement of your difficult work and of your determination to continue to allow Nature to assist you on your chosen life path. Read over the ceremony carefully. Feel free to change or insert any additional information or practices that you feel will enhance and personalize the ritual, so that it is more meaningful for you.

Tonight's Preparation

The dedication ceremony supplies are listed here so that you can be prepared for your final rite of passage into HedgeWitchery.

Mortar and pestle (for grinding herbs)

HedgeWitch cleansing herbal mix—dried or fresh lavender, rosemary, chamomile, lemongrass, and lemon verbena (this is also used in the first night rite)

Spring water

Incense and incense holder (your choice of scent)

HedgeWitch dedication candle: A special candle of your choice to be used for the final ceremony

Appropriate candle holders

Altar stone on which to do your workings

Four altar candles for the final ceremony: Green, black, gold, and white

A cauldron in which to burn your wish

Your signature herb

Your magick key (real or charm)

Bell or chimes

Other herbs/flowers (fresh or dried) of your choice

Empty bowl (for mixing water and herbs)

Empty bottle to store tonight's power potion—this should be a gold-colored bottle with a good sealing cap, if at all possible

Fresh flowers, if you so desire

Your magick symbols: How you represent these in your ceremony is entirely up to you. I drew mine with indelible black marker on small white stones. Some students drew them on notecards and arranged them near the dedication altar, others embroidered them on their ritual clothing or on an altar cloth. During the ceremony, you will touch each symbol. Some students simply opened their HedgeWitch journal and touched the symbols drawn there.

Chamomile, bergamot, ginger, and rosemary (powdered or crushed—for the power potion)

Morning dew collected from outside (for the power potion) or your favorite magickal oil or perfume

Your HedgeWitch journal

Fourteenth Night

I am always connected to Spirit. Spirit fulfills my every need and my every desire. I know that Spirit lives within me.

Welcome to Your HedgeWitchery Dedication Ceremony!

In this ceremony, we begin with an empty altar (other than the stones you may have left there from the mountain ritual). All supplies should be close at hand for their placement as indicated within the ritual. Right before you begin, write one wish in primal language on a small piece of paper. You will burn this during tonight's ceremony.

Rite of Passage

Ring your bell or chimes to match your personal magick number. Light incense, and place this on the eastern corner of your altar. Mix together the HedgeWitch power potion herbs in a bowl. Add spring water and three drops of morning dew. If you have not collected morning dew, you can use three drops of your favorite magickal oil or perfume. Pour this mixture in your HedgeWitch power potion bottle. Hold your hands over the bowl and repeat the power potion blessing:

Power Potion Blessing

HedgeWitch power I invoke
Heaven's prayers like sacred smoke
Clear the way to manifest
That desire which I think best!
Holy vial of glass and gold
Allow my treasure to unfold
With candle spark and vibrant flame
I conjure that which I dost name!
Sacred vessel, create the field
Pattern rise and thought congeal
Coalesce and make it right
Spirit, lend thy holy light
To conjure this most special brew
Of my desire and morning dew!
Power grows and comes to me
As I will, so mote it be!

HedgeWitch Power Potion Herbs
* chamomile
* bergamot
* ginger
* rosemary

Sprinkle a little of this potion on yourself, saying: "I am cleansed, consecrated, and regenerated in the name of HedgeWitchery!" Once you have cleansed yourself, sprinkle the remaining water on the altar and around the room or area in a clockwise direction. Place any fresh flowers on the altar now. If they will not fit on the altar, place to the right and left of the altar, on the floor, or on their own pedestals.

Stand by your altar with knees slightly bent, feet about two feet apart. Take thirteen slow, even breaths—in through the nose and out through the mouth. Raise your hands like a gentle wave and flip your fingertips to the sky as you inhale, and bring hands down to chest level and push out toward your altar as you exhale. Do not begin the HedgeWitch circle conjuration until you feel steady, secure, and well-balanced—completely comfortable in what you are about to do.

> *"I conjure thee, O HedgeWitch circle"* (put right hand up to the sky and left toward the ground—slowly bring both hands to an imaginary ball in front of you and believe that you have brought the power of the sky and the power of the earth together)

> *"Through charge of earth and sky, I create a leafy hedge of positive energy"* (make the imaginary ball in your hands larger and smaller by moving your hands in and out at least three times, breathing in as you move your hands out and breathing out as you move your hands in)

> *"And manifest a field of unlimited possibilities herein!"* (open your arms as if you are flinging the energy out around you like a protective circle, visualizing the leafy hedge of protection exploding around you in a riot of delightfully colored leaves, flowers, and hedge)

> *"As above, so below! This circle is sealed!"*

Stamp your foot on the ground to seal.
Ring your bell or chimes three times.

HedgeWitch Charge

Rub your dedication candle with HedgeWitch herbal mix—either the mix you learned to make on the first night or your signature herbal mix. Place a bowl of clear spring water on the altar, preferably on the left side. Place your magick key on the altar, near the center. As you put it there, consider what this key means to you. Set up the candles (green, black, white, and gold) that represent the HedgeWitch colors. Do not light the candles at this time.

Breathe deeply and slowly thirteen times. Shift your mind into the power of the earth, sea, and sky. Draw a figure eight on the ground. Imagine a gateway at the center of the eight. Step into it. Wait until you touch the still point of quiet. The hair on your arms may begin to rise. Speak the charge loudly, and as you say each element of HedgeWitchery (wind, fire, etc.), think of the lessons you have learned in the past several days. Allow your voice to flow with power!

Wind of Spirit, inner fire
Bring the change that I desire
Earthly gifts of stable ground
Sky to bring the spirit down
Rain to nourish, sun to light
Mountain guards and moon for sight
Lightning sparks to make connection
Thunder roils to merge perfection.
Wood and stone and nature's breath
Inner magick coalesce
Metal bends and shapes and cools
Still-point silence—HedgeWitch rules!

Your Dedication

Speak the dedication:

> *From this day forward, I pledge to study the ways of herbal witchery*
> *for the betterment of myself and others on my life journey.*
> *Honor is the law. Love is the bond. So be it!*

Ring your magick bell or chimes three times.

Place your HedgeWitch journal in the center of your altar. Light the four altar candles (green, black, white, and gold). Hold your hands out in front of you, palms up. Now light your personal dedication candle. Envision a spiral of energy building in each palm. Take your time. Each time you breathe in, you are gathering power; each time you breathe out, the power in your palms grows. When you feel quite strong, touch the representation of your first symbol (wind), then place your hands over your heart and repeat the first line below, inhaling and exhaling slowly to reap the benefits of all that you draw in with your breath. Repeat each subsequent line, following the same procedure (touching the symbol, putting hands over heart, announcing the power, and breathing in the energy, exhaling slowly).

> *I take into myself the power of wind (breathe deeply)*
> *The power of fire*
> *The power of earth*
> *The power of sky*
> *The power of rain*
> *The power of mountain*
> *The power of lightning*
> *The power of thunder*
> *The power of metal*
> *The power of stone*
> *The power of sun*
> *The power of moon*
> *The power of wood*
> *The power of silence*
> *Which combine to make the power of One! It always works. Always a blessing!*

Remember to smile! Dip your finger in the spring water and draw the figure eight on your third eye to seal these powers within yourself. Ring your bell or chimes fourteen times.

Your Rebirth

Take apart the stone pile you created on the mountain night. As you remove each stone, say: "I am reborn in power and perfection. From this day forward, I have the ability to accomplish anything I desire." Place these stones under your altar or near it. You can reuse them again later, if you so desire. Burn the conjuring bag and its contents in your cauldron. (This can be done outside at a later time, if you feel it will smoke up the house too much.) When the flame has died, state clearly: "I am reborn!" Ring your magick bell one time.

Your Wish

Place your wish that you wrote before the ceremony underneath your magick key but on top of your HedgeWitch journal on the altar. Take a deep breath, and exhale slowly. Hold your hands over the key and wish, saying:

> *Power of the east, winds of sacred birth*
> *Gather all your forces and bring desire to earth.*
> *Power of the south, winds of hot creation*
> *Separate the earth by fire, refine this incantation.*
> *Power of the west, winds of down below*
> *Bubble up to meet the sky and make the pattern so!*
> *Power of the north, winds of sacred treasure*
> *Solidify my own desire and formulate the measure!*
> *Power of Spirit, winds of dusk and dawn*
> *Align the planets in their places, words convey the song!*
> *Power of myself, the winds of my demand*
> *Thrice I speak to penetrate and bring about my plan!*
> *It always works. Always a blessing!*

Clearly speak your desire three times in primal language. Say thank you, and smile! Then burn the wish paper in your cauldron. Ring your magick bell three times.

HedgeWitch Closing

Stand with your feet about two feet apart, knees slightly bent. Gather the circle into a ball of energy in front of you. Visualize the leaves, branches, and flowers you created in your mind condensing back into a beautiful ball of energy, and then clap your hands together, saying:

> *Thanks be to the spirits of earth and sky;*
>
> *Thou art released to thy natural form!*
>
> *Peace with the gods*
>
> *Peace with nature*
>
> *Peace within.*
>
> *It always works.*
>
> *Always a blessing.*
>
> *Thank you!*

Smile.

Allow all candles used this night to burn completely or light them every night for a few moments until the candles are all gone. Pour any remaining spring water outside, asking for blessings from Spirit. Sprinkle any remaining herbal mix on your doorstep to keep negative energies from entering your home. Put your HedgeWitch symbol representations in a safe place. If you drew them on notecards just for this evening's ritual, burn them and scatter the ashes. Write of tonight's experiences in your HedgeWitch journal, then draw a design, or sigil, that best represents tonight's ritual. This symbol means sacred ceremony and the combined power of all the other symbols.

You are about to embark on the wonderful life of a HedgeWitch! Open your arms, and welcome this positive energy. Spirit will teach you, if you only listen!

Your HedgeWitch Sacred Symbols

Over the past two weeks, you have created fourteen sacred symbols that are specifically meaningful for you. Here's the complete list:

First Night—Wind—My connection to Spirit

Second Night—Fire—My personal creativity

Third Night—Earth—Richness and abundance of the universe

Fourth Night—Sky—My unlimited opportunity

Fifth Night—Rain—My good health and healing

Sixth Night—Mountain—My stability and treasures within the self

Seventh Night—Lightning—My personal power, confidence, and balance

Eighth Night—Thunder—My power of thought and action

Ninth Night—Metal—My flow and harmony within Spirit

Tenth Night—Stone—My gratitude

Eleventh Night—Celestial Power—My light within

Twelfth Night—Wood—Knowledge, wisdom, and education

Thirteenth Night—Silence—The still point of manifestation

Fourteenth Night—The symbol of my personal transformation and combined power of all my symbols

We can now use our symbols in a variety of ways, such as meditative tools, divination lots, spell activators, and affirmation vehicles.

Your Symbols as Divination Tools

Inscribe your symbols on stones, small pieces of wood, or clay, and store them in a small bag. To divine, place a glass of spring water (this is your offering to the gods, spirits, angels—whatever you believe in), a small bowl of blessed water, your magick key, your magick bell, one white candle, and a bowl of your favorite herb mixture on a clean table top or divination cloth. Light the white candle. This represents bringing inspiration and peace into your life. Take your stones out of the bag and sprinkle them with a bit of the blessed water from the bowl.

Roll the stones in the herbal mix, and brush off the stones. Place stones back in the bag. Ring your bell or chimes corresponding to your personal magick number. Repeat the following charm or incantation of your choice:

HedgeWitch Divination Charm

I close my eyes and touch the spirit
Of things both seen and not.
And in this place of perfect peace
I bless and cleanse these lots.

Then say three times:

I receive and understand the answer.
It always works. Always a blessing!

Remember to smile! Finish with:

Peace with the gods
Peace with nature
Peace within. Thank you!
It always works. Always a blessing!

Smile.

Ask your question, and then draw a single sigil from the bag. For example, let's say you are working on a very difficult problem that just refuses to resolve itself, and you are seeking to find the way to best handle the situation. The sigil you pull from the bag will tell you which HedgeWitchery correspondence will most help you find the right way for you. Once you pull the sigil, read over the work you performed in your journal for that night or check this book on the explanation. Sometimes, even though we think we know something, we overlook important information. Repeat the affirmations that match the symbol. If necessary, release the suggested item for that day (there's always junk to remove in our lives), and if the situation calls for it, do that night's ceremony as a mini spell. If you are concerned about timing, what day (first, second, third) did this sigil originally represent? That's approximately how many days or months it will take to resolve your problem, or perhaps it indicates the time needed to build what you desire. I would be careful, though, in tying yourself to timing, because if you do, you could be stalling what you really desire. A single-draw sigil can be done each morning to help you better design your day or at night to help you with dream interpretation.

You can also spill all your sigils like runes on the center of the table. Those lots facing up apply to the situation. Those with hidden sigils do not. Those lots facing up and in the center of the table are the most significant. Those to the right indicate energies that helped to create the present. Those to the left are helpful guides to the future. Cleanse the lots with the blessed water and dry them before you return them to the bag.

Your Symbols as Spell Activators

You can draw your symbols on candles, petitions to deity, or even work them into a stitchery design for a friend! Use the general HedgeWitch conjuration on page 107 as an empowerment charm. Refer to this book and your journal for what herbs you may wish to use for the working. Reword the affirmation to fit the circumstance. For example, if you desire to do a healing for a friend (let's call her Margaret), first write down (in primal language) exactly what you want: "I want Margaret to enjoy good health." Say this statement at least three times. Then, you could make something nice for Margaret—perhaps a card, bookmark, flower arrangement, or design a perfume, magickal oil, or soap just for her, somehow incorporating your healing rain sigil in the gift. Not only are you giving Margaret your good wishes, you are also sharing your talent, and therefore your chi, or personal energy of harmony. While you are physically making the gift, repeat rain's affirmations, changing the wording to fit Margaret (adding her name, for example), or choosing an affirmation that is more suitable to her circumstances. Just remember, Margaret's destiny will not be changed simply because of your efforts. To make any change in oneself, one must believe. You are merely a vehicle of assistance should she reach out for that energy.

Other Ways to Use Your Magickal Symbols

You can meditate on a specific symbol to continually align your mind and body with the harmonious powers of the universe. Turn your symbol into a beautiful painting, stitchery, or other creative project, repeating the affirmations that match the symbol or creating your own affirmations. Carry the symbol with you throughout the day to continually keep the pathway

to that energy open. Make a mandala of all your symbols for meditation out of fiber art or canvas. You could even design separate drum beats (for drummers) or dance moves (if this is your talent). Into car parts? Fine. Match a car part to each symbol.

Your symbols can also be used as talismans to draw a specific desire to you, as all the symbols you created follow the law of attraction. Let's say you need to pay a bill, and you don't have the money. Activate the earth symbol, using its affirmations, and draw it on a dollar bill. Rub it with chamomile herb (inexpensive and plentiful—you could even use chamomile herb tea from the grocery store). Roll the dollar bill toward you, speaking the affirmations several times. Clearly formulate in primal language exactly what you want, and then repeat what you have formulated aloud three times. Remember to say thank you, and smile. Put the dollar bill in your pocket and carry it with you until your desire is met.

Use your symbols to continually encourage harmony in and around the home. Create stepping stones for your garden or outdoor altar area that carry each individual symbol, or make a mini altar with a stepping-stone mold and concrete, and decorate it with your personal sigils. Decorate indoor and outdoor flower pots, garden flags, or tools with your sigils. Because you have designed your symbols, they carry great personal power!

section
④

Love, Health & Beauty

tips, formulas &
techniques

HedgeWitchery
Within and Without

All of the recipes in this section use organically grown herbs. Your formulas will be especially powerful if you have grown most or all of the herbs yourself in your own herb garden, but if this isn't possible, look for the highest-quality herbs and spices during your magickal shopping. Use primal language to find the best selection!

HedgeWitch Brews

A HedgeWitch brew is a combination of herbs, spices, salts (sometimes), essential oils, and water. These brews are for cleansing the body and freshening the air—they are not for ingestion. You may wish to empower the herbs with the following charm, written in primal language (remember, primal language uses the fewest amount of words possible, still gets the point across, and is positive in nature):

Remember, remember, the oldest of herbs

The fruit of the vine, the root and the words.

You have the power of infinity.

You have the power of healing and good health.

You have the power to attract abundance and good fortune.

You have the power to move in any direction.

Awaken, awaken! Bring my will to perfection!

It always works. Always a blessing!

Sunshine Brew

This amazing formula has many uses! The liquid can be added to soaps and floor washes, and the dried herbs can be included in your own incense recipes or burned alone on an incense charcoal tab. I created the formula to vibrate to good health, wealth, and success. Be sure to empower the finished brew with your magickal bell (tuning forks) and your own special prayer.

    2   tablespoons dried chamomile

    2   tablespoons dried bergamot

    2   tablespoons dried ginger

    2   tablespoons dried rosemary

         Mortar and pestle

    1   cup distilled water

    1   paper coffee filter

    1   clear glass bottle or jar

Grind the herbs with mortar and pestle just enough to break them up and release their aroma, not enough to pulverize them. Boil one cup of distilled water. Take one half of your herbal mixture and place in center of a paper coffee filter. Twist filter tightly. Place filter in the cup of hot water. Remove after one hour; throw soaked herbs away. Refrigerate sunshine brew, and be sure to label DO NOT DRINK. To use, empower at sunrise or at noon. Add a crystal to the brew for more power.

Ginger, chamomile, rosemary, and bergamot are all considered body-safe herbs; however, anyone can have an allergic reaction to an herbal additive. Always check a small area of your skin first before using any herbal product.

Spring Sunshine Brew Floor Wash

To one gallon of warm water, add:

1   cup sunshine brew

Juice from one squeezed lemon

Juice from one squeezed lime

1   herb bouquet of your choice (see page 254)

Excellent as a spring-cleaning floor wash to encourage good fortune and harmony in the home.

HedgeWitch Tub Teas

Relaxing in a warm, magickal bath does wonders for the body and mind! Tub tea formulas consist of botanicals, bath salts (sometimes), and a large tea bag made for the bath (these are available from many herbal suppliers on the Net and in some health-food stores). If you don't have these paper bags, use a small, clean cotton drawstring bag. Here are some great recipes to encourage magickal stress relief!

Aura-Cleansing Tub Tea

Lavender

Rosemary

Lemongrass (shred to release aroma)

Chamomile

6–10   drops lavender essential oil

Sea salt

Mix equal parts of dried lavender, rosemary, lemongrass, and chamomile. Add lavender essential oil, and fluff herbs. Fill remainder of bag with sea salt. This is an excellent recipe for aura cleansing, especially for a ritual bath before an important ceremony. This mixture can also be used in a cleansing ritual.

Healing Salts & Minerals Tub Tea *

¼ cup Epsom salts

½ cup sea salt**

½ cup European mineral salts

**Note: To scent any sea salt mixture, add twelve drops of body-safe fragrance to one cup of salt mixture.

Body Toning Tub Tea

1 cup dried chamomile

½ cup dried peppermint

¼ cup dried comfrey

¼ cup dried lemon peel

¼ cup dried rose hips

¼ cup dried rosemary

¼ cup dried sage

¼ cup dried, crushed ginger

Note: In some areas of the United States, comfrey is considered illegal because, if taken internally, it is now thought to damage the liver. It is still sold for topical use in many states. Substitute dried rose petals if this applies to you. For more power, scent with body-safe patchouli fragrance.

Zen Tub Tea

½ cup dried lavender buds

½ cup chamomile

½ cup oatmeal

½ cup green tea

¼ cup orange peel

¼ cup rosemary

¼ cup lemongrass (shred to release aroma)

8 bay leaves (minced)

* the recipes on this page will make 4 to 6 tub teas

HedgeWitch Soap Making

Making your own soaps with empowered herbs can be an extremely rewarding and magickal experience. The recipes in this book rely on melt-and-pour soap bases that can be purchased at your local craft store or online. This type of easy carrier allows you to make lots of fragrant soaps in a single afternoon and can be a great magickal project practiced with a circle of friends or your children (as long as you monitor the hot soap and you do the pouring). When shopping for a glycerin soap base, look for formulas that permit good suspension of herbs, as most herbs will sink to the bottom of the mold unless the soap is poured just at the moment of setting (which can be tricky). Here are the general supplies you will need for all of the recipes:

Soap cauldron (can be purchased at local craft store) or microwave (if soap directions say you can use this)

Desired fragrance (sweet scents help to instill good feelings and harmony within the body)

Small plastic baggies or shrink-wrap system for packaging after soap has cooled

Sharp, smooth-blade knife (for cutting soap base into small, 1-inch blocks)

Pyrex measuring cup (4-cup size)

Wire whisk (only to be used for soap)

Droppers (for adding scent and color)

Rubbing alcohol in spritzer bottle (removes bubbles from the poured soap)

Ladle (if using a soap cauldron)

Mortar and pestle or spice grinder

Soap molds (you can also use silicone muffin molds)

X-Acto knife (for trimming soaps if you over-poured the mold)

Wire curing rack (for handmilled soaps)

In soap making, timing is essential. If you whisk too long, then your soap will begin to gel in the measuring cup to the point where you won't be able to pour it. If this occurs, it must be re-melted before pouring. Re-melting soap with fragrance can destroy the integrity of the aroma. Expect to make a few mistakes when first learning to make your own soap; however, you will quickly get the feel of this super-simple process! Goat's milk, coconut, and shea butter bases do not have good suspension and require that you whisk your formulas until they thicken but are still warm enough to pour.

Basic Melt-and-Pour Soap-Making Instructions

- Heat your soap base as indicated by manufacturer. (Be careful not to overheat or you will destroy the integrity of the soap base.)

- Add color per manufacturer's instructions.

- Add fragrance or essential oils per manufacturer's instructions. Hint: For every pound of soap use three teaspoons of fragrance (this does not apply for essential oils).

- Add herbs.

- Add any other inclusions—water for handmilled, jojoba carrier or other oils; vitamin E (a preservative), etc.

- Whisk mixture until it begins to thicken.

- Pour into molds.

- Spritz each soap while still warm with alcohol to remove bubbles.

- Allow to cool completely in mold.

- Remove from mold.

- Air-dry (length of time depends on what type of base you are using). Glycerin can be packaged after one hour.

HedgeWitch Body-Safe Dried Herbs for Soaps

There are a large number of body-safe dried herbs that you can include in your soaps, although some of them, such as chamomile, sage, and teas, will bleed over time. This doesn't hurt the soap but may make your soaps unsightly. Adding ¼ teaspoon of vitamin E to each pound of your soap mixture will help to retard this process by preserving the herb. Although some individuals add rose petals to their soaps, I don't recommend it because rose petals have a tendency to turn black over time. Here's a list of herbs you can include in your magickal soaps!

Allspice

Almonds

Barley

Basil

Bergamot

Bladderwrack (sea kelp)

Brown sugar

Calendula (marigold)

Cardamom

Chamomile

Chocolate

Cinnamon (just a bit!)

Coffee

Coriander

Cornmeal (for garden and deep grime removal soaps)

Dill

Eucalyptus

Ginger

{more...}

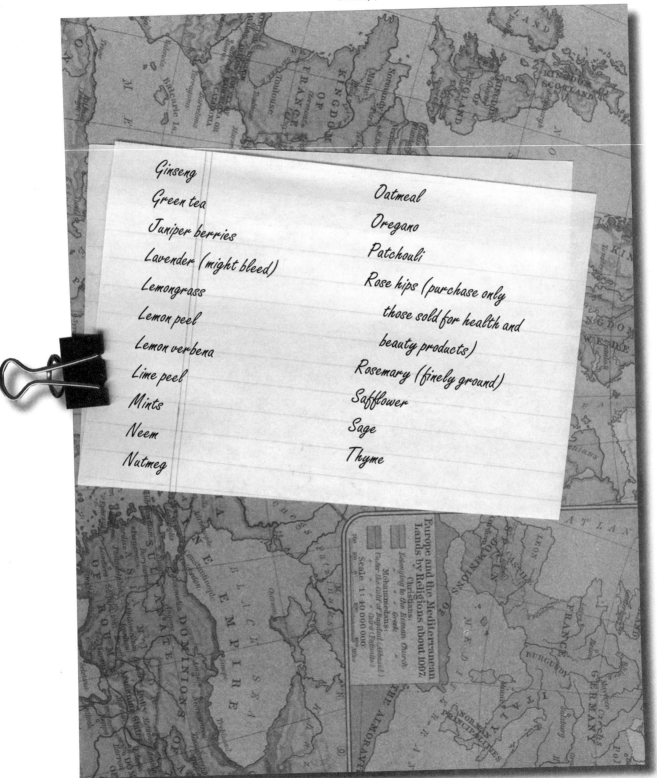

Ginseng

Green tea

Juniper berries

Lavender (might bleed)

Lemongrass

Lemon peel

Lemon verbena

Lime peel

Mints

Neem

Nutmeg

Oatmeal

Oregano

Patchouli

Rose hips (purchase only
those sold for health and
beauty products)

Rosemary (finely ground)

Safflower

Sage

Thyme

Note: Take special care when making soaps for allergy-sensitive individuals. Ingredients like almonds, cinnamon, and honey may have adverse effects on some individuals.

How Much Soap Base to Melt?

If you don't want to melt as much soap base as the recipe calls for, fill your soap mold with water. Pour the water into a measuring cup and mark the water line. That's how much soap you'll need! Pour out the water and dry the cup and the mold. Cut your soap base like cutting a block of cheese and place in Pyrex measuring cup. If you need only a small amount, cut a few pieces of base at a time and heat. If you are using a microwave product, wave first at fifteen seconds and then nine-second intervals. Once the soap is melted, adjust your other ingredients (dye, fragrance, botanicals, butters, oils) to match the amount of soap you are using.

Note: Do not overheat the soap base. If a base is cooked too long, it will smell funny and most likely crack when cooled.

Charming Soap and Other Beauty Products

Intoning prayers and charms during any project focuses the mind on a positive future and fills the item you are working on with clean, bright energy. How you empower these items is entirely up to you, as your good will is the primary catalyst. Here are a few magickal tips on project empowerment:

- If the recipe calls for water, use empowered spring or distilled water.

- Always stir herbs, sauces, waxes, etc., in a clockwise direction.

- Choose chants, charms, and repetitive words that are positive in nature. Think about what you do want, not what you don't want.

- Work in a clean, orderly environment.

- Pennsylvania Dutch *Braucheries* (magickal people) used similes in their conjurations. They chose something they knew to be true, and then equated what they desired to this truth as well. For example, if they believed that the sun rising in the morning was an absolute truth, then they might say: "As surely as the sun rises each day, so, too, shall I have great health, wealth, and beauty." Try making your own magickal similes; just be careful what you say you believe! Choosing the words you speak aloud carefully is a wonderful magickal exercise for the mind and something we can continually endeavor to practice, no matter how long we've concentrated on our spirituality!

- Use the highest-quality ingredients in your soaps and body-care products.

- Bells and tuning forks work wonders during project formulation whether you are making soaps, beauty brews, candles, or knitting that afghan! The clear tonal sounds remove unwanted negativity and clear the mind.

General Soap and Beauty Product Charm

As surely as beauty fills the world with blue skies and sunlight
With vibrant colors and fragrant flowers
So, too, will this project be filled with love, good health, and beauty.
It always works. Always a blessing!

Remember to smile! Repeat this charm nine times as you are working, or as many times as you feel necessary.

Sunshine Brew Glycerin Body Soap

4 cups melt-and-pour glycerin soap base

2 tablespoons sunshine brew (p. 136)

Ground sunshine brew herbs (dried)

Yellow soap dye (optional, but if you do not use dye for this recipe, your soap will appear a faint, murky yellow-green)

Soap molds or square Pyrex dish

4 vitamin E gel capsules

Grind sunshine herbs into a finer mixture—especially the ginger; this should be powdered. Follow soap-melting instructions as given on the package. Once soap has melted, with ladle, transfer soap to your Pyrex measuring cup. (If you melted the soap in the cup in the microwave, transfer won't be necessary.) Whisk in desired amount of color and scent by following instructions given with those products. Add the two tablespoons of sunshine brew, and whisk. Add desired amount of herbs. Some individuals like very few herbs in their soaps, where others like a more generous amount—just remember that herbals can clog your drain if they are too large or you use too much. Break vitamin E gel capsules and add the liquid to your soap mixture. Vitamin E will help to preserve the chamomile. Makes approximately ten 6-ounce soaps.

Brown Sugar Soap

A favorite harvest and Yuletide gift, this soap smells luxurious and encourages good fortune! Soap will be a country-prim brown color due to the brown sugar.

2	cups goat's milk soap base
2	tablespoons brown sugar
2	tablespoons toasted oatmeal, finely ground
	Vanilla fragrance
1	teaspoon jojoba oil
¼	teaspoon ground nutmeg
8	vitamin E gel caps

Toast oatmeal on cookie sheet in your oven. Allow to cool. Grind fine. Melt soap base. Add all ingredients except gel caps. Cut gel caps and pour liquid into mixture. Whisk until mixture begins to thicken. Pour into molds. Cool. Remove from mold, and allow to air-dry for at least twenty-four hours. Package. Makes approximately five 6-ounce bars of soap.

Garden Soap

This excellent soap mixture is perfect for cleaning up after a day of gardening, messing with your favorite car, or playing a hard game of softball!

2 cups goat's milk or coconut soap base

1 tablespoon cornmeal

½ teaspoon chamomile

½ teaspoon lemongrass

½ teaspoon lemon peel

½ teaspoon orange peel

¼ teaspoon rosemary

Gardenia or chamomile fragrance

4 aloe vera gel caps

Grind ingredients as finely as possible. Melt soap base. Add herbal ingredients. Cut aloe vera gel caps and add liquid to mixture. Whisk until just about to gel. Pour into soap molds. Cool. Remove from mold. Air-dry twenty-four hours. Wrap.

Honey Oatmeal Goddess Soap

2 cups coconut soap base

½ cup toasted oatmeal

½ teaspoon honey

¼ teaspoon cinnamon

¼ teaspoon nutmeg

Spiced apple fragrance

Toast oatmeal on cookie sheet in oven. Grind fine. Melt soap base. Add ingredients. Whisk until just about to gel. Pour into soap molds. Cool. Remove from mold. Air-dry twenty-four hours. Wrap.

Kitchen Witch Hand Soap

This soap recipe is a great formula for kitchen cleanup! The mixture of tea tree oil and botanicals provides a wonderful, natural anti-bacterial formula.

4   cups glycerin soap base

2   teaspoons dried basil

2   teaspoons dried oregano

2   teaspoons dried parsley

2   teaspoons dried sage

10   drops tea tree essential oil

4   vitamin E gel caps

    Lemon, lime, or orange fragrance

    Dye to match fragrance

Grind herbals together. Melt soap base. Add tea tree oil and desired fragrance. Add dye. Cut gel caps and pour liquid into mixture. Add herbs. Whisk until near gel. Pour. Cool. Remove from mold. Wrap after one hour.

Come to Me Love Soap

2   cups goat's milk soap base

2   teaspoons dried patchouli

¼   teaspoon honey

½   teaspoon jojoba carrier oil

    Equal parts of jasmine and rose fragrance

    Red or pink soap dye

Finely grind patchouli herb. Melt soap base. Add herb, honey, jojoba, fragrances, and dye. Whisk until near gel. Pour in love-themed mold. Cool. Remove from mold. Air-dry on rack for twenty-four hours. Store in Saran Wrap to help hold the scent.

Cleopatra Beauty Soap

    2   cups goat's milk soap base

    1   cup shea butter soap base

    2   tablespoons fine sea salt

    1   tablespoon powdered milk

        Frankincense and jasmine fragrance

    4   drops cypress essential oil

Melt soap base. Add ingredients. Whisk until near gel. Pour into heart-shaped molds. Allow to cool. Remove from mold. Air-dry for twenty-four hours on rack. Wrap.

Goddess Caffeina Glycerin Soap

The coffee and chocolate provide their own aroma and coloring to the soap. This makes a great kitchen hand soap.

    2   cups glycerin soap base

    1   tablespoon bergamot

    2   tablespoons fresh, finely ground coffee beans

    1   teaspoon powdered chocolate

Grind coffee just before making soap to capture the magnificent aroma! Melt soap base. Add coffee, chocolate and bergamot. Whisk until near gel. Pour into molds. Allow to cool. Remove from mold. Air-dry for one hour. Wrap.

Medicine Woman Formula

I created this formula for healing work of all kinds. A bit complicated, it employs nine herbs, two fragrances, and two essential oils. The formula can be used for soaps or healing sachets.

    Herbs: Rosemary

             Ginseng, powdered

             Eucalyptus

Calendula

Lemongrass, shredded to release aroma

Chamomile

Thyme

White Sage

Neem

Fragrances: Body-safe nag champa and evergreen

Essential oils: Tea tree and lemongrass

Mix equal parts of dried herbs. Grind. For soaps, grind to a powder as much as possible. For sachets, grind just enough to release aroma. Add fragrances and oils, just enough to lightly scent. Toss. Store in air-tight container until used in soaps or sachets.

Lime & Roses Victorian Love Soap

1 cup goat's milk or coconut soap base

1 cup shea butter soap base

1 teaspoon rosemary herb, ground fine

1 teaspoon lime peel, ground fine

½ teaspoon body-safe rose hip powder (don't grind your own, purchase specially formulated rose hip powder specifically for the body, as some rose hips will cause severe itching when ground)

10 drops lime essential oil

Rose fragrance

Green and yellow dye (just enough to color the soap a lime green)

Rose petal sachet (for packaging)

Melt soap bases together. Add herbals, essential oil, fragrance, and dye. Whisk until just about to gel. Pour into heart- or rose-shaped molds. Allow to cool. Remove from mold. Air-dry for twenty-four hours. Wrap with a sachet of dried rose petals.

Honey-Rum Prosperity Harvest Soap

2 cups goat's milk or coconut soap base

1 teaspoon honey

1 teaspoon jojoba oil

½ teaspoon patchouli, ground

¼ teaspoon nutmeg, ground

¼ teaspoon allspice, ground

⅛ teaspoon cinnamon, powdered

Bay rum body-safe fragrance

Orange soap dye

Melt soap. Add ingredients. Whisk until just about to gel. Pour into pumpkin-shaped molds. Allow to cool. Remove from mold. Air-dry on rack for twenty-four hours. Wrap.

Yule Wassail Glycerin Soap

Wrapped in festive paper with ribbon, this makes a great Yule gift.

4 cups glycerin soap base

1 teaspoon dried orange peel

½ teaspoon nutmeg

¼ teaspoon cinnamon

½ teaspoon cloves

Red dye

Apple fragrance

Cinnamon sticks, whole (do not grind)

Rubbing alcohol in spritzer bottle

Grind herbs and spices into a fine powder. Melt soap base. Add herb mixture, red dye, and apple fragrance. Whisk. Put one cinnamon stick in each soap mold. Spray lightly with alcohol (this will allow the soap base to adhere to the cinnamon stick). When soap is just about to gel, pour into each mold. Allow to cool. Remove from mold. Air-dry for one hour.

If you want to suspend a cinnamon stick in the mold, try the following:

1. On first pour, fill mold only partway.

2. Let soap cool in mold until it is lukewarm but not cold. If the soap is too cold, your second pour will split off when you take it out of the mold.

3. Put one cinnamon stick in each mold.

4. Spray cinnamon stick and soap surface with alcohol.

5. Completely fill the mold with reheated soap base.

When the soap has cooled, the cinnamon stick will appear suspended inside the soap bar, making for a very pretty and unusual soap.

Basic Handmilled Soap

Handmilled soaps are often expensive due to the amount of curing time. They are called handmilled because you stir the mixture by hand with your whisk until the mixture gels slightly, which can take from ten to fifteen minutes. Some soap makers use a hand-held, battery-operated mixer to make the soap mixture fluffier. Handmilled soaps take at least two weeks (or more, depending on weather conditions) to dry. The soap mixture is usually poured in a loaf pan and then cut with a sharp knife after curing. The basic recipe is very simple:

½   cup soap base (coconut, goat's milk, shea butter, or a mixture of the three)

2   tablespoons distilled water

2   tablespoons olive oil or jojoba carrier oil

Color, fragrance, and botanicals are added as desired. To make enough to pour into a loaf pan, increase:

4   cups soap base

12   tablespoons distilled water

12   tablespoons olive oil or jojoba carrier

Handmilled soaps are harder, which means they last longer in the bath or shower. This is due to the inclusion of the water during the soap-making process. Unlike other soaps, they are not packaged in plastic, as this destroys the integrity of the soap. Instead, they are wrapped in paper or placed in a cardboard soap box for gift-giving.

Handmilled Zen Soap

Make the basic handmilled formula (smaller ½-cup size). Add:

- ¼ teaspoon dried lemon grass (grind to release aroma)
- ¼ teaspoon dried sage, ground
- ¼ teaspoon powdered lime peel
- 4 drops lime essential oil
  Lavender fragrance

Whisk until just about to gel. Pour in soap mold. Allow to cool. Remove from mold and place on wire rack. Let cure for at least two weeks.

Note: For a very unique gift, place a lucky Chinese coin in the mold before pouring in the soap base. Spray coin with rubbing alcohol before pouring the soap to help the coin adhere to the soap. When ready for gift-giving, tie decorative raffia or a green ribbon around the soap.

HedgeWitch Body Powders

Soothing body powder is super easy to make—all you need is cornstarch, essential oils, and maybe a body-safe fragrance or two! Body powders may also be used in magickal applications such as loading candles, sprinkled in conjuring bags or strewn on your doorstep to welcome health and good fortune. Simply fill a jar that can be tightly capped with one of the recipes below. Cap. Shake. Allow to sit for three days. Each day, repeat an affirmation or chosen prayer while holding your hands over the jar. Shake. By the third day, you'll have a delightfully scented body powder! Powdered herbs can also be added to the cornstarch base. Use the body-safe herbal soap list on pages 141–142 to whip up your own designer powders. What's great about HedgeWitch powders? You know exactly what's in it, because *you* made it! The recipes below can also be turned into matching magickal soaps by omitting the cornstarch and using one cup of melted soap base, or by factoring ten drops of essential oil to one four-ounce bar of soap. Blend essentials first and then add to melted soap in the desired quantity.

Haunting Witch Body Powder

- 10 drops patchouli essential oil
- 10 drops body-safe rose fragrance
- 10 drops body-safe jasmine fragrance
- 2 tablespoons cornstarch

To make this recipe more powerful, add an additional tablespoon of cornstarch and a body-safe pheromone oil blend that can be purchased over the Internet.

Summer Spice Body Powder

- 10 drops ylang-ylang essential oil
- 5 drops sandalwood essential oil
- 5 drops clove essential oil
- 5 drops nutmeg essential oil
- 5 drops orange essential oil
- 2 tablespoons cornstarch

Woodland Nymph Body Powder

15 drops pine essential oil

5 drops cypress essential oil

5 drops patchouli essential oil

5 drops sandalwood essential oil

2 tablespoons cornstarch

Aura-Cleansing Body Powder

10 drops lavender essential oil

10 drops lime essential oil

5 drops rosemary essential oil

5 drops lemon essential oil

2 tablespoons cornstarch

Sunrise Glow Body Powder

15 drops grapefruit essential oil

10 drops lime essential oil

5 drops allspice essential oil

5 drops tangerine essential oil

2 tablespoons cornstarch

Healing Glow Body Powder

10 drops eucalyptus essential oil

10 drops lime essential oil

5 drops myrtle essential oil

5 drops sandalwood essential oil

2 tablespoons cornstarch

Money-Drawing Body Powder

- 10 drops spearmint essential oil
- 5 drops chamomile essential oil
- 5 drops calendula essential oil
- 5 drops patchouli essential oil
- 5 drops sweet bay essential oil
- 2 tablespoons cornstarch
- 2 tablespoons finely ground chamomile

Love Potion Body Powder

- 15 drops allspice essential oil
- 5 drops patchouli essential oil
- 5 drops clove magickal oil
- 5 drops honeysuckle fragrance
- 2 tablespoons cornstarch

Steady Income Body Powder

- 10 drops peppermint essential oil
- 10 drops spruce magickal oil
- 5 drops bergamot magickal oil
- 5 drops sweet bay magickal oil
- 2 tablespoons cornstarch

HedgeWitch Stitchery

Whether you're into needlepoint, cross-stitch, knitting, crochet, embroidery, crewel, quilting, or making clothes and household goods with your trusty sewing machine, the art of stitchery creates an incredible energy that can be focused in a specific direction with little effort. HedgeWitch stitchery definitely falls into the category of love, health, and beauty: stitching for yourself or someone else is truly an act of love through your dedicated time; stitching puts you in a meditative place that is conducive to good health and healing; and your work is an act of beautification for yourself and others. When stitching, your mind infuses the project with your special magick with every movement of the needle. The repetitive nature of the work allows you to slip into a light, meditative state, soothing the nerves and allowing a field of harmonious opportunity wherein anything can be manifested. Whether you are making a small project, like a gris-gris bag to hold your HedgeWitch herbal sachet, or something that will demand a lot of time and effort, such as designing a marriage quilt for your son or daughter, here are a few ideas on how to make your sewing projects the most powerful they can be!

Empower Your Tools with Primal Language Intent

Needles, scissors, seam guides, pins, and the like may occasionally be blessed with a holy water spray or smudged with a fragrant herbal incense. If you have a large family, sewing supplies are not considered solitary ownership, no matter how loud you proclaim it so. Anyone in any mood could have used your tools prior to your magickal project. Even if you tell your kids that those thirty-dollar scissors for paper crafts or embroidery are off-limits, frankly, they are too hard to resist (so small and handy, you know?). For some reason, teenagers think those razor-sharp points are really screwdrivers and try to use them as such—that, or "What do you mean I can't cut that bamboo skewer for roasting my marshmallows? It worked, didn't it?" Keep your tools free of negativity as best you can, and put them away after each use. Remember to empower your tools with primal language intent, as explained earlier.

Organize Your Supplies

Yarn, thread, canvas…many stitchers collect a compendium of odds, ends, unfinished projects, and supplies for proposed projects (it's a shopping weakness, like when you went in for one spool of thread at your favorite store last month and came home with the most *darling* pattern and of course *all* the supplies for it). Take a lazy, rainy afternoon and organize what you have. Give away any project that you know you will never do. Throw out old, unfinished projects that brought a great deal of frustration. This item will only attract continued anxiety and create stress every time you happen to run across it. Any project that has gathered dust is also a magnet for negativity. If you still want to keep the project but the original bag is discolored and yucky, place the items in a new bag, clearly labeled. Throw out tangled thread and yarn. Again, these tangles will trap negative energy. If you really want to save it, sit down and untangle it, then store it neatly.

Where You Stitch

Most of us do not have dedicated sewing rooms, but, even if you do, you may wish to try some of these helpful hints. One of the many advantages of stitchery is that it is very portable. Therefore, you may find yourself anywhere (bus, train, subway station, waiting in a doctor's office) while working on your project. Before you begin to stitch on the road, take three deep breaths, inhaling through the nose and exhaling through the mouth. Close your eyes, and surround yourself with white light. You might try saying the stitcher's charm three times before you begin:

Stitcher's Charm

Needle up and needle down
Bringing thought to form
Bless this work and guide these hands
Harmony is born.

If you are working at home, try to stitch in a clean area. An environment free of dust and clutter promotes the movement of positive chi, surrounding both yourself and your work with harmonious energies. Stitching by an indoor fountain is very soothing and encourages healing energies. If you can't stitch by a real fountain, try listening to meditative music or music that promotes the type of energy you wish to capture in your project.

Although soft lighting is preferable for most magick and meditation, it is not so in enchanted stitchery! You need excellent light, both for color choice and the good health of your eyes. Straining will actually muddy your work in terms of energy.

If it doesn't present a hazard, try working by a highly scented candle chosen to match your intent, or place a bowl of herbal potpourri or a scented oil burner near your working area. Fresh flowers are also an option; however, as soon as they begin to wilt, remove them, as dead flowers symbolize dead chi. Working near a hearth fire in the wintertime promotes the cozy feeling of safety and security. Stitching outdoors in the summer brings the harmonious spirit of nature right into your work, especially if you sit in a garden or sacred site.

Stitching with Others

Group stitchery falls into the environmental category. Whether you wish to devise a particular ritual that can be used every week or month, or wish to flow with the seasons, a mini rite before stitching and a nice closure when everyone is finished for the evening promotes magickal togetherness. An enchanted stitching circle of friends and relatives weaves you into the tapestry of this time-honored activity.

Your Good Health While Stitching

Take numerous breaks: Get up and stretch every thirty minutes, especially if you are lucky enough to spend the entire day stitching. Move around, do a little deep breathing, exercise your hands to avoid future problems. By taking breaks, your body, your mind, and your magick will be fresh when you resume.

Placement of your stitching chair: Yep, the actual placement of the chair can affect the energy of the project. Your back should never be facing a doorway or open shelving, as both can affect your personal chi. If you plan to expand your magickal library, a few feng shui books on magickal placement will be very helpful, not only in setting up your craft or sewing room, but also in placement of your chair, and the eventual hanging of your special craft pieces. If you do a lot of stitching, I believe there are two things you must be willing to buy the best of: your chair and good lighting.

Choosing Projects, Designs, and Colors to Match Your Intent and Your Time

Stitchers always take extra care in choosing just the right project for just the right person, but now I want you to think of the process of attraction and hone your choice from there. Let's say you want to make a purse for your daughter. You know she's having money problems, so choose colors or fabrics that are rich in texture and design—reds, purples, golds, greens, and yellows are well-suited to prosperity magick. Toads, frogs, and goldfish have been traditionally linked to good fortune, as have sunflowers, marigolds, chamomile, and maples. Granted, you will want to follow her taste, but sometimes presenting something just a bit different than the norm is welcomed by the recipient, especially if that person understands magickal energy and knows the gift was made specifically to draw something special into their lives. Shapes, too, have their own magickal significance. For example, a circle is for unity, a triangle for focused energy (which way will it point in your design? To the center pulls from the outside in; from the center out pushes energy outward). Oak leaves symbolize good health and longevity. Willow symbolizes relieving the mind from stress. A waterfall symbolizes healing. The rites you performed in Section 2, as well as the tea-leaf-reading information in Section 5, list several shape and symbol correspondences that you might like to use.

Let's say your husband loves cars—maybe he fixes them or even races them. You've found the design for a cross-stitch for his office wall, and you want to make it more magickal. Why not design a bind rune or your personal symbol for success, and draw it on the unworked canvas? When the project is finished, you won't see the symbol—but you will know it is there. If you have a flair for designing patterns yourself, you can even incorporate the symbol right into the design.

If you are extremely busy, yet you *really* want to make something for your ailing aunt, you can look longingly at that afghan pattern or sixteen-by-twenty-inch cross-stitch all you want; but…sigh…don't go there. You know your schedule and how much time you can invest. It is far better to stick with smaller projects that can be completed quickly, rather than fuss and stress over that knitted scarf that seems to be taking *forever* because you decided to use a complicated pattern with many colors! Remember, if you add frustration to the work, you've actually stitched frustration into it!

Holiday Stitchery Tips

Plan ahead. Here are a few simple tips for beginners and experts that will help to ensure your projects are finished by the intended event or holiday:

Beginners

Let's say you want to cross-stitch a cool design for your mother, and you've even found what you want to do—but you've never cross-stitched anything in your life, or if you have, it was twenty years ago. Do at least two small projects first, before you jump into the big one. These "test-drive stitcheries" will teach you a number of things, including:

- Whether or not you like this type of stitchery

- How long it takes you to finish a small project

- How to integrate stitchery in your busy life

- What supplies or tools you should have when you start that special project

For example, over the summer I taught myself to knit. I had grand designs on my first project and became frustrated quickly (and with sore fingers to boot) because I wanted a beautiful finished piece the first time by a particular day. After a few days of ripping and re-knitting, I decided that I would just knit. No project, no intent—just knit. And purl (tough for me at the time). And knit some more. I knitted for two weeks with different yarns, needle sizes, etc., sitting on my back porch—no television, no DVDs—just nature, me, and the stitchery. No project in mind, just learning and enjoying the meditative feeling of knitting. By the third week, I was ready for my first project, and this time I finished it in a few days. During my practice knitting, I realized I needed a few supplies I hadn't picked up when I started, such as a knit gauge, rubber ends to secure my knitting when I wasn't working on it, a stitch counter, and additional needle sizes. I also realized that I disliked working with plastic or wooden needles—my work flowed better with the metal ones. Sure, I had some mistakes, but I was able to fix them and produce something very nice. With counted cross-stitch, I chose small designs—a bunch of smiling carrots on a baby's bib, a bookmark for success. From there, I stitched a larger project with little trouble. Again, I discovered supplies I needed that I didn't have—a good pair of scissors, tapestry needles in various sizes, a seam ripper. I found I didn't like working with the hoops like I had learned long ago—this time I invested in stretchers when it came to working a bigger project.

Now that you know about how long different-sized projects take you, we can go on to the more advanced tips.

For the Experienced Crafter

Buy a magickal calendar or almanac showing moon phases and astrological events (Summer Solstice, etc.) that is reserved *only* for your craft or stitching projects. Write in all your personal important dates (or highlight them), such as birthdays, anniversaries, and holidays. Put stars on the dates that apply to projects you wish to complete. Let's say that this year you would like to needlepoint Yule stockings for various members of your family. Choose a "to be done by" date for this project. This date would be at least two full weeks *before* the special day—more if your item must be sent out to be blocked or finished. Since Yule is around December 21, we should have our stockings completed at least by the end of the first week of December. Yule being so busy, you might want to back that date up even more—say, the last week of November. Now, consider how long it takes you to normally do a particular project. Three weeks? A week? Six weeks? Only you will know by your schedule. Count back that number of weeks on your calendar, and then check the astrological correspondences around that date—anything cool nearby for magickal planning? Select your start day, and write: BEGIN YULE STOCKING FOR FAMILY. Or you could do something like this: AFGHAN FOR CHARLIE—PROSPERITY. I realize this sounds elementary, but you've just added more power to your work by listing a start date and the intent, *and* you've allowed yourself plenty of time for the project. If you do many projects, keeping a calendar will help you to remember what you bought for whom.

Rule of stitchery thumb: always give yourself plenty of time to complete a special project.

For Big Projects, Learn to Work Two Seasons Ahead

I realize this can be a pain. The problem with working way in advance lies in specialty supplies and, perhaps, your mindset. For example, let's go back to those Yule stockings, and let's say I know the size I want to make, but I want a unique design. Given my time allotment, this means I have to start in June to be sure that I'll have this project done by the first week of December. Here's where we run into a problem or two. First, few local stores will start showing patterns for Yule in June. Instead, the stores will be filled with designs that match the current season. Secondly, you may not be in the mood to deal with Yule—heck, you just finished paying the bills for *last* Yule! To solve the first issue, either shop on the Net or, at the end of any given season, pick up projects for the following year. You can also go to trade shows featuring stitchery that are held throughout the year in various parts of the country. To keep the Grinch out of your work (since it's June), change your perception on the flow of the seasons. Remember, each season seamlessly slides into the next and builds on what has gone before. This means that if you want to dedicate your Yule stocking on Summer Solstice, all the better! You'll find that if you get into the habit of thinking two seasons ahead, other projects in your life will finish quickly and easily as well. The psychological upside to this way of planning allows you to skip over worrying about current issues in your life that have managed to root themselves in the current season. Instead, you are looking ahead and creating positive thought patterns for the future.

Here's a quick rule of stitchery thumb for seasonal work:

Big Projects

- Begin summer-completion items at Yule.

- Begin fall-completion items at Spring Equinox.

- Begin winter-completion items at Summer Solstice.

- Begin spring-completion items at Autumn Equinox.

Small Projects

- Begin Candlemas-completion projects at Samhain.

- Begin Spring Equinox-completion projects at Yule.

- Begin Beltaine-completion projects at Candlemas.

- Begin Summer Solstice-completion projects at Spring Equinox.

- Begin Lammas-completion projects at Beltaine.

- Begin Autumn Equinox-completion projects at Summer Solstice.

- Begin Samhain-completion projects at Lammas.

- Begin Yule-completion projects at Autumn Equinox.

Embellishments and Accents

Although you may choose some of these items (buttons, zippers, charms, ribbons, etc.) when you first design or purchase your materials, leave room in your budget to review the project when almost completed. By then, you'll be able to "feel" if something extra-special is needed. Remember, your thoughts during the stitching process have changed, enhanced, or possibly negated your original intention. Hold the piece in your hands, and think about what you wish to attract. Then go shopping or digging in that sewing stash of yours. What you need will be there. The great thing about stitching is that you can add items not associated with sewing to the lining or incorporate an unusual embellishment. Let's say you knitted a purse for your daughter, and you choose to line the inside with a colorful cotton print so that it will last longer for her. You can stitch a packet of dried herbs (just a bit) in the lining (cinquefoil, marigold, and chamomile for money and prosperity) and add lucky Asian coins as a fringe or as part of the closure. Perhaps you made a special project for a new baby that will be framed and hung in the baby's room. Sew up a small bag containing life everlasting herb, lavender, and rosemary, and attach it to the back of the framed project. If you don't have a compendium of magickal herbs handy, no problem! Dried organic teas can be a quick and easy choice for empowerment. There are so many blends on the market, you'll be able to find something that closely matches your intent.

The Day to Begin Your Project

General timing applies to enchanted stitchery just as it affects any other magickal work. Choose which pattern of timing works best for you. Some people like to work with the moon phases, others the days of the week, and some with astrological timing. Rather than fret about which timing is best, work with the timing that is most comfortable to you. If you need to learn more advanced timing, the opportunity will come, and you'll integrate the information easily. Trust the design of the universe to bring you what you need when you need it. If you are unfamiliar with any timing vehicle, try the days of the week:

Sunday	Success
Monday	Intuition, emotion, women, children
Tuesday	Action
Wednesday	Communication, knowledge
Thursday	Expansion, spirituality, legal issues
Friday	Love, fast cash, education, beauty
Saturday	Structure, closure, senior citizens

Although this explanation is brief, it will get you started. You'll find more information on magickal days at the beginning of Section 5. The best timing to set that first stitch is dawn of your chosen day.

Your Very First Stitch

Okay, so you've chosen your project, picked your day, and have all your supplies. Should you just start stitching? You can, but try this and see how it works for you:

On a flat, cleaned, empty table, lay out your supplies (instructions, tools, thread, material, embellishments), placing the main piece (such as your cross-stitch Aida cloth) in the center of the table. We use the clean, flat table to signify the vast universe of opportunity.

Ring a bell or chime eight times, signalling the mastery of the physical plane. Tuning forks are super great for this, too. The idea here is to remove all negativity from your tools and supplies—from the manufacturer to the clerk at the store or even to family members who have fingered through your things. By removing the negativity, you have presented a fresh vehicle to the universe.

Light a white candle and pass the light over all the items on the table. This is done to connect your project with Spirit (that which you feel runs the universe). You can intone your favorite prayer or just say a simple blessing. If the project is for someone other than your-self, say: "This project is for (whomever). May they receive the purity of unconditional love through my work."

Close your eyes, and visualize the finished project. Then see yourself giving the project to whom it is intended. Visualize yourself and the other person smiling happily. Envision the person using the item with a smile on their face, then physically smile yourself, open your eyes, and say: "It is done! It always works. Always a blessing!" Smile. You are now ready to stitch the magickal way!

When you have completed your project, follow the exact same formula. Clear and clean the table. Place the finished item in the center of the table (wash and block first, if necessary). Ring the bell eight times. Pass a new, lit candle over the item for the renewed connection to Spirit. Intone your prayer, charm, or statement. Visualize yourself and the recipient happy and empowered. End with a physical smile. Say: "Thank you! It is done!" Your item is ready to be given to that special person.

Stitching the Magickal Way

When the needle points to the sky, you are pulling in the energy of Spirit. When it returns to the cloth, you are bringing that energy down into the project. When the needle points down to the earth, you are drawing in earth energy (extremely powerful when you wish to manifest things on this plane). When it comes back up through the cloth, you are bringing that energy into the project. Likewise, when knitting, your needles are working with sky ener-gy, but your yarn is a representation of earth energy—together, just as in stitching cross-stitch or needlepoint, you are creating balance in the work.

When Beginning a Project

Cleanse and consecrate all tools, threads, canvas, yarn, and so on, with either holy water or sacred smoke. Bless everything with your overall intent. By intent, I mean love, money, health, success, or you can be more exact. Remember, magickal stitchery works only on attraction. Refrain from negative wording or intent. Think of what you *do* want, not of what you don't want. Infusing your stitchery with negative intent will only boomerang. There is no escape.

Create an affirmation or short stitchery poem to match your intent—something that can be said quickly and easily at every stitch, or if this is too much, at the end of every row. Keep your language simple, direct, and straightforward. Use nouns or single-action verbs (your best bet), such as healing, success, prosperity, happiness, serenity, peace, tranquility, harmony, love, security, joy, compassion, safety, luck, unity, opportunity…even a simple thank you carries great power.

During Your Project

Try to stay as upbeat as possible. If things are going well for you, concentrate on the positive aspects of whom the project is for. People suffering from terminal illnesses and depression can find great solace in needlework due to its meditative qualities. Take advantage of this energy if you are in this situation, working the stitches to promote healing for yourself and for others. Sharing positive thoughts and actions is the epitome of caring.

If you become frustrated during the construction of a project, renew the process you first used when you began your work—the clean table, the white candle, the bell, the prayer, the visualization, etc. When you open your eyes, laugh, and say: "This is so easy!" Surprisingly enough, this works wonders! If the problem seems particularly testy, just set the piece aside for a day or two. Begin again when you are in a better mental place.

Sometimes your frustration may have nothing to do with the piece itself, but revolves around a problem in your own life. For example, let's say you are knitting a simple shawl, but your yarn keeps tangling, to the point that you are sure you will scream, scream, *scream*! Stop! This is the universe telling you that you have some tangle in your life you aren't paying attention to, and this is the shortest and best way to show you. Think about what this might be, acknowledge the fact, put the project down, and take a walk or do something physical that does not relate to your project. In this way, you won't be weaving negativity into your work. Come back to the project when your mind is clear and focused. You may be delighted that you have also thought of a solution to your present "tangle."

Big Projects

To me, big projects are items that take more than five days to complete. This could be crocheting an afghan, knitting a sweater, sewing a quilt, stitching a large cross-stitch pattern, etc. It doesn't hurt to burn a lovely candle while working, occasionally ringing the bell or tuning forks and repeating your prayer of intention. This will keep you and the work in the mindset of opportunity.

Storing Your Project While Working

At the end of each stitching session, take a few moments to relax. Bless the project before you put it away. Repeat your original intent and visualization, and remember to thank the universe for the time you were able to spend doing something you love.

Stitchers have a variety of ways in which they store their projects while working. Some have fancy, special bags, where others just put the project back in the original plastic bag from the manufacturer. I do something a bit different. I purchased ten inexpensive canvas bags to use for various projects. Before I begin a project, I launder the bag and include the bag on the table during my original blessing. If the project is for someone else, I will put their picture in this bag. If I don't have a picture, I write their name on a three-by-five-inch card and place that in the bag. Sometimes I add a potpourri pillow or herb sachet to the bag, along with a charm or two. When I'm not working on the project, all supplies and the project are stored in the bag. I also store this bag in the area of the room that relates to my intent—a feng shui principle. For example, if I decided to make a quilt for my granddaughter, then I might place the bag in any of the following positions: for her education, northeast; for her prosperity, southeast; for her general success and artistic abilities, south; for my love for her and her mother, or a good relationship with her (grandmother to granddaughter), or marriage possibilities, southwest; help from good mentors, northwest. Too complicated? Just remember to store the work with love—your intent is absolutely the key.

I Really Should Be Doing Something Else!

Sometimes allowing ourselves time to actually enjoy working on our creative stitchery can be very difficult. Right now I'm knitting a healing shawl in soft, baby blue yarns. Yet when I sit down to knit, I think: "I should be doing the dishes. I should be finishing that writing project. I should be doing laundry. I should be sweeping out the basement. I should pay that phone bill. I should be cleaning the bathroom shower (ugh!)," etc. It's never just one "should-be"—your mind will create quite a dance line if you let it. To appease this nagging, before you begin stitching, do one thing you've been putting off all day (or even all week), and then settle in for some happy stitching! Stitch for a half-hour, then get up, move around, and do something else you've been putting off. Now that you've taken a healthy break, go back to stitching! By releasing the tasks you must do, you are actually creating a mind-healthy, magickal time slot that can be filled with what you desire—stitching!

Integrate Your Family

This is a big one. Whether it is just you and your partner, or you have rooms bulging with kids—few, if any, humans can tolerate your attention to what you are doing if they believe it is taking away attention from themselves. Rather than suffer for years in silence, here are a few tips to better integrate your family and your crafting:

- Refrain from stitching during heightened family hours. These might be breakfast, lunch (perhaps), dinner, right after school lets out, bath time (for younger kids), etc. I know you might be saying "Well! That doesn't have to be said!" However, we humans have a habit of subconsciously trying to carve out our own territory during less-than-hospitable times. For example, dinner takes a half-hour; you need only put it on the stove and then take it off when it is done, and so you sit down to catch a few stitches—and suddenly the family won't leave you alone. The problem here is that everyone in the house is hungry, and when people are hungry, they demand attention.

- Teach your craft to your children or partner. Of course, not all are interested, but by at least showing family members how something is done, they often learn an appreciation for it. You never know, some may simply love it! Likewise, learn the hobby of your spouse or partner. In this way, you will appreciate what they like to do, too.

- Focus your projects on the family, especially in the beginning. Over the years, I've done a lot of crafting—jewelry, clay art, painting, etc. I learned the hard way to focus my first projects on them. For example, when I learned jewelry making, I asked my daughters to select beads, findings, and clasps that appealed to them, and made a bracelet or necklace for them before I began other projects. I found that if they benefited early from my crafting, they were less likely to disturb me when I did projects for others. Although my kids are now grown, my oldest continues to do counted cross-stitch, and my youngest son can braid hemp like an expert.

- Family members may also enjoy the shopping experience if they know the project is specifically for them. One woman's husband was furious that she'd taken up such a "pansy" activity like knitting, citing the expense of the yarn, the "waste" of her time, etc. Wisely, she took him shopping, saying, "My skill isn't very good. But eventually I would like to make something for you. What would you like?" He considered this for a moment and said, "You know, my grandmother made beautiful afghans. I'd like one of those." She smiled and said, "Fine. Let's look at the different weights of yarn and colors. What appeals to you?" He spent an hour eagerly looking through all the books at the store for the pattern he wanted, and then another hour on yarns and colors. He made no complaints on the smaller projects she chose to do first, understanding that for what he wanted, she had to build her skill. Eventually, she completed the afghan, and he proudly displayed it to friends and family members, saying, "Yep! She made this just for me!"

Your Signature Is Your Seal of Positive Chi

Don't forget to sign your work. Although it may not be a big deal to you, it may be something forever cherished by the recipient of your work. Your signature, or designer logo, carries your personal chi *and* the intent of the piece. During the final blessing, be sure to lay your hand over your signature and fill it with white light.

The Finished Project

Before you hand over your hours of work stitched with thoughts of love and success to the intended recipient, present the project to the rising sun on the day of giving. Thank the universe for your time and skill, and reaffirm the intent of the piece along with your visualization. This is an important closure for you and takes only a few moments of your time, allowing you to connect with Spirit in a celebratory way. If the project is for yourself, ask for continued blessings, and enjoy the beauty of your creation!

Raise Your Energy By Learning a New Type of Stitchery

A great way to welcome new, fresh, dynamic energy into your life is by learning something new. Turn an old magick in stitchery into a powerful vehicle of change! Whether it be photography or stitchery, fixing a car or learning to speak a new language, knowledge always brings new opportunities.

Last fall and winter, I taught myself to knit. As the winds howled and the snow swirled, I knitted and knitted and knitted! Such a wonderful, magickal way to spend those cold winter days and nights. I made several blankets, three mohair shawls, purses, a baby sweater, scarves, hats, a shopping bag, neat cell phone carriers, a stuffed rabbit, a pillow, and a huge, snuggly warm kimono coat. In the spring, I took a trip to Mannings outside of East Berlin, Pennsylvania. What a marvelous place! Yarn, yarn everywhere! Looms, spinning wheels, and books galore; I was in textile heaven! Among my treasured purchases snuggled a "learn to crochet" kit. I'd conquered beginning knitting, and now I wanted more, though I wasn't sure if I wanted to learn to crochet—it seemed like such an old-lady type of thing. Did I really want to go there? Yet there were patterns I'd seen that looked so neat, new, and retro-hip…hmm…dare I? Did I want to invest the time it took to learn to knit into learning to crochet? I'd already tried once over the winter—I spent two days and got nowhere with the crochet thing. Did I want to try again? Maybe this type of practice just wasn't for me…

Yet that crochet pattern…it called to me. Truly, it did! And I have a thing about patterns and energy…

So this time I started on a new moon, and I just tried making a block using a single crochet stitch. I didn't have any particular project in mind, just the idea of learning the stitch. I used a bigger hook than called for so I could see the mechanics of the stitches…and lo and behold, I did it! On my first real project, I had trouble keeping the edges even, so I used a big, fat safety pin to mark where I should be making the last stitch and the turning chain; after that, it was onward and upward! In no time at all, I'd made two pillows, a purse, two belts, and started on a big ripple afghan for my granddaughter. In just two days, I'd finished my first project and moved on to the others.

Okay, I had the mechanics down…now for the magick. For me, I've found in most cases crochet goes faster than knitting, which means I can make more things for more people in the same amount of time if I crochet rather than knit. Granted, knitting works specifically well for some things, but when it comes to creating a fast magick item, such as a healing gris-gris for a friend, crochet seems to work up quicker. Here's how I now begin all my crochet projects:

1. Focus on the intent. I write down on a notecard specifically what I desire, along with the person's name. For example, if I wanted to make a gris-gris for Sharon, I'd write her name, along with the energy I wish to draw into the work, such as healing of her right elbow after surgery. Or, if I were making a blanket for a child, protection and good health all year through, and so on. I keep this card with the project until completion, then burn it with sacred herbs after the project has been washed and prepared for the blessing ritual.

2. Choose the pattern and the yarn to match the intent and the person. Let's say Sharon's favorite colors are pink and green, and she loves heavily textured things. I'd go with her favorite colors, a unique, textured yarn, and perhaps a more intricate pattern. Waved afghan patterns are perfect for drawing in the positive flow of the universe and so are especially nice for sleep-oriented magick for children as well as adults.

3. Cleanse the yarn and the hook you will use, and dedicate them specifically to the project at hand. Use the procedure that is most comfortable to you.

4. Begin the project with the timing that suits the intent. Use the moon phase and the moon in the signs as your guide.

5. Consider the foundation chain number. Use the magick in numbers if at all possible. For example, a three-count ripple pattern is perfect for almost all projects. Eleven count makes a nice larger ripple and is very magickal as well. What will your foundation chain number factor down to on the scale of one through nine? Is this the energy you wish to instill in the project? If necessary, can you possibly change the foundation chain number without ruining the pattern?

6. Each time you sit down to crochet, light a white candle to acknowledge the light of Spirit, and place a glass of empowered water close to the

project. This water should be filled with your blessings and intent. Give the water to a plant when you are done with the project for that day or evening.

7. Use the simple HedgeWitch formula on page 40 before you begin the project. Be sure you have your statement of intent ready before you do this.

8. Finish the HedgeWitch formula with the chant below. Say the project chant nine times, and then begin to work.

   Crochet Project Chant

   > *Magick circle*
   >
   > *Pull it through*
   >
   > *Loop the thought of (healing, prosperity, good fortune, protection, etc.)*
   >
   > *To bring to you*
   >
   > *Handle hook*
   >
   > *To catch the thing*
   >
   > *Manifest in sacred ring of (healing, prosperity, good fortune,*
   >
   > > *protection, etc.)!*

9. When laying down the foundation of the project, try this chant, to be repeated nine times:

   Foundation Chain Chant

   > *Sacred fiber*
   >
   > *Spun to make*
   >
   > *Unfolding path*
   >
   > *That I (she, he) will take.*
   >
   > *Lines of (hope, joy, healing, prosperity, happiness, etc.)*
   >
   > *Loop to bring*
   >
   > *A chain of (hope, joy, healing, prosperity, happiness, etc.)*
   >
   > *From thought to thing!*

10. Remember that the turning chain with every row represents the slowing of energy that occurs when a thought manifests into a thing! The turning chain helps to "set the work" each and every row you make and therefore becomes the most powerful stitch of the row. Say special prayers on this loop to add additional energy to the piece, and then end with "It always works! Always a blessing!"

Finish the project as I recommended on page 169 or choose your own magickal way to complete the item. You can use the above chants for knitting as well as other stitchery projects by changing the wording to fit your activity. By mixing this type of stitchery and magick together, I found peace of mind and a contemplative, relaxing way of using some of my spare time. Best of all, my efforts brought joy to the recipients, which is by far the most exquisite benefit of all!

OMAR

section
⑤

Hearth, Home & Garden

tips, formulas &
techniques

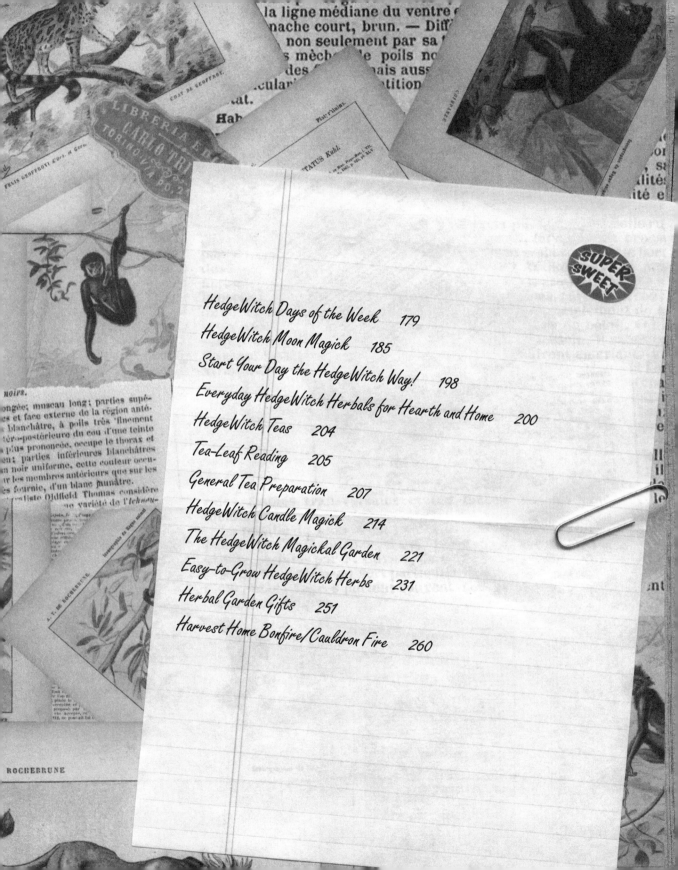

HedgeWitchery in Daily Life

The art and science of HedgeWitchery moves throughout your daily life if you only allow it to do so. Every day can be magick-filled if you so desire. You have the ultimate choice! This section of the HedgeWitch material provides tips, techniques, formulas, and recipes that can be used to enhance and fulfill your life in enchanting ways … every day!

HedgeWitch Days of the Week

Every day of the week provides opportunities for magick! The following list gives you general energy correspondences and ideas on what tasks might be best performed. Having a sense of task-defined order can free your mind from worrying about all those little items that seem to inundate us if we don't pay attention.

Sunday

Rest and play: Sunday is ruled by the sun, bringing vibrant, successful and positive energy to any application or task. Above all, the sun symbolizes harmony in action, making Sunday a great day for family activities, enjoying the world around you, and having fun. Celebrating the light of the sun, Sunday provides great timing for working with gold jewelry. Light a white or yellow candle this day for future success in your life. Take time to enjoy your favorite hobby; it's a perfect day to finish projects meant for loved ones! Add a sundial to your magickal garden and ask for weekly blessings every Sunday.

Sun-related garden plants: Plant, tend, harvest, or use these plants on their favorite day: angelica, bay, carnation, celandine, chamomile, eyebright, ginseng, juniper, lovage, marigold, palm, peony, rosemary, rue, saffron, St. John's wort, sunflower, tea, witch hazel.

Work on issues regarding . . . prominent people, superiors, employers, executives, personal illumination, personal power, persons worthy of trust, men ages 30–45, good health, life force, success.

Sunday's colors: yellow, gold/purple, gold, scarlet, purple, bright red, orange

Monday

Water and flow: Monday is ruled by the moon, bringing the powerful element of water into play. In magick, we know that water conveys the energy we put into it, helping our work to flow into the goals we wish to achieve. Monday is a great day for working with water—washing the car, doing the laundry, taking a long, luxurious bath or shower. It's also a great day to make magickal perfumes, oils, floor washes, and air fresheners! Designing silver jewelry also vibrates well with Monday's energy. Given the moon's representation of our emotions, this is a good day for a longer-than-usual meditation, creating new affirmations that fit what we truly want in life, and considering the flow of our emotional well-being. It's a good day for painting, developing new dance steps, or composing music. Monday is also considered the primary day for workings for women (mothers, daughters, grandmothers, female friends, female partners, etc.). Light a white or blue candle on this day for emotional well-being. Add an outdoor water element to your magickal garden!

Moon-related garden plants: Plant, tend, harvest, or use these plants on their favorite day: aloe, lemon balm, cabbage, cucumber, eucalyptus, gardenia, gourd, grape, honesty, jasmine, lettuce, lily, mallow, moonflower, poppy, potato, purslane, turnip, willow.

Work on issues regarding... mothers, women in general, the public and the public eye, change, your feelings, liquids, runaways, lost items, the sea, short trips, your perception on various issues.

Monday's colors: colors spotted or striped with white, cream, opalescent, pale yellow, pale green, pale lavender, pale blue, pearl, silver, white

Tuesday

Fire and energy: Tuesday is ruled by Mars, the planet of success, action, and derring-do! Fire and metal are the featured energies on this day. Save Tuesday for dealing with difficult people and issues, cultivating the warrior energy within yourself and channeling that emotion in the right direction through positive action. It's a good day to buy small tools or have old ones repaired and cleaned. Also a day for contacting mentors (who are ruled by the element of metal) and people of strength who may be able to help you. Baking, working with wax, firing pottery, or forging alliances all fall under Mars energy. Celebrating the element of fire, this is a great day to make HedgeWitch grubby, or overdipped, herbal candles. Tuesday is also considered the primary day for workings for men (fathers, sons, grandfathers, male friends, and male partners). Light a white or red candle on this day for personal success through action! Add a fire element to your outdoor magickal garden, such as a new grill, burn pit, offering cauldron, etc. Make use of it every Tuesday!

Mars-related garden plants: Plant, tend, harvest, or use these herbs on their favorite day: basil, cactus, carrots, chili peppers, coriander, garlic, holly, horseradish, mustard, nettle, onion, pennyroyal, pepper, peppermint, pine, radish, shallot, snapdragon, thistle, woodruff, wormwood.

Work on issues regarding... energy, sex, leadership, weapons, fire, assertiveness, doctors (especially surgeons), sewing, personal transformation, sports, winning, baking, cooking.

Tuesday's colors: colors that shine—crimson, fiery red, lemon yellow, red ochre, rust, saffron, scarlet

Wednesday

Chatter box! Wednesday is ruled by Mercury, that quicksilver planet of thought and communication. Take care of all written stuff today—letters, e-mails, cards to friends and family, notification on a move or other important events in your life. Send birthday cards, holiday cards, and flowers to those you love! It's a good day to compose the next entry in your blog, the next entry in your journal, study, take a written test, or communicate clearly through words. Research and gathering information also relate to Mercury energy, as well as designing scrapbook pages, bookmarks, altered books, and photo albums. Keep forgetting to send out your bills? Make Wednesday the day for such things. Today, send that book you promised to someone and never got around to doing. Wednesday is also a great day for giving things away, as you are sharing your love and personal energy with every gift you give. Light a white or silver candle on this day for mental growth and success in communicating with others. Add wind chimes, bells, flags, and ribbons to your outdoor magickal garden. Petitions to Spirit outdoors on Wednesday are perfect ways to use Mercury energy.

Mercury-related garden plants: Plant, tend, harvest, or use these herbs on their favorite day: beans, bergamot, caraway, celery, clover, dill, fennel, fern, goat's rue, horehound, lavender, lemongrass, lemon verbena, marjoram, mint, parsley, savory.

Work on issues regarding . . . communication, books, letters, e-mails, messages, questions, blogs, writing in general, transport, contracts, bargaining, neighbors, research, young people, students, office employees, salespersons, tricksters.

Wednesday's colors: dusky silver, light blue, azure, dove, light grey, clear, or new color blends

Thursday

To market, to market! Thursday is ruled by Jupiter, the Great Benefic, a planet of long-term good fortune and expansion, and also attributed to personal spirituality. Running errands that involve the transaction of large sums of money, charity, and your spiritual pursuits might be a great way of turning this day into a fulfilling use of your time. Jupiter's job is to attract positive growth and good fortune, so this is a great day to start a new hobby, expand your garden by adding a spiritually related statue, or put in that new foot path. A great day to shop for large-ticket items, expanding your favorite collection, and another great day for gift-giving. Jupiter represents both fire and water (modern and classical astrological correspondences), making this a primary day for healing work. It's a wonderful day to make healing sachets, herbal washes, and aura-cleaning products. Light a purple or white candle today, and welcome healing energies into your life.

Jupiter-related garden plants: Plant, tend, harvest, or use these herbs on their favorite day: anise, borage, chestnut, cinquefoil, clove, dandelion, endive, honeysuckle, hyssop, maple, pumpkin, sage, sarsaparilla, sassafras. It's a great day to add new plants and expand your outdoor or indoor garden.

Work on issues regarding . . . good luck, expansion, good fortune, higher education, abundance, long trips, divination, gambling, professionals, the wealthy, lawyers, judges, horses, foreigners, middle-aged men.

Thursday's colors: red and green combined, sea green, deep blue or purple, violet, ash, lime, forest green, green and gold combination

Friday

Just for pretty: From entertainment to personal beauty and fixing up the place, in all you do, Venus energy can be used dynamically for achieving the higher vibrations of love. Fridays are great days for personal beauty enhancements, making the home and garden an art-inspired sanctuary, building your altar, healing through love, and, of course, fast cash workings. Entertainment and get-togethers with friends and family also fall under the power of seductive Venus. Arts, crafts, and just plain being creative share in Venus pursuits. Make body powders, soaps, perfumes for love, passion sachets, love amulets, gemstone jewelry, and decorative clay pieces. Venus often represents the element of earth and growth, hence the occult association of the color green. Light a white, green, or pink candle today, and attract beauty into your life! Bring your garden inside! Work with potted plants today.

Venus-related garden plants: Plant, tend, harvest, or use these herbs on their favorite day: African violet, apple, barley, birch, blue flag (iris), cardamom, catnip, coltsfoot, columbine, corn, crocus, daffodil, daisy, geranium, hyacinth, lilac, magnolia, mugwort, myrtle, orchid, plantain, rose, sorrel, spearmint, strawberry, thyme, tomato, tulip, valerian, vervain, wheat.

Work on issues regarding . . . alliances, love, gifts, money, harmony, relationships, marriage, what you value, your resources, moveable goods, lost objects (especially those lost at a social affair), parties, young women, your best friend, wife, pleasures, arts of all types, luxury items.

Friday's colors: any color that shines; white; purple; blue; green and brown combination; sky blue; copper; brass

Saturday

Heavy duty day: Saturday is ruled by Saturn, the planet of limits as well as rewards through hard work. Saturday's tasks may include cleaning out the garage, the basement, the attic, or those overflowing closets. It's often a day for choosing appliances such as stoves, air conditioning units, refrigerators, etc., where partners can shop together and take their time choosing what is right for them. It's a good day for picking up clutter, vacuuming, washing windows, rearranging furniture, and banishing all negative items and emotions by the act of releasing and attracting good energies through positive tasks and aromas. Make furniture polish and carpet fresheners today. Light a white or brown candle today for drawing miracles! Erect a trellis, build a retaining wall, design a rock garden, or make major renovations to your outdoor garden on this day.

Saturn-related garden plants: Plant, tend, harvest, or use these herbs on their favorite day: amaranth, beets, boneset, comfrey, ivy, lobelia, morning glory, mullein, pansy, patchouli, solomon's seal, yew.

Work on issues regarding . . . removing obstacles or limitations, lifting restrictions, hardscaping the garden, old people, debts, poverty, real estate, construction, karma, plumbers, fathers, overcoming delays.

Saturday's colors: black, dark green, dark brown (for miracles), wood colors, dark blue

Note: Those herbs listed are the ones that are most commonly found in yards and gardens in the northeast. Feel free to substitute your own native plants.

HedgeWitch Moon Magick

How to Tell If the Moon Is Waxing or Waning

Magickal people use the moon as a vehicle for focus and order, flowing with the energy of the moon to accomplish particular tasks. Earlier in this book, you learned that:

Full moons equal the harvest of any given thing and are the perfect balance of opposites.

New moons are a time to begin new projects and take a fresh approach to any situation.

Waxing moons represent building and growing, giving more energy to a particular focus.

Waning moons herald closure, putting the last touches on a project, and the elimination of ideas, projects, and desires we no longer need.

The full moon and new moons are easy to tell when looking up at the sky. But what about the waxing and waning moons? You can use an almanac like the *Farmer's Almanac* or one of Llewellyn's many excellent magickal almanacs, check out the daily newspaper under the weather section, surf online, or you can simply step outside and look up at the sky, using the following guideline: When does the moon rise? The time the moon rises will indicate if it is waxing or waning. If the moon rises in the daytime, then it is waxing. If the moon rises in the nighttime, it is waning.

Circumference of the Moon

The second technique is to look at the circumference of the moon. If the outer edge is fullest toward the east, the moon is waxing, or growing towards the full moon. If the outer edge is fullest towards the west, the moon is waning to a new moon. If the circumference appears to be more horizontal than vertical, use the highest point of the moon as your guide.

Flowing by the Full Moon

Trying hard to find a schedule to get everything done this year? Try using the monthly full moons as harvest times for particular projects, using the name of the moon as a focus for your activities. Here are some suggestions:

Note: These moons apply to the Northern Hemisphere.

Historical Moon Names

January: Nursing Moon, Milk Moon, Wolf Moon—Concentrate on family activities this month. Take care of all wellness/health appointment scheduling for the coming year for yourself, family, and pets.

February: Storm Moon, Fasting Moon, Weaning Moon—Change your eating habits to match a more healthy way of life. You might choose to go on a diet, or perhaps slowly begin to adjust your diet, removing or adding one food type at a time. Go through those automatic payments and determine if there is something you could do without (magazines, memberships).

March: Seed Moon, Chaste Moon—Excellent time to start new projects and begin a new job or family activity. Great month for teaching yourself new skills. Choose which plants you will grow in your garden this year, and consider any hardscaping plans.

April: Mating Moon, Hare Moon—Focus on your partner this month. Review your behavior and what you can adjust in your own activities that will satisfy yourself and bring harmony to your partner. When the last frost hits, begin planting your garden.

May: Dyad Moon, Journey Moon—Try getting all those errands done this month that you've been putting off. Take several short weekend or day trips. Enjoy the season by visiting places you've never been.

June: Mother's Moon, Mead Moon—Take care of any issues relating to females this month, including mothers, friends, sisters, daughters, etc. If you are interested in feng shui, activate the southwest corner of your home with an altar dedicated to the mother of the home.

July: Father's Moon, Wort Moon—Take care of any issues relating to men this month, including fathers, friends, brothers, sons, etc. If you are interested in feng shui, activate the northwest corner of your home with an altar dedicated to the father of the home.

August: Nesting Moon, Barley Moon—Time to look over your winter wardrobe and household supplies. Prepare now for the winter. Mend or sew blankets, hang heavier curtains, etc. Decide what type of winter wear you would like to purchase this year.

September: Harvest Moon, Wine Moon—Tie up large projects with a sure completion by November (if the project is very large).

October: Blood Moon, Sorting Moon, Culling Moon—Time to sort through and clear out the attic and the basement, garage, closets, kitchen cabinets, etc.

November: Snow Moon, Death Moon—Remove any "dead-energy items" from the home. For example: compost dead flowers or plants, repair broken windows, and throw out torn carpets, broken furniture, etc. Make sure all clutter is removed (magazines, books, papers, clothing on the floor or under beds, extraneous junk).

December: Dark Moon, Birth Moon—Sort through seasonal decorations and throw out the torn, broken, or old things you'll never use again. Take advantage of holiday pre-season and after-season bargains. Go through next year's calendar and mark off special dates, magickal times, etc., and block off areas for specific projects.

Full Moon Magickal Oil Formula*

- 6 drops gardenia fragrance
- 2 drops lemon essential oil
- 2 drops sandalwood essential oil
- 1 ounce jojoba carrier oil (can use sweet almond oil)

*for heavy cleaning work,
add 1 drop camphor essential oil

Full Moon Herbal Charm for Attraction

You will need:

> White candle
>
> Cotton
>
> Gris-gris bag
>
> ⅛   teaspoon lemon peel
>
> ⅛   teaspoon yellow sandalwood
>
> ⅛   teaspoon wild lettuce
>
> ⅛   teaspoon Irish moss
>
> Your desire written on a small piece of paper
> (with berry magickal ink—see page 258)
>
> A lock of your hair
>
> White or silver cord
>
> Mortar and pestle

Choose a specific deity from the list provided on pages 193–194. Research this deity fully before petitioning. Using primal language, write your desire with berry magickal ink on a piece of paper. Place all items under the full moon for one hour.

When you are ready to perform this working, light incense and pass over all items. Spread the cotton like a small nest. Grind herbs together to make a powder. Place the ground mixture in the center of the cotton. Put your hair on top. Roll cotton and herbs around your folded petition (fold very small, toward yourself). Secure with white or silver cord. Place in gris-gris bag. Sprinkle bag with full moon magickal oil or your enchanted perfume, as explained in Section 2.

Place gris-gris bag beside white candle. Rub candle with sandalwood herb and hold up to the moon like a wand. Beckon, in your own words, the power of the full moon to enter the candle. Petition the deity chosen, paying special attention to your previous research. Light the candle and pass over the gris-gris bag seven times. Place candle in holder and repeat your desire seven times, remembering to use primal language and saying thank you when you are finished. Allow candle to burn completely. Carry gris-gris with you until your desire is achieved. Burn when your request has been granted. Note: Various flowers can be added to your altar along with favorite items associated with your chosen moon goddess to increase your connection with divinity.

Did you know: In early times, the sun was attributed to the Goddess, and the moon attributed to the God?

Full Moon Magick Water

Magickal waters are used to cleanse and empower objects, people, and sacred areas. Try this great no-salt recipe using magickal herbs!

	Spring water (or white rum; see below)
⅛	teaspoon water lily root
⅛	teaspoon lemon peel
⅛	teaspoon poppy petals
1	clear bowl
1	round mirror (about 6 inches)
1	moonstone
	Mortar and pestle, optional
1	white candle and candle holder

On a full moon, either grind herbs to a powder with mortar and pestle or leave whole, as you desire. Place clear bowl of spring water on top of a mirror where you can catch the light of the full moon in the water. Add herbal ingredients and moonstone. Stir water with finger, wooden stick (type of wood can be chosen by magickal correspondence), thin copper tube, or braided sterling silver wire. Both types of metal (sterling is a mix) are excellent for energy flow. Stir water nine times in a clockwise direction. Take three deep, even breaths before blessing and empowering, making sure your feet are firmly on the ground, shoulders straight yet relaxed. Rub white candle with a little sandalwood herb. Light candle. Place candle in the water so that the flame burns safely out of the water. Hold both hands over the water and candle, then speak any of the herbal empowerment conjurations given in this book that match your intended desire. When you are finished, seal the work by ringing your magickal bell to match your personal lucky number. Store water in a fluted potion bottle in refrigerator until needed throughout the month. Make new water each month. This magickal water is to be used for adding power to any working, esbat rituals, or harvest spells, so you may wish to indicate your desire accordingly.

Hint: Full moon water carries extra power if made in your own magickal garden. As a special touch, float carnations or moon flowers in the water for at least one hour.

Note: Salt is unnecessary in this formula, as the lemon peel and water lily root are natural herbal cleansers. For a healing moon formula, add eucalyptus herb. For divinatory pursuits, add eyebright herb. To move a particular spell along, use white rum instead of water (just don't put it near a fire!). If you use white rum, you can steep the herbs for an entire month to make the brew more magickal, but don't drink it!

Prayer Beads

Prayer beads are a vehicle used to focus the mind on a single intent by saying an affirmation or prayer as you touch each bead. Ideally, to focus the mind completely, the affirmations should be intoned for a minimum of sixty-five seconds. HedgeWitch prayer beads use twenty-eight beads on a string, with twenty-eight corresponding to one moon cycle (full moon to full moon). Your beads can be used in a variety of ways—there is no limit to their creative use.

You will need:

- 28 beads (your choice)
- 2 5-yard pieces of hemp or cord (your choice of color; larger beads will require longer cord)
- Full moon water
- White candle
- Sandalwood herb or full moon oil
- A positive affirmation of your choice that fits your lifestyle

Fold cords in half and make a knot, leaving four dangling ends. On a full moon, cleanse and bless all supplies. Rub white candle with sandalwood herb. Keep candle lit as you work. String one bead onto the two center cords. Tie a plain knot with the two outer cords so that the bead sits within the cords, stabilized by the knot underneath, or use a macramé knot such as the square knot. Each time you string a bead or add a knot, repeat your chosen affirmation out loud. Add another bead. Knot. Continue until your project is completed. Sprinkle beaded cord with full moon water. Place beaded cord in the moonlight. As the month progresses, you can use the beaded cord for a variety of prayers and spell work. Re-empower every full moon. Additional charms can be added throughout the year—you can even add buttons! (That's an Old Pennsylvania Dutch custom.) Your beads can become a year's worth of magick. Retire them at the end of the year, or continue to use them the following year.

Note: Wooden beads with large holes work best. Add a sterling silver charm to the top or bottom (or both) of your newly made prayer beads. Hang beads on staff, over altar, or carry in purse or pocket.

Dark Moon Prayer Beads

Use only black or midnight blue beads. Use black cord. These beads are for banishing negativity and releasing our fears or worries. Touch each bead, saying: "I let go of _____," naming whatever is upsetting you at the time. "I am free! I am filled with harmony, happiness, and peace of mind. I am cleansed! Thank you!" When you have finished touching all the beads and repeating your mantra, place prayer beads under the full moon to cleanse them after your working.

Window Dressing

Lengthen cord and add additional colorful beads and bells. Use as a decoration on windows, doors, or over altar. Beads with dots and wild patterns are thought to ward off negativity, confusing the evil energy, making it lose its power. Bells cleanse the atmosphere of anger and negative intentions.

For Magickal Gardeners

Make your HedgeWitch prayer beads while sitting in your garden, allowing the natural touch of Spirit to flow through your fingers. If your basil or hyssop is flowering, add those tiny petals, too!

Full Moon Meditation/Affirmation

For a full month, repeat this affirmation each morning and upon retiring at the end of the day, beginning on the first day of the full moon:

> *In stillness, I find illumination.*
> *By looking within, I learn the mysteries of the universe,*
> *for therein lies the portal of understanding!*

As you look within yourself, you will discover an amazing gateway to divine energy! Practice filling yourself with white light many times during the day. After one month of practice, you may find yourself happier, calmer, and healthier! Consider this inner light the illumination of Spirit, as we see in the face of the full moon. You may find that adding the sound of a singing bowl or tuning forks (particularly B, associated with the second chakra) is helpful in your full moon work. The "Om" sound also resonates well, whether you use a tuning fork or your own powerful voice.

Full Moon Scrying Bowl

Just like tea-leaf reading (see section starting on page 205), scrying bowls also use the intuitive mind and symbol association to find answers to questions, solutions, or creative ideas. Gazing calmly into a bowl of colored water or a black mirror is like looking directly at the still point of the universe, where opportunity always exists and the answers are always there. Scrying is normally done in a quiet place with low light and pleasant aromas—no interruptions to scatter one's thoughts or intensify worries or negative emotions. The full moon and Wiccan high holidays are traditional scrying times. Before you begin, you may wish to invoke a particular moon goddess for assistance or focus directly on Spirit.

Here is a list of full moon goddesses:

> *Aido Hwedo (Haiti)*
> *Amaterasu (Japan)*
> *Aphrodite (Phoenician)*
> *Arianrhod (Wales)*
> *Astarte (Semitic)*
> *Copper Woman (Native America)*

Demeter (Greece)

Freya (Scandinavia)

Hathor (Egypt)

Hera (Greece)

Hina (Polynesia)

Ishtar (Babylon)

Isis (Egypt)

Kwan Yin (China)

Lilith (Hebrew)

Luna (Etruscan)

Luonnotar (Finland)

Mawu (Dahomey)

Parvati (India)

Selene (Greek)

Tiamat (Semitic)

Venus (Rome)

When scrying, the practitioner often positions a candle near the bowl to capture the reflection. You may also take the bowl outside to capture the reflection of the full moon during the scrying process. As in tea-leaf reading, shapes that seem to float across the water are deciphered using word association; therefore, full moon scrying becomes a very personal endeavor.

Here is a recipe for a divination water bowl, enhanced by the correspondences of empowered herbs. You will need:

1	clear bowl (about 3 inches in diameter works well)
1	bottle of India ink
⅛	teaspoon water lily herb
⅛	teaspoon poppy petals
	Spring water
1	cotton gris-gris bag or tub tea bag

⅛ teaspoon eyebright (or one of the herbs listed in appendix 4
associated with divination or mental acuity)

⅛ teaspoon ancestral grave dirt (optional—
used to invoke the honored ancestors)

Mortar and pestle

Pen and paper

Magick bell or chimes

Directions: Grind water lily, poppy, eyebright, and grave dirt (from beloved ancestor's grave) with mortar and pestle. Pour in cotton bag or tub tea bag. Tie or seal. Place in bowl of warm water. Set water under full moon for an hour (it is best if the moon is reflected in the surface of the water). Remove. Add India ink to water until water is completely black. Set under full moon for another hour (it is best if it can reflect the light of the moon). Seal the moon energy in the water using your magick bell or chimes.

Instructions for scrying: When you are ready to use the water, light your favorite incense and the white candle. Call upon a moon goddess, Spirit, or your sacred ancestors for blessings and assistance. You may wish to use this simple scrying charm by holding your hands over the water and slowly speaking the following words:

HedgeWitch Scrying Charm

Magick water, speak to me…
Tranquility (pause)
Harmony (pause)
Creativity (pause)
Positive activity (pause)
So mote it be. Thank you!
It always works. Always a blessing.

Smile. Now ask your question. Stare into the dark surface of the water. If your vision seems foggy, this is good! Write down any and all mental impressions, but don't make any formulations at this time unless they are crystal-clear to you. Sleep on the information you have received, and the following day, when your mind is clear, in a quiet place, review the impressions. Review again the following week. Practice makes perfect! Do not store water; make it fresh each full moon.

Note: Water formula without ink can be used to paint the back of a prepared magick mirror to heighten its power.

To heighten your scrying experience, you may wish to employ other full moon correspondences, such as an oil or incense that relates to the moon; moon colors; or use moon powder (below).

Full moon color associations: silver, dark blue, light blue, white, lavender

Moon powder: Use this for scattering around magick candles and placing in poppets and gris-gris bags to enhance the power of any working. Grind together sandalwood, lemon peel (better if you have dried it yourself), and poppy. Add a pinch of bladderwrack. To increase fragrance, you can add three drops of any of the following full moon oils, as it suits your purpose: sandalwood essential oil, lemon essential oil, or lily fragrance.

You might also like to heighten your experience by placing your personal magickal symbols created in your HedgeWitch rites around the scrying bowl, or choose one particular symbol to assist in activating the water.

How the Void Moon Affects Your HedgeWitch Workings

Many HedgeWitch practitioners pattern their magickal work and daily tasks by the phases and the signs of the moon, following a magickal almanac for their information. From setting posts in the ground to breeding animals, from baking to canning, from hair cutting to going to the bank for a loan, the almanac and its advice are considered invaluable. These "best times" were calculated on the position of the planets in the heavens on a given day/night and the phase of the moon, as well as the sign the moon might be visiting. The moon passes to a new astrological sign approximately every two-and-a-half days, allowing the moon to visit each astrological sign at least twice a month. The moon's path isn't calculated by a calendar but by precise mathematical data, which means the moon switches signs any day or night according to her predestined movement. As the moon moves through the heavens, she communicates with the other planets (called *aspects*) while visiting the various signs. From the last conversation she has before leaving a sign to the first conversation she has in the next sign is called moon void-of-course. The moon is putting a busy signal on her phone, if you will, and isn't taking any calls. This window of dead air (so to speak) can last from a few minutes to several hours. It, too, is mathematically calculated. In classical astrology, a void moon means "nothing will come of this"—meaning actions taken during this time will most likely result in nothing. Important actions begun during the void moon are often based on poor judgment, missing information, inaccurate evaluations, and wasted effort. Daily tasks, however, don't seem to be affected by the moon void, other than producing an irritating delay or false starts, affecting our patience more than anything else.

Moon voids can be extremely useful. For example, it is a time when loopholes can be found and used. If you really don't want to go to Aunt Susie's house on Saturday, make your plans during a moon void. Most likely, something will occur later on to prevent you from going. Moon voids are a great time for meditation, reflection on goals, and a good old-fashioned power nap!

Try to avoid scheduling important meetings or signing sensitive documents during these times unless you want these things to come to nothing. Pay particular attention to phone calls and other missives received during moon voids—this will tell you the importance of the information, as well as the outcome of the issue. Try not to purchase any important items during a moon void, as the items may either be broken, torn, missing pieces, or break easily in the next few weeks. Spell work, magickal recipes, and formulations are best done with an eye on moon voids. If the void lasts only a few minutes, this won't affect your working; however, if the void lasts several hours, you may wish to reschedule making that special love or healing formula!

Start Your Day the HedgeWitch Way!

Sunrise provides perfect timing for communing with Spirit. Greeting Spirit with the sun puts you in a positive psychological mindset that will help you move throughout the day. It seems that no matter what goes wrong, if you have connected with Spirit each morning, you can handle whatever comes your way. As you did on the first night rite, use the spiritual affirmations given for that day at the moment of sunrise for at least thirty days, or try the quick sunrise meditation below. You will be amazed at the results!

Quick Sunrise Meditation

Supplies: One glass of clear water; one white candle; your magick bell; your chosen affirmations for the day; your morning drink (coffee, tea, juice).

Timing: Sunrise; if you are unsure of the time, check your local newspaper, an almanac, or the Internet for the exact time.

Position: Best done if outside, facing the rising sun; however, as this is not always possible, at least face the east, with a view of the sun.

Preparation: Mornings can be super busy, so a bit of forethought may be in order to fit your meditation into your schedule. You might have to get up a little earlier than usual, move your shower time around, or set out your clothing the night before rather than searching for it at the last minute. College students may wish to have everything packed for their first class of the day the night before rather than rushing around in the morning. Maybe you are a person that is stuck in transit as the sun rises—that's okay. Work around this by doing your meditation while it is still dark, but facing the east. When the sun does rise, silently repeat your affirmations. You can always welcome the energy of the sun into your life, no matter where you are!

Meditation: Settle yourself comfortably, facing east. You can be sitting or standing; the choice is up to you. Light the white candle and place the clear glass of water beside the candle. The candle represents your willingness to connect the flame within yourself to the living flame of Spirit. The water represents the ocean of possibilities for the new day. Root

Witches say that if bubbles appear in the water throughout the day, Spirit will grant all your wishes and is pleased at your observance.

As the sun rises, close your eyes and let the light of the sun wash over and through you. Breathe deeply several times. I always begin by saying, "Thank you for my healing," as a proactive approach to a healthy mind and body. Then I say several things I'm grateful for, because when you are grateful, a feeling of pleasure and relief washes over your body. Visualize white light flooding through and around your body. Allow yourself to feel that perfect connection with Spirit. You might next intone the names of your chosen divinity. For example, if Egyptian gods and goddesses fill you with a sense of peace and power, repeat those names that match the sun, or simply allow the general connection of Spirit to take place. This is entirely up to you.

Next, repeat your chosen affirmations for the day. These can be different every day, or you can use the same ones all the time. I usually start my affirmations by saying, "I am at peace with the gods; I am at peace with nature; I am at peace within; I am at peace with the world and everything in it," and then I move on to affirmations that are pertinent to my present situation. For example, when writing this book, my affirmations went something like this: "Spirit flows through my fingers to create peace, prosperity, and healing for others through my words." I finish by saying, "Peace with the gods; peace with nature; peace within. Thank you!" and smiling. Ring your magickal bell in your personal number.

If you have time, drink your morning juice, coffee, or tea while enjoying a few moments in the sunshine. With every swallow, believe you are drinking in the power and purity of the rising sun. Sit quietly and just observe the waking world. Keep any plans or thoughts of the coming day out of your mind; save those for later. For now, just *be*!

Extinguish the candle. If you can, leave the glass of water where you placed it for the day. At sunset, pour the water on the ground (or in a houseplant), repeating your affirmations and saying thank you.

For magickal gardeners: Place the candle and water on a special stone in your garden, and walk your garden at sunrise, enjoying this sacred space.

Everyday HedgeWitch Herbals for Hearth and Home

The following mixtures and recipes encourage connecting with Spirit and Nature with every task at hand, helping you to live in harmony every day!

Furniture Polish

10 drops ylang-ylang essential oil

5 drops lemon essential oil

5 drops lime essential oil

2 ounces jojoba carrier oil

Blend ingredients and store in airtight container. Makes a marvelous magickal furniture polish! Rub on with a soft, clean cloth. Then polish with a separate soft, clean cloth.

Carpet Freshener

60 drops lavender essential oil

20 drops orange essential oil

10 drops eucalyptus essential oil

10 drops spruce essential oil

½ cup bicarbonate of soda

Mix all ingredients in glass jar that has a tight lid. Cap tightly and shake thoroughly. Set aside for at least twenty-four hours to allow the oils to blend. Sprinkle over carpet. Leave for fifteen minutes. Vacuum.

Carpet Freshener for Good Luck and Prosperity

30 drops lime essential oil

30 drops orange essential oil

20 drops patchouli essential oil

10 drops clove essential oil

10 drops cedar essential oil

Mix all ingredients in glass jar that has a tight lid. Cap tightly and shake thoroughly. Set aside for at least twenty-four hours to allow the oils to blend. Sprinkle over carpet. Leave for fifteen minutes. Vacuum.

Air Fresheners

Natural air fresheners help to elevate our mood and can be used in place of incense in ritual. Use spring or distilled water as your liquid base. For all air fresheners, fill a four-ounce spray bottle, then add essential oils. Tighten cap. Shake well. The longer the mixture ages, the stronger the scent becomes. For ritual use, age your freshener for at least seven days before using, shaking bottle every day. Store in a dark place.

What's terrific about these fresheners? You know what's in them!

Sacred Woodland Air Freshener

A wonderful formula for creating sacred space, meditation, and for drawing good fortune.

- 40 drops pine essential oil
- 20 drops cypress essential oil
- 20 drops sandalwood essential oil
- 20 drops cedar essential oil
- 4 fluid ounces spring water

Money-Draw Air Freshener

- 40 drops peppermint or spearmint essential oil
- 40 drops bergamot essential oil
- 10 drops patchouli essential oil
- 10 drops cedar essential oil
- 10 drops calendula essential oil
- 10 drops allspice essential oil
- 4 fluid ounces spring water

Healing Glow Air Freshener

40 drops lime essential oil

40 drops eucalyptus essential oil

10 drops sandalwood essential oil

10 drops clove essential oil

10 drops rosemary essential oil

4 fluid ounces spring water

Harvest Spray Freshener

Spray at front and back door during the months of September and October (or your fall-related months in the Southern Hemisphere) to welcome an abundant harvest and good fortune. You can also use this same formula (without the water) to scent your harvest potpourri.

40 drops ginger essential oil

30 drops allspice essential oil

10 drops clove essential oil

10 drops dill essential oil

10 drops cinnamon essential oil

10 drops orange or tangerine essential oil

10 drops apple fragrance

4 fluid ounces spring water

Devil-Be-Gone Spray Freshener

This formula is terrific for a child who is afraid of the dark and things that go bump in the night, and for nervous pets during thunderstorms!

- 40 drops lavender essential oil
- 40 drops sandalwood essential oil
- 10 drops sweet bay essential oil
- 10 drops rosemary essential oil
- 10 drops chamomile essential oil
- 10 drops marjoram essential oil
- 4 fluid ounces of spring water

Merry Yule Spray Freshener

Welcome good fortune into the home by spraying the house with this mixture every day from the first of December through the Winter Solstice. Spray around a Yule bonfire to encourage good fortune in the home during the deep winter. You can also use this same blend (without the water) to scent your holiday potpourri.

- 40 drops spruce or pine essential oil
- 10 drops cedarwood essential oil
- 10 drops eucalyptus essential oil
- 10 drops sandalwood essential oil
- 10 drops allspice essential oil
- 10 drops clove essential oil
- 10 drops cinnamon essential oil
- 10 drops orange essential oil
- 10 drops cypress essential oil
- 4 fluid ounces of spring water

HedgeWitch Teas

The marvelous thing about blending your own tea is that you can use your recipes for other magickal endeavors as well. Load a bit of a dried special blend into a candle or use in sachets, incense, and even soaps! Experiment with different proportions until you find a blend that's just right for you.

Herbs you can grow or process yourself that are great for teas include anise; bee balm; calendula flowers; chamomile; cinnamon basil; crushed and dried berries (blueberries, strawberries, raspberries, etc.); dried apple slices; dried lemon, lime, or orange peels; fresh lemon balm; lemon thyme; lemon verbena; orange mint; peppermint; pineapple mint; rose geraniums; rosemary; sage; summer or winter savory; spearmint; and thyme.

To make your own magickally brewed herb teas, use a heaping teaspoon of each dried ingredient or three teaspoons of each fresh ingredient per cup. Add approximately ¼ or ½ teaspoon of dried fruits or spices and increase the quantity for a bolder cup of tea. Heat water to boiling and pour over herbs, allowing a five-minute steep time. Warm the cups and the pot before making the tea to enhance the flavor of your special brew.

Apple Abundance/Love Tea: Black tea, dried apples, and dried orange rind, flavored with honey. (A great attraction tea! You can also add apple mint for a bit of zest.)

Healing Glow Tea: Lemon balm, chamomile, and dried orange peel. Add a touch of sage or rosemary during flu season.

Prosperity Money Tea: A variety of mints (your choice; see appendix 4 for a listing) with a touch of bee balm and chamomile.

Note:

A food dehydrator is a great investment for home-grown herbals

Tea-Leaf Reading

The process of reading tea leaves is primarily an intuitive one based on symbol interpretation and word association. Some practitioners use the leaves to foretell the future, whereas others employ the process for spiritual and creative assistance. Therefore, tea-leaf reading can be a divinatory process or used as a practical psychological tool, showing you what energies you are specifically drawing toward you. If you don't like what you are attracting, change your circumstances—it is as simple as that! Taking notes can be extremely helpful, especially if you are working in a spiritual or creative venue.

Supplies Needed for Tea-Leaf Reading

Loose tea

Clean spoon

Hot water

Teacup with saucer (preferred)

Paper towel or napkin

Sweetener

Table decorations

Incense (optional)

Candles (optional)

Tea Blend Choices for Readings

Various blends of teas can enhance the focus of the reading. You may wish to choose a matching incense as well. Here is a list of different blends and their associations:

Chamomile: Dreams and wishes

China Black: General

China White: Spiritual

Cinnamon Spice Tea: Action, movement, and creativity

Citrus Teas: Good fortune and business

English Breakfast Tea: Beginnings and new ventures

Fruit Teas: Matters of the heart

Green Tea: Health issues

Herbal Teas: Use magickal correspondence depending upon the herb chosen

Herb and Citrus: Aura cleansing

Holiday Teas: Blends that are available only during specific seasons with aromas traditionally matching the intended holiday. These teas are great for affirmations involving holiday projects, parties, and shopping.

Jasmine Tea: Matters of the heart

Mint Teas: Study, education, learning, and wisdom

Mint and Chamomile Blend: Money and prosperity

Tea-Leaf Conjuration

Repeat this conjuration nine times over the steeping tea, or use your own words of empowerment.

Herbs of earth and sun and rain
Speak to me of life and gain.
Sacred brew, treasured leaves
Reveal your secrets unto me.
Thank you!
It always works. Always a blessing!

General Tea Preparation

Method 1

1. Heat water to boiling.

2. Stir dry, loose tea clockwise three times.

3. With spoon, put loose tea to taste directly into cup. If tea spills outside the cup, this is a good omen.

4. Pour hot water slowly over tea. Allow tea to steep.

5. Querent (person asking question) should pass finger over rim of cup three times in a clockwise direction before drinking, and then make a silent wish. This wish should be formulated in primal language, as discussed in Section 1. Querent should then drink the tea.

Note: The only drawback to this method is trying to drink around the floating tea leaves.

Method 2

1. Heat water to boiling.

2. Stir dry, loose tea clockwise three times.

3. With spoon, put loose tea to taste into the water in the pot. If tea spills during transfer, this is a good omen.

4. When steeped, pour tea into cup.

5. Querent should pass finger over rim of cup three times in a clockwise direction, and then make a silent wish formulated in primal language. Querent should then drink tea.

Note: Fewer leaves flow into the cup with this method.

Method 3

1. Heat water to boiling.

2. Place strainer over cup.

3. Stir dry, loose tea clockwise three times.

4. Put leaves in strainer.

5. Pour water over leaves. Let set five minutes or to taste.

6. Set strainer to the side. Do not throw away leaves.

7. Querent should pass finger over rim of cup three times in a clockwise direction, and then make a silent wish formulated in primal language. Querent should then drink tea, leaving one teaspoon of liquid in the bottom of cup.

8. Use teaspoon to scoop one helping of wet leaves from strainer into cup.

9. Swirl cup nine times clockwise.

10. Drain, then dump the residual liquid on saucer, trying not to remove any of the tea sediment from the cup (see more detailed instructions below).

Dumping the Residue Tea Water

Once the querent, or seeker, has drunk the tea, the reading is about to begin. The querent should swirl the residue three or nine times, and state aloud the purpose of the reading. This should be done in primal language, as explained in Section 1 of this book; the more defined the question or statement, the more defined the answer. Querent hands cup to the reader. As reader, do not turn the cup. Take the cup as it is handed to you, as this has its own significance. Gently pour any remaining liquid onto a napkin or paper towel, trying not to remove any of the tea sediment.

Reading Position and Placement of Symbols

The top of the cup (rim) relates to things, ideas, or events that will manifest in a few hours or are currently present in the life of the seeker. The middle section of the cup indicates a few days away. The bottom of the cup signifies the root of the question as well as the ultimate future for this query. Read clockwise from the handle of the teacup. If your cup has no handle, read from the twelve o'clock position around in a clockwise manner. Some readers believe that the dregs closest to the reader represent real issues, whereas the dregs and their associated symbols closest to the querent stand for thoughts, wishes, and dreams.

If you are reading for others just for fun, make sure the tea-leaf-reading area is well lit, filled with pleasant, natural aromas, and very colorful. These props aid the mind to reach for its fullest potential. In HedgeWitchery tea-leaf reading, the reader is really the orchestrator of the event, allowing the querent's intuition to blossom (not the reader's). When the seeker, not the reader, identifies the symbols and does their own word association, they are an active participant in the reading, which allows for a more fulfilling experience.

Omens While Pouring the Tea and During the Reading

Bubbles across top of the cup: Good fortune, money on the way; prosperity and happiness

Stalk bits or leaf pieces floating to top: Visitor or news on the way; hard stalk=man; soft stalk=woman. Place stalk on the back of the hand. Tap hand until leaf or stalk drops. The number of taps it takes for the stalk to drop is the number of days it will take until the seeker receives news or a visit.

If the querent requests sweeteners:

Honey: They are actively working to attract things into their life.

Artificial: Concentrating on dieting and health issues.

Raw sugar: Working to touch Spirit and the inner self.

Processed sugar: Possible resistance to change.

No sweetener: Possible concentration on health issues or living a constrained life.

If the querent is splashed with hot water: A sudden shock may be forthcoming, and it is highly possible the querent is not truly interested in the reading.

Foam across the top of the cup: Busy life and much activity ahead.

Tea too strong: New friendship or partnership on the horizon.

Tea too weak: Querent is working on "endings" in their life.

Spilled liquid or tea: Seeker is surrounded by unhappiness.

Querent who requests strong tea: Likes a full-bodied, adventurous life. Always on the go. Likes to take charge and be in control.

Querent who requests weak tea: Tentative individual, plagued with worries, problems, accidents and unfortunate circumstances. Possible health (body or mind) problems.

Querent who requests whiskey in tea: High stress; however, some readers pour a cup of tea for "the spirits" and add whiskey as an offering. This tea is never drunk, but sits steaming on the table until the reading is completed. Tea is poured outside on the ground at the end of the reading.

Querent who breaks or cracks teacup: Desperately desires to escape current circumstances.

Tea-Leaf Symbol Key

Acorn: Good fortune; growth

Arrow up: Success; action

Arrow down: Working within; don't miss a good opportunity

Bag, box: Constraint

Ball, circle: Movement; protection from negative influences

Beetle: Change

Bell: Good news; happiness

Birds flying: Information arriving

Butterfly: Freedom; new, exciting experiences

Candle: Transformation; clarity

Cat: Mystery

Chain: Business success or success in a current goal

Clouds: Happiness; success ahead

Crescent: Spirituality

Cross, equal arm: Gateway to prosperity and happiness; protection

Diamond: Gift; partnership; marriage of like ideas

Door: Opportunity; looking for good fortune or a needed change

Dots: Busy time ahead; pathway to success

Egg: Birth, beginnings; new project

Eye: Wisdom; healing; knowledge

Fan: Beauty; flirting

Fire: Lust; passion; zeal

Flowers: Gifts; nature spirits

Frog, toad: Good fortune; money

Glass: Social opportunities; parties

Hand: Your desires are unfolding as you think about them

Hat: Change

Heart: Love; harmony

Hourglass: Patience

Kite: Wishes; hopes

Knot: Problems; blocks; scattered thoughts

Leaves: Success (usually by the end of the season)

Lightning: Sudden event; power; bold thoughts

Lines, straight: Travel

Lines, wavy: Career luck

Mask: Secrets; hidden opportunities

Mountain: Stability; treasure within

Rectangle: Business luck

Ring: Proposal

Shell: Treasure; travel over water

Shoe: Move of house or job

Snake, single: Gossip

Snake, double: Healing or the root of the matter

Spade, shovel: Growth and achievement

Spiral: Power

Star: Wishes granted, good timing to make decisions

Sun: New beginning; personal success

Table: Family happiness and abundance

Tree: Unity and growth

Umbrella: Protection; new buildings; renovation

Wings: Guardian; spirituality

Empowering Your Tea for Creative Potential

1. Clearly state your intention as the water begins to boil. Be sure to use primal language (remember, primal language uses the least amount of words, yet clearly gets your point across in a positive way); for example: "I want ideas to make my work creative, interesting, and useful to myself as well as others."

2. Prepare tea as indicated in the general instructions.

3. Position empowered crystals (optional) around cup.

4. Decorate tea-leaf-reading area to match your desired intention. For example, if you are making Halloween or Yule cards for gift giving, place some of your supplies in the tea-leaf-reading area.

5. Breathe deeply several times, relax, and sink comfortably into your chair, feet flat on the floor. Hold your hands over the teacup. Form a triangle with index fingers and thumbs touching. Breathe softly into the triangle formed by your fingers, your breath just touching the surface of the liquid. As you breathe on the tea, visualize white light entering the liquid. Now visualize spirals of energy leaving the palms of your hands and entering the liquid as you intone an affirmation of power. For example: "My work will be creative, interesting, and useful to myself and others."

6. If you desire, light incense that matches your purpose. Pass the incense over the cup three times. Rub a light blue candle with a bit of the same brand of dry tea you are using. Light candle and repeat your affirmation. Pass light of candle over your cup three times. Scatter a bit of the dry tea around the candle holder.

7. Read the tea leaves, then set the cup out to dry. The following day, place the dry tea, a bit of the cold candle wax, and one of the crystals in a gris-gris bag. Carry with you as long as you work on your current project. Burn bag when work is successfully completed.

HedgeWitch Candle Magick

Grungy Candles for Attraction

Country prim (as it is now called) fits right in with HedgeWitch magick, and grungy candles, a representation of this type of candle art design, are very easy to make. These primitive candles are perfect for attraction magick due to the wide variety of herbs, spices, and scents you can choose to create just the right magickal formula! Grungy candles take about two hours to make (from the initial wax melting to completion), and you can use dollar-store tapers, pillar candles, or highly scented votives to begin, or you can dip candles you have poured yourself. Grungy candles employ a technique called "overdipping," where you dip the cool candle into the hot wax several times, building up a beautiful shell around the original candle. With grungy candles, the shell contains clumps of herbs and spices, making the surface bumpy and misshapen. Therefore, no matter what the candles look like, they are perfect country prim!

Supplies Needed

A double boiler: This is a double pot: the bottom pot holds water that boils and heats the contents of the second pot that sits atop the bottom pot. Warning: The water must *never* boil dry during your candlemaking process. You must use a dedicated double boiler for making candles, as you cannot melt wax directly on the stove: a flash fire may occur. Also, once you heat the wax, the pot can't be used for future food preparation.

Your choice of candles: Pillars, votives, or tapers that can be dipped in the double boiler. Be sure your candles aren't bigger than your pot!

Wax or candy thermometer

2 to 4 pounds of candle wax: You can actually melt down already colored and scented brown candles, depending upon the diameter of your chosen pot.

Brown candle dye: If you can't get candle dye, do not use crayons: melt a variety of colored candles in shades of red, orange, green, and blue to create the brown color you desire.

Your choice of candle scent: If your candle is already highly scented, you don't
need to use an additional scent unless you want to.

1 pound of good, strong ground coffee

Powdered cinnamon, nutmeg, and cloves: At least ½ cup of each.

Baker's parchment paper

Spray candle gloss (optional)

Good needle-nosed pliers: You will use these for dipping the candle by firmly
holding the wick with the pliers.

Directions

Fill the bottom pot with water (not so much that it will boil over and not so little that it
will boil dry). Fill the top pot with the cold, broken wax. Insert the candy thermometer. Melt
the wax on medium heat (the boiling water will eventually melt the wax) until you reach a
temperature of 170 degrees. This part of the process takes the most time and must be constantly monitored due to danger of flash fire. (Granted, I've made thousands of candles and
never had a flash fire, but you must be cognizant of what *could* happen at all times. Do not
walk away from the melting pot. If someone calls, knocks at the door, or you must leave the
area, *turn off the heat.* You can always turn it back on again. This is not a project you can walk
away from!) Once the wax has reached about 170 degrees, add your color and scent as directed
on the package. Either turn the heat down or off—your choice. The trick is to maintain that
170-degree temperature *and* keep the pot from boiling dry.

While your wax is melting, mix the ground coffee and spices together in a bowl. Set out the
candles you wish to dip. Cover your working area with parchment paper. Bless your ingredients, and with primal language, state the purpose for your finished candles. Just as when you
make cookies, place parchment paper on a separate table where your finished candles will cool.
Pour ½ to ¾ cup of the coffee and spice mix in the center of the parchment. Spread it out a bit
with your fingers (not too thin).

To Dip Candles:

Firmly hold the wick with the pliers and immerse the entire candle in wax (this is where
the importance of the pot size and amount of wax is evident). The wax must cover the dipped

candle. Raise the candle above the wax and let it drip a bit, then move over to your working area. Roll warm candle in the coffee and spice mix. Never put your fingers in the hot wax, as serious burns can occur. If the candle slips out of the pliers' grip, fish it out with an old spoon. Once rolled in the coffee and spice mix, set the candle aside (still on the working area). Do the next candle in the same manner. When you have dipped all your candles once, check your temperature and then dip them all again and roll them in the coffee and spice mixture. Repeat this procedure—dip, roll, and cool—five to sixteen times, depending on how thick you want your grungy shell. Renew the coffee and spice mixture as necessary. If the wax becomes too cool or too hot, the shell will begin to bubble and crack, which you really don't want, so watch that temperature carefully. If you've done this and they *still* crack and bubble, it could be that your thermometer is off. Atmospheric conditions can also cause this phenomenon. The cracks and bubbles won't hurt the finished product, it just looks better if they aren't there. Also, the more dips, the more possibility of bubbles and cracking.

When you are finished dipping all the candles, turn off the heat. *Do not* pour the remaining wax down the drain; this will completely block your plumbing! Either allow the remainder to cool in the pot to use at a later date, or pour the wax outside on the ground. Place your dipped candles on the cooling paper. Allow to dry undisturbed at least twenty-four hours. Do not touch the candles while they are drying, as you could smear off the dipped shell or crack the shell. After twenty-four hours, spray the candles with manufacturer's candle gloss (available at most craft stores) for a lovely sheen.

Magickal Uses of Grungy Candles

The recipe given here corresponds to attraction energies. The coffee and cinnamon are for movement, and the nutmeg and cloves represent good fortune and an excellent harvest of any project. The traditional brown "grungy" color invites the element of earth, prosperity, stability, abundance, treasure, and miracles. These candles make wonderful gifts throughout the harvest and winter season, especially if you use apple, vanilla, or pine-scented candles. Seven tapers bound together with a checkered ribbon and a magickal good fortune tag designed by yourself would be a welcome gift! Burn one a day for seven days by a rooster statue to encourage prosperity and good fortune.

Herb Candle Variation: Clear Wax Dip

For striking candle designs, omit the brown dye, leaving the dipping wax clear. Dip the candle once, then carefully press dried herbs and flowers into the wax. Dip again. Wait sixty seconds. Dip again. Wait sixty seconds. Dip a third time, and set aside to dry.

Caution: Too many dried herbs can turn your burning candle into a fireball! To burn a candle packed with dried herbs, use *only* a fire-safe cauldron.

Tip for Magickal Gardeners:

During the height of your growing season, harvest flowers and petals just after the morning dew has dried. Press petals and leaves between paper towels inside heavy books. When dry (this can take several days or weeks, depending upon your choice), use these pressed florals on candles or in scrapbooking projects. You can heat-laminate dried florals if they are not too thick. I made several bookmarks for prosperity one year using dried marigold and sunflower petals, a bit of glitter, and a heat-laminating machine.

HedgeWitch Painted Herb Candles

You will need: a double boiler; one pillar candle; two to three votives with color that matches pillar; herbals to decorate the pillar—choose herbs, flowers, leaves, etc. that are very thin; an old paintbrush.

Instructions: Melt votive candles in double boiler. Do not let the wax go over 170 degrees. With this type of project, we really just need the wax to melt to liquid. Choose whether you wish to apply your herbals randomly or if you would like an overall pattern or special design. If you choose to make a design, try arranging your herbals on white paper first. When you are ready to apply the herbals to the pillar, dip paintbrush into hot wax. Dab hot wax onto pillar where you wish to place your first herbal. Quickly place herbal onto hot wax area. Immediately dip the paintbrush into the hot wax again, and apply a thin coat of wax gently over the herbal. Continue adding herbs and flowers until your design is completed. Apply one last thin coat of wax over entire candle. Allow to completely cool. For gift giving, tie a ribbon or raffia around the candle. If the wick is long enough, you can add beads and other baubles to create a striking gift. Empower candle at sunrise or noon for ultimate fire power!

Hand-Dipped HedgeWitch Taper Candles

You will need: a double boiler that is six inches taller than the length of the candle desired; candle thermometer; two or more pounds of wax, depending on the desired length of candle; scent and fragrance; candle wicking; chopstick or thin dowel rod cut to eleven or twelve inches; steel nut (for weight); powdered herbs; wooden stirring spoon.

Instructions: Melt wax to 170 degrees. Add scent and color per manufacturer's instructions. Add ¼ to ½ teaspoon of powdered herb to wax. Stir. (The herbs often will settle; this is okay. In these herbal candles, we are infusing the wax with the power of the herb.) Cut wicking to the desired length of candle plus three inches. Fasten steel nut to one end of the wick. Tie the other end of the wick in the center of the chopstick or dowel rod. Dip the wick into the hot wax while holding the chopstick. With smooth motion, pull the wick straight up and out of the hot wax. Count to five in an easy cadence. Dip again.

Count to five. Dip again. Repeat this procedure until you reach the desired thickness of candle. If outer wax begins to bubble, your wax is either too cold or too hot. If you leave the candle in the hot wax too long during dipping, you will melt off the previous layers. When finished, hang candle to cool. Candles should not touch each other when hanging and should hang free (not touching anything). Candle suppliers sell special spinning racks, or you can improvise.

HedgeWitch Dipping Charm

Try this easy magickal charm when dipping candles. Remember to state your purpose clearly in primal language as you learned in Section 1 before you begin.

> (Dip candle) *One—the magick's begun*
>
> (Dip candle) *Two—my wish comes true*
>
> (Dip candle) *Three—I attract it* (meaning your desire) *to me*
>
> (Dip candle) *Four—I open the door* (meaning you welcome and accept your desire)
>
> (Dip candle) *Five—the thing* (what you asked for) *is mine!*

Keep repeating chant until you reach the desired thickness of candle.

*The trick with all of the HedgeWitch candle recipes given in this book is to continually monitor the temperature of the wax *

Holiday Heat-Gun Tissue-Paper Candles

Tissue-paper candles bring a whole new level to creating fast magickal gifts for the busy HedgeWitch. In just fifteen minutes (or less) you can create unusual designer candles suitable for sharing or using yourself! The trick to these types of candles is to just barely heat the surface of the candle around the edges of the tissue paper without burning the tissue with the heat gun and seriously melting the candle or seriously burning your hands. Therefore, this isn't a project for young children.

You will need: pillar candles in colors of your choice; tissue paper in colors that match your intent, or you can also use tissue papers with designs such as leaves, pumpkins, flowers, etc.; heat gun (I use an embossing gun); candle gloss (optional—can be obtained at your local craft store or craft candle supplier)

Instructions: Tear tissue paper in various small shapes. Lay one piece of torn tissue on candle. Heat edges of tissue just enough to where you see the wax glisten (this will take only a few seconds). Move around the edges of the tissue evenly with the heat gun. If the wax begins to drip, wipe drip off lightly and quickly before it solidifies. Once all the edges are adhered, heat center of tissue lightly, just enough to allow the tissue to begin sinking into the wax. Apply the next piece of tissue in the same manner. When you are satisfied with the design, set the candle aside to cool completely. For a professionally finished look, spray candles with candle gloss. Tie ribbon or raffia around candle for a gift-giving finishing touch! Empower cooled candles with tuning forks or bells.

How these candles burn: In my experience, the outer tissue forms a shell and the center of the candle burns down completely. However, every candle is different, and to be safe, I would burn them in a fire-safe cauldron.

The HedgeWitch Magickal Garden

One of the easiest ways to connect to Spirit through nature is to dive into the wonders of your own enchanted garden! From planning in February (in the Northern Hemisphere) to planting after the first major frost, to growing and harvesting, your magickal garden will provide thousands of hours of peace and enjoyment. Even if you have never gardened in your life, there is nothing so difficult that you can't accomplish it, if you only try! If you can't work outside, try building your own rock garden inside, using potted plants and herbs. Begin small, and watch your garden grow! Here are some magickal tips to help bring you an amazing connection to nature.

Planning: Start small, and build. What type of environment suits you best—an Oriental feel? Celtic? Victorian? Walk your property. Your focal point sets the stage for the future of your garden, as well as your outside life. Choose one small area to change first. Close your eyes and visualize what you might like to have. Use primal language (see Section 1) to formulate what you desire. Look through magazines, garden catalogs, and books.

Take several trips to various local greenhouses. Ask questions! In designing my garden, I chose two focal points: a meditative statue of Buddha for the general yard and toads for prosperity in my raised-bed herb garden. Even though we had a dry year, my garden and yard flourished! I even built a toad habitat, and the week after I did so, I received a large check in the mail I wasn't expecting. By providing for nature, nature provides for you!

Watch the path of the sun: Different areas of your property will have different access to light throughout the year. By learning the light, you will know what will suit your plants best and where you can change their placement, if necessary, later on.

Plant tags: Plants from the greenhouse normally come with a tag that explains light, temperature, and water requirements. Seed packets also carry this information. However, I found that these mini write-ups aren't always accurate, and the only way you will know this is your experience through the growing season. When trying a new plant in your garden, why not put it in a pot first and see how the plant behaves in its prospective placement? If it does well, transplant it where you originally placed it, but if not, move the plant rather than throw it out. A plant can lose quite a lot of leaves and still be revitalized in a different location. For example, I bought patchouli and Chinese sunflowers last year and put them in pots rather than directly into the ground. I'm glad I did! The patchouli tag said it took full sunlight. The Chinese sunflowers said they required indirect lighting. In both cases, this wasn't how the plants reacted. The patchouli did horribly in full sunlight, but when I moved it to partial shade, it grew beautifully. The Chinese sunflowers did well at first and then began to die. I cut out all the dead foliage and moved these plants to a more lighted area. They did beautifully and bloomed into October.

Your Garden Matches Your Life

Working in your garden provides an easy, open pathway to Spirit. Yes, at first your mind is full of the other parts of your life, but as you work the soil and study and care for the plants, everyday problems slip away and your energy naturally starts to vibrate with that of the earth. By caring for your garden, you are also caring for your life. If something is wrong in your garden (not enough water, a particular weed, a bug infestation), this often equates to what is going on in your own life. By correcting the problem in your garden, you will naturally move to correct the difficulty in your life outside of your garden. You and your garden are actually vibrating together and are really companions throughout the seasons. Here are a few intuitive tips that might help you when problems occur in your garden:

Overwatering: You are overindulging yourself or someone else in a particular area of your life.

Underwatering: You are being too stingy with yourself or someone closely related to you.

Japanese beetles and other chewing bugs: These are a major pain, and some years, of course, in some areas will be worse than others. Let's say you've taken appropriate gardening steps to solve this problem, but for some reason, those darned beetles left your garden alone but went after your marigolds. Japanese beetles and other chewing predators (deer, rabbits, bugs) indicate that you have allowed negative thoughts to chew away at your personal harmony. Release the negativity, as explained in Section 2 of this book (such as the Rite of Wind), as you take appropriate action to remove the beetles from your marigolds.

Slugs: Lure them into the sun with a mixture of beer and grape juice—and at the same time, consider where in your life you've been lazy and negative.

Weeds: Your schedule is way too busy, and you've allowed things that mean nothing to take up your valuable time. Think about what you can release, and be sure to give yourself time to peacefully meditate and commune in your garden.

Creeping vines: You've allowed one particular negative issue or fear to infiltrate your entire lifestyle. Release this issue and make active, aggressive changes to bring harmony into focus.

Fungus and root rot: You are ignoring your real feelings. Get in touch with them!

White flies and aphids: You can actually use a DustBuster to suck these babies up, or try the soap-spray recipes given on pages 248–249. In life, however, the appearance of these nasty critters may mean that your thoughts are scattered and rather than accomplishing one thing, you are destroying many good things in your life.

What is that bug? Not all bugs in the garden are bad ones! If you see a new, unusual bug in your garden, take a picture of it and research the critter on the Net or visit a local green-house and ask. Good bugs such as mud wasps and ladybugs actually help to keep your garden healthy. A new bug in the garden means a new opportunity is coming to call. If the bug is helpful to your garden, consider this a good omen. For example, late in the growing season I found amazing, fat caterpillars on my parsley. At first, I was alarmed, but after researching them, I discovered that these caterpillars would turn into beautiful swallowtail butterflies and they don't eat enough to destroy a parsley crop. Not long after, I received a terrific opportunity in my life.

Forgetting to fertilize: There is something in your life you are refusing to do, and because of this refusal you are not allowing new and fresh opportunities to help you grow. Get out there and fertilize!

Never say: "I don't have any luck with . . ." and name the plant. Granted, you have to be aware of the particular environment a plant needs to survive. You can't put a jungle plant outside in the desert without some sort of dramatic hothouse, but in regards to plants native to your environment, there is always a way to raise it, and in doing so, you bring a special measure of Spirit into your life. When I was a little girl, my grandmother had the most beautiful Boston ferns on her porch every year. When I first tried to raise them, they died; so, for years, I passed by these plants longingly at the nursery but never purchased them, fearing that once again I would waste my money. Once I developed the Hedge-Witch guide and worked through the material myself, I decided I would be daring and try once again. I bought two beautiful ferns and re-potted them immediately, using organic soil and fish fertilizer, then I blessed them and put them on the back porch. Each week I monitored their progress, moving them on various occasions to different locations on the porch until they seemed happy and settled. By fall, I had the most gorgeous ferns! I learned that people are like plants—we need to change our environment when necessary to that which is most conducive to our personal growth. Now and then, we need a bit of fertilizer (new information) to boost our productivity!

When you are troubled, work in your garden: Connecting with nature can be one of the most healing activities you will ever try. By concentrating on growth, maintenance, and harvest (depending upon the time of year), you are allowing your mind, body, and spirit to commune directly with Spirit. Sometimes it will take at least thirty minutes for you to get into the swing of nature, but that's okay. Keep at it until your troubles melt away and you are totally concentrated on the garden task at hand. When you are finished for the day, you will find a renewed sense of healing and purpose.

Remove dead and diseased leaves: Just like in your own life, there are times when your garden plants will need what I call a magickal haircut. Many times a plant isn't dead, even though it looks like it is past all saving. Remove dead, dying, or diseased leaves, apply a remedy if necessary (for example, an organic bug killer), give it a little water and fertilizer, and move the plant to a better location, if necessary. Our lives need to be maintained the same way, especially if we remember that change can always be made to our advantage. Dead-heading flowers, or taking off the dead blooms, encourages new growth in the plant. Dead-heading in our lives can be very advantageous, too. Learn to release so that new growth can take place.

Keep the paths in your garden free of weeds: If you want a bright, clear future ahead, keep those garden paths clean and free of weeds! As you remove the weeds in your garden, you are psychologically removing the blocks in your outside life. Solutions will come easy and quickly to you!

Share your harvest! Incorporate the harvest of your garden into the lives of others by giving away some of the fruits of your labor. As you release by gift giving, so will you benefit with new growth in the future! As you work in your garden, in your mind set aside specific plants that will help others. If you can, show them the plants while they are growing. Last year I grew eucalyptus for my daughter because she makes beautiful fall and winter wreaths. Eucalyptus is a plant well known for healing. During that summer, she was able to extricate herself from a chronic medical problem, and by fall, she had benefited from the relief of healing.

As another example, I bought six sickly ceremonial sage plants at the beginning of the season. Until I understood the nature of patience, I lost three of them. But with determination I decided that the remaining three were going to grow and be productive because I wanted to share the dried leaves with a particular friend in October. To enhance the growth of these plants, I placed palm-sized stones at the base of the plants that were engraved with the words *luck, prosperity, wealth,* and *happiness.* I paid special attention to fertilization and watering. During this time, I didn't know that the person I'd intended sharing these plants with was having a really hard time in life, and in the beginning of the season, around the time I purchased the plants, he was having a "sickly" financial period. By the end of the season, just about at harvest, my ceremonial sage plants were doing beautifully! It was then I'd heard of his tough spring and difficult summer. But by fall, things had really turned around for him! Your thoughts while tending plants for future harvest for a particular person will benefit that person throughout the entire growing season. You must simply believe.

HedgeWitch Scarecrow Timing—
Spring Butzeman Garden Magick

The beloved scarecrow—called a *butzeman* in Pennsylvania Dutch—normally conjures up golden harvests, sparkling autumn skies, and pumpkins plump for the carving, yet its empowerment and placement were always part of spring rites and an intricate piece of HedgeWitchery garden magick. Like many enchanted vehicles from the Old Country, there were specific rules on how to prepare and handle one's garden guardian. A protective and good fortune device, the butzeman didn't secure just the garden, it protected the prosperity and welfare of the entire family. Here are the rules, should you care to follow them:

1. When building your scarecrow, always use natural fibers and old clothes—never use clothes from an enemy to dress your scarecrow!

2. Sew or stuff protective charms in the arms and sleeves of the device. From runic sigils to specially blessed charms, trinkets, and dried herbs, each choice should be associated with your true desires.

3. Like it or not, the energy of the butzeman is often used to create protection through humor—think of it as the light of laughter.

4. A healer's scarecrow should contain both comfrey and horehound.

5. It is bad luck to erect your scarecrow before Easter.

6. It is bad luck to erect your scarecrow on May Day.

7. Never, ever wear any item that has been worn by a scarecrow—this is thought to bring death to the household.

8. Your scarecrow must be given shade on the longest day of the year to ensure luck and prosperity.

9. Finally, and most importantly, your scarecrow *must* be burned before November 1, preferably on Halloween Night of October 31. Every single part of the butzeman *must* be destroyed—the clothing, the charms, even the pole he rests on. If this is not done, bad luck will plague the entire family.

Many magickal practitioners from the Old Country believe the butzeman was used to hold magick for the homestead securely in place, and it was generally agreed by all members of the community that it was capable of conjuring good weather for the well-being of the farm or garden. For example, if it is too dry, place a glass of water at the base of the pole. If it is too wet, retire the butzeman to a dry spot or cover it with an umbrella so it can conjure the return of the sun. It can be dressed in any manner you desire, although its clothes should not be torn. If the clothes tear over the summer months, they should be mended. The butzeman can even be given special things on special days or hold a sign to welcome visitors—however, anything given to the butzeman must be burned at the end of the season and not taken back into the house. Above all, your scarecrow must always be treated with respect, because it carries the spirit of HedgeWitch magick!

Butterfly Garden Magick

When working healing magick for others, we send out a visualization of light, love, peace, and good fortune. Like beautiful butterflies, these vibrations of our thoughts float in quantum fashion to an end conclusion of happiness, success, and wholeness. If you are having trouble visualizing what you need, then try sending your thoughts on the wings of butterflies. Hedge-Witchery works by the law of attraction. Don't think of what you *don't* want—think about what you *do* want! If you need information, wish to promote a healing, or desire wealth in your life, simply go outside, face the east at 7:00 AM (the time of healing power), and think about what you want. Throw your right hand out to the horizon. As you extend your hand, imagine that your thoughts are beautiful butterflies, winging their way out into the universe to capture what you desire and bring it back to you. Surround your butterflies with beautiful white, sparkling light, then close your eyes and say thank you three times (and truly believe you are saying that because you have already received your desire). Once you begin using this technique, don't be surprised if you are often visited by beautiful butterflies, see images of them in places you frequent, and hear about them in conversation. This is Spirit's way of telling you that your prayers have been answered. Remember, your pure thoughts are angels with golden wings that by the nature of their very being can accomplish anything! If you have something very special you want to create, visit a local butterfly garden and make your wishes there among the thousands of gorgeous butterflies!

Keep These HedgeWitch Tips in Mind When Creating Your Own Butterfly Garden:

Butterflies simply adore bright colors—the more vibrant, the more butterflies you'll attract! They seem to especially love deep purples, bright yellows, sizzling reds, and hot oranges, particularly with single petals, as these flowers are easier for butterflies to obtain nectar from. Mix the flowers in your garden with an attractive variety of annuals and perennials to ensure pretty flowers (and magickal butterflies) all season long.

Butterflies don't mind lots of sun, but they do get thirsty, just like our bird friends. An attractive birdbath in the center of your butterfly garden will help to lure them in, and don't forget the host plants—those herbs and flowers that provide food for butterfly caterpillars. Often called nature's pruners, these catepillars never eat enough to destroy the host plant.

Want to create your own butterfly garden? Here are the plants that naturally attract lovely butterflies:

Anise

Aster

Azalea

Basil

Bee balm

Bugle

Butterfly weed

Carnation

Chrysanthemum

Coltsfoot

Cosmos

Dill

Echinacea

Heartsease

Honeysuckle

Hyssop

Impatiens

Lavender

Marjoram

Mints

Musk mallow

Purple loosestrife

Rosemary

Rue

Sage

St. John's wort

Sunflowers

Thyme

Valerian

Yarrow

Zinnia

Herbs that encourage butterfly larvae to lay eggs and provide food:

Cowslip (Primula veris)

Fennel (Foeniculum vulgare)

Foxglove (Digitalis purpurea)

Horseradish (Armoracia rusticana)

Musk mallow (Malva moschata)

Nettles (Urtica dioica)

Parsley (invites the beautiful
    swallowtail)

Rocket (Eruca vesicaria, subsp. Sativa)

Sweet violet (Viola odorata)

Wild strawberry (Fragaria vesca)

*Other herbs and plants that attract
    butterflies include borage, marigold,
    selfheal, and catnip.

Easy-to-Grow HedgeWitch Herbs

If you choose to grow your own herbal garden, these great herbs have a compendium of uses, are super easy to maintain, and can be used for both cooking and magick! The information in this section is taken directly from my experience with my own organic herb garden, grown in six large raised beds and one ground bed during the spring, summer, and fall of 2007. Weeding, watering, and a bit of organic liquid fish fertilizer was all it took for a bountiful harvest, even though the summer was comparatively dry. You'll notice that my space-between-plants requirements are a little larger than most herb books, because by harvest, all of my plants were huge, and I had plenty to share with friends and family. In planting, I set two beds aside as the "no eat" beds. These were the herbs I wished to grow specifically for magickal purposes, which included hyssop, lavender, white sage (for incense), eucalyptus, myrtle, patchouli, and horehound. These herbs are not listed below. I also grew a variety of vegetables, including broccoli, green and hot peppers, tomatoes, pumpkins, and cucumbers. For floor strewing, I grew chamomile and rue in separate areas of the property, as rue has a habit of not playing well with others. Rue is sometimes called Queen Mother of the Garden, and she likes to rule her own little area.

Basil

Growth and care: Requires a sunny area. There are a wide variety of basils, so choose a few to widen your culinary cabinet! Purple leafy basil is a must if you wish to make lavender-colored vinegar for hostess or holiday gifts. African basil and sweet basil are also wonderful choices. Basil likes more than its share of water, especially if you have it planted in a raised-bed environment. Planting basil with tomatoes creates a healthy combination for both plants; however, be sure you put enough room between your basils and your tomatoes, as the tomato plants tend to try to overwhelm the basils. Basils can turn into large, leafy bushes by the end of the growing season, so take this into consideration when planting. Prune all season long to use in your magickal cooking. Cut off flower heads before they flower to keep the flavor in the leaves. Harvest in the morning after the dew is dry for best flavor. Basil tends to lose some of its flavor in the drying process. You can freeze basil, but you must blanch it first or the leaves will turn black. Basil is thought to repel flies and mosquitoes, and it improves the growth and flavor of other vegetables except for cucumbers, rue, and snap beans. Basil will probably be the last plant you put in your garden each year, as it is extremely fussy about temperature—it hates to be chilly. To nurse a difficult basil plant back to health, re-pot, take out of direct sunlight, and choose a warm area with strong, indirect light.

Fertilizer requirements: light application of your choice (I used organic fish fertilizer)

Space between plants: 18 to 24 inches

Incompatible planting with: cucumbers, rue, and snap beans

Compatible with: peppers and tomatoes

Magickal basil: Above all, magickal basil is thought to promote harmony in the home, soothe unhappy feelings, and blend energies to reach a happy conclusion. Used for good luck, wealth, and love spells.

Culinary basil: Use in pesto, tomato sauces, salads, vinegars, omelets, soups, corn, cream cheese, eggplant, peas, white beans, zucchini, pasta, and red meats.

Goes well with: chives, garlic, marjoram, oregano, mint, parsley, rosemary, thyme

Parts used for food: fresh and dried leaves; buds from flower spikes are often used as garnish

Bay

Growth and care: Light requirements for Bay seem to depend upon your climate and location. If you plant in a tub, you can easily move it until you find just the right spot where it seems happy. Bay can actually grow into a small tree if you let it. Requires semi-shade and may need to be brought indoors in tough winter areas until the plant has reached several feet high. If you are going to let your bay grow large, you may prefer large tub planting, as the plant will eventually require several feet of space. Once your bay takes off, you can harvest leaves for cooking throughout the summer months.

Fertilizer requirements: light application of your choice (I used organic fish fertilizer)

Space between plants: 3 feet

Incompatible planting with: (see below)

Compatible with: As it grows into a tree, bay is not particularly compatible with anything, unless you give it lots of space to grow.

Magickal bay: Popular in spells for divination, seeing clearly, and understanding the information you are receiving. Also used for protection, cleansings, banishing ghosts, doing well in physical activities, and wish magick.

Culinary bay: Use leaves in herbal bouquets and marinades as well as soups, stews, lamb, game, lentils, rice, chicken, beef, and casseroles. (Two to three leaves flavor a dish for four to five people.)

Goes well with: allspice, garlic, marjoram, oregano, parsley, sage, savory, thyme

Parts used for food: fresh and dried leaves (soak dried leaves in water first)

Chives

Growth and care: Chives are a perennial warm-season herb that like a rich, well-drained soil and lots of water. Very resistant to bugs and diseases, chives are easily grown indoors as well as out. Chives enjoy full sun to light shade and can be divided each spring to encourage new growth. Chives are best frozen but can be dried, though they do lose a great deal of their flavor in the drying process. To preserve chive flavor, layer your cuttings alternatively in a glass jar—one inch of kosher salt, then one inch of chives, packing down each layer with a spoon. Use dried chives and salt in cooking. Chives are great in vinegars as well. Plant chives with roses to keep those blooms of love disease-free! Chives can be harvested all summer long.

Fertilizer requirements: light application of your choice (I used organic fish fertilizer)

Space between plants: 6 inches

Incompatible planting with: beans

Compatible with: carrots, celery, grapes, peas, and roses

Magickal chives: Used in spells for good health, cleansings, and protecting love. Mix with dried hot peppers and rose petals to keep your partner close!

Culinary chives: Salads, cheeses, breads, butters, dressings, and as food decoration over fish (cut and sprinkle over food right before serving). Flavor your potatoes with a mixture of chives, parsley, and rosemary while cooking.

Goes well with: basil, parsley, and tarragon

Parts used for food: stems and flowers

Dill

Growth and care: Can grow very tall, so companion stakes are well worth your investment. Dill functions as an annual in areas with hard winters, but it may be a perennial if your climate is conducive. Dill will re-seed itself throughout the growing season, so make sure your dill patch has plenty of room to grow! Dill enjoys full sun. Harvest the seeds for pickling and the feathery leaves for cooking. Can reach 4 feet in height and 24 inches in breadth. May require extra watering in dry weather. Dill isn't called an abundance herb for nothing. Your dill will seed all over the place—in other beds, on the path, among other plants. It can be a social nuisance.

Fertilizer requirements: light application of your choice (I used organic fish fertilizer)

Space between plants: at least 18 inches

Incompatible planting with: carrots, fennel (will cross-pollinate), tomatoes

Compatible with: fruit trees and cabbage

Magickal dill: As dill re-seeds itself, this herb is great for endeavors of long life, preservation of hearth and home, protection on the job, and cultivating opportunity.

Culinary dill: Seed heads are used in pickled cucumbers and herbal breads and butters. Fresh dill leaves are great for fish and other seafood, cabbage, cauliflower and cucumber dishes, beef, beans, potatoes, lentils, and spinach, as well as light sauces. Great for vinegars.

Goes well with: Leaves—basil, garlic, horseradish, mustard, and parsley. Seeds—combine with garlic and ginger.

Parts used for food: fresh and dried leaves, seeds

Lemon Verbena

Growth and care: Can reach a height of 6 feet and will bush out if pruned repeatedly, growing into a graceful shrub. Can be a perennial if winter is not too cold. Likes full sun and can be a good outdoor container pot herb. Lemon verbena has an intense, fresh lemon aroma, but the taste is less strong. Until about a hundred years ago, the plant was considered for its merit in potpourris and garden aroma. Lemon verbena is still used today in the more expensive perfumes. Now, however, it is used in teas and fatty meat dishes as well as a light flavoring for fish. In my experience, this plant takes a little over-average water and lush, organic soil.

Fertilizer requirements: light application of your choice (I used organic fish fertilizer)

Space between plants: 24 inches

Incompatible planting with: none

Compatible with: plants arranged in garden for aromatic and meditative qualities

Magickal lemon verbena: Used in love spells and potions, workings for personal strength, attracting passion for any person or thing, and banishing nightmares. Steep lemon verbena in hot water, cool, strain, and use to asperge sacred space.

Culinary lemon verbena: teas, fatty meats such as duck, flavoring for desserts and drinks, pork chops, chicken, fish, stuffings, marinades

Goes well with: basil, hot peppers, chives, lemon thyme, mints, garlic

Parts used for food: leaves, fresh or dried

Marjoram

Growth and care: Winter-hardy only in the South. Requires full sun and well-drained soil and can be harvested throughout the growing season. Some varieties make attractive border plants. Marcelka marjoram is similar to oregano and has an aromatic hint of pine—great for mushroom sauces! Sweet marjoram is wonderful for salads, vinegars, and Italian cuisine. Pinch out regularly to ensure bushy, compact plants.

Fertilizer requirements: light application of your choice (I used organic fish fertilizer)

Space between plants: 12 inches

Incompatible planting with: cucumbers

Compatible with: sage and vegetables

Magickal marjoram: A well-rounded herb used in workings for love, protection, health, happiness, strength, wealth, and money. Create a money sachet using marjoram, chamomile flowers, and marigold petals in a green bag decorated with a bee motif to attract fast cash!

Culinary marjoram: Use in stuffings, sausage dishes, pasta, pizza, and sauces, as well as root vegetable, mushroom, and bean dishes. Marjoram should be added in the last few minutes of cooking so that the flavor is not lost.

Goes well with: basil, bay, hot peppers, garlic, parsley, rosemary, sage, thyme

Parts used for food: fresh and dried leaves; flower knots are also edible

Mints

Growth and care: Mints have a tendency to overtake any garden, so planting them in pots really is the best choice. Extremely hardy, most mints have a strong aroma, grow rapidly, and spread underground runners. As perennials, mints need plenty of water and prefer a rich soil in a shady area. Mints can reach 16 to 20 inches in height and are a primary choice for teas and money magick.

Fertilizer requirements: light, if at all, application of your choice (I used organic fish fertilizer)

Space between plants: best if potted

Incompatible planting with: none, but see growth and care, above, for caution about planting mints in your garden

Compatible with: broccoli, cabbage, peas

Magickal mints: Most commonly used in money spells, but you will also find magickal mint in safety and travel workings, love potions, cleansings, study aids, and stress-relieving formulas. Mix with lavender and chamomile for a nice, no-stress herbal sachet. Check out appendix 4 for a list of different types of mint.

Culinary mints: Teas, jellies, and salads. Great flavoring for lamb as well as carrots, eggplant, tomatoes, potatoes, zucchini, chicken, pork, Asian dipping sauces, and desserts.

Goes well with: basil, cloves, dill, ginger, marjoram, oregano, parsley, pepper, thyme

Parts used for food: fresh and dried leaves, flowers for salads and garnishes

Oregano

Growth and care: Perennial warm-season plant that is a stronger, more peppery version of marjoram. Some oreganos are creepers, keeping close to the ground, and make good border plants, where others such as the autumn flowering variety can grow into a small bush. Oreganos enjoy full sun and are not usually harvested until the plant begins to flower, as this is the time of highest flavor content; however, oregano snippets can be taken all season long for cooking requirements. If happy, some types of oregano will bush to the diameter of a barrel!

Fertilizer requirements: light application of your choice (I used organic fish fertilizer)

Space between plants: 18 inches

Incompatible planting with: none

Compatible with: beans, cucumbers, and squash

Magickal oregano: A great money-draw herb. Much like marjoram, this herb is used in a variety of workings for love, lust, good health, protection and general happiness.

Culinary oregano: Italian cuisine, sauces, red meats, beans, potatoes, duck, shellfish, cauliflower, corn, lamb, mushrooms, spinach, squash, veal, venison and root vegetables such as turnips and carrots, soups, stews and roasts. Add oregano near the end of cooking to retain flavor.

Goes well with: basil, bay, garlic, parsley, rosemary, sage, thyme

Parts used for food: fresh and dried leaves and flower knots

Parsley

Growth and care: Cool-season biennial that usually does well under winter conditions and is probably the easiest herb to grow on our magickal list. Parsley enjoys full sun to partial shade and does well if your summer is drier than usual, although you should take care to water during that time. Can be harvested all season long—the more you cut, the more the plant will bush out with fresh, new greenery and grow 18 to 20 inches in height.

Fertilizer requirements: light application of your choice (I used organic fish fertilizer)

Space between plants: at least 18 inches

Incompatible planting with: none

Compatible with: asparagus, corn, peppers, and tomatoes

Magickal parsley: Used in magickal growth and birth workings; also used in cleansings and for protection against accidents at home and while traveling.

Culinary parsley: Great as a garnish. Use in soups, stews, potatoes, herbal bouquets, eggs, fish, lentils, rice, and sauces.

Goes well with: basil, bay, chives, garlic, lemon balm, marjoram, mint, oregano, pepper, rosemary, tarragon

Parts used for food: fresh and dried leaves; fresh stalks for soups and stews

Rosemary

Growth and care: Although rosemary is a perennial herb, it doesn't take well to hard winters. Rosemary will grow in bushlike form and can reach 6 feet in height in excellent conditions. This is the most-used herb in our home, from magick to making soaps to cooking. To dry, hang cuttings upside down. When dry, remove leaves and keep them whole in storage. Throw away stems. Grind dried leaves right before use for best flavor and aroma. Rosemary requires full sun and good drainage and will do well during a dry summer if watered occasionally. If raised indoors, rosemary can be harvested year-round.

Fertilizer requirements: light application of your choice (I used organic fish fertilizer)

Space between plants: 24 inches

Incompatible planting with: cucumbers

Compatible with: cabbage, beans, carrots, and sage, as both sage and rosemary require the same type of well-drained soil.

Magickal rosemary: Extremely versatile herb used in workings for love, protection, cleansings, mental acuity, lust, healing, restful sleep, stress removal, and retaining one's youth.

Culinary rosemary: Use with pork, lamb, game, and beef. Great for marinades, flavoring oils, or vinegars. Use sparingly in herbal breads and butters. Excellent if cooked with potatoes, mushrooms, rabbit, veal, and winter squashes. Not diminished by long cooking so is great for stews and oven-baked casseroles.

Goes well with: bay, chives, garlic, lavender, mint, oregano, parsley, sage, savory, thyme

Parts used for food: needlelike leaves, young sprigs and stems, flowers

Sage

Growth and care: Sage is certainly not fussy when it comes to soil content and prefers sun and well-drained soil. Sage is a natural antibacterial and has been used as a preservative for meats, poultry, and fish. There are several varieties of sage, each with their own unique flavor, so I suggest planting several to see which you like the best. We grow white sage for incense and broad-leaf sage for meats and stuffings. As with rosemary, when dried, remove leaves and throw away stems. Do not crush leaves until you are ready to use them. Sage takes approximately two full years to grow into a shrub. White sage is edible and makes an excellent addition to herbal mixes—just use sparingly, as this particular sage is extremely potent in taste and aroma. Pineapple sage can be placed in the bottom of a cake pan to scent a plain cake. Variegated golden sage is very mild, should you not like a more robust flavor. Tricolor sage also has a gentle aroma.

Fertilizer requirements: light application of your choice (I used organic fish fertilizer)

Space between plants: depends on variety you choose

Incompatible planting with: cucumbers and onions

Compatible with: rosemary, carrots, marjoram, strawberries, tomatoes, and lavender, as they require the same type of soil

Magickal sage: Used in workings for wisdom, wishes, knowledge, strength, long life, and immortality through your actions or talents.

Culinary sage: Poultry, beef, stuffing, stews, poultry, tea, apples, beans, onions, sauces, herbal breads, and butters. Strong flavor, use sparingly.

Goes well with: bay, celery, marjoram, parsley, savory, thyme

Parts used for food: fresh or dried leaves, flowers for garnish

Savory

Growth and care: There are two types of savory: winter, which is a perennial, and summer savory, which is an annual. Winter savory has more aromatic leaves, where the summer variety is much lighter and a bit peppery. Savory doesn't dry well, but it can be frozen. Savory is called the poor man's sauce and is a must-have to empower and cook beans!

Fertilizer requirements: light application of your choice (I used organic fish fertilizer)

Space between plants: 18 inches

Incompatible planting with: none

Compatible with: beans, onions, and sweet potatoes

Magickal savory: Used in spells to obtain secrets, answers to questions, general knowledge, and mental acuity. Also used in love spells and potions.

Culinary savory: Beans, beets, cabbage, peas and other veggies, sausages, lamb, pork, game, oil-rich fish, bean and potato salads, and stuffings. Strong flavor.

Goes well with: basil, bay, garlic, marjoram, mint, oregano, parsley, rosemary, thyme

Parts used for food: dried and fresh leaves, fresh sprigs, flowers for garnishes and salads

Tarragon

Growth and care: Choose only French tarragon if your plant will be used for culinary purposes. This was the touchiest of the plants on my list. It doesn't like high-acid soil and is fussy about needing water, even though they say it needs little. It was worth the fuss, though it was my least-yielding plant. Tarragon likes full sun to partial shade and doesn't take well to being moved. Tarragon can reach a height of 36 inches—mine didn't, topping out at 10.

Fertilizer requirements: light application of your choice (I used organic fish fertilizer)

Space between plants: 18 inches

Incompatible planting with: none

Compatible with: vegetables

Magickal tarragon: Use for harmony in the home, protection, and cleansings.

Culinary tarragon: Excellent in vinegars, chicken, egg dishes, and salad dressings. Also good in soups, salads, stuffings, sauces, fish, cheese, mushroom, seafood, potatoes, and zucchini. Strong flavor.

Goes well with: basil, bay, chives, dill, and parsley

Parts used for food: fresh leaves and sprigs

Thyme

Growth and care: Like basil, oregano, and marjoram, there are several types of thymes that you can choose to grow. Some grow into upright shrubs, where others creep along the ground. Thymes are cut as needed before the plant blossoms around midsummer. Thyme can be dried, but it doesn't freeze particularly well. Requiring full sun to partial shade, thyme requires average watering, although I found in a dry summer, thyme will suffer more than the other herbs, so keep it well watered if the rainman forgets your neck of the woods.

Fertilizer requirements: light application of your choice (I used organic fish fertilizer)

Space between plants: depends on the variety you choose

Incompatible planting with: cucumbers

Compatible with: cabbage, lettuce, eggplant, potatoes, strawberries, and tomatoes

Magickal thyme: Used in workings for courage, long life, health and healing issues, cleansings, love potions, dream magick, restful sleep, and gaining knowledge.

Culinary thyme: Casseroles, soups, root vegetables, stuffings, lamb, onions, potato, rabbit, mushrooms, sausage, fish, vinegars, herbal breads and butters, chicken, and stews.

Goes well with: allspice, basil, bay, hot peppers, clove, garlic, marjoram, nutmeg, oregano, parsley, rosemary, savory

Parts used for food: dried leaves, fresh sprigs, flowers for garnish

Herbs That Do Well in Pots and Containers

Can't go to the expense or don't have the room for an outdoor garden? Here is a list of herbs that do well in pots. If you are using plants rather than seeds, an hour before planting, soak the root ball in a tub of water.

Basil

Fennel

Horseradish

Hyssop

Lemon balm

Lemon verbena

Marjoram

Mints

Myrtle

Nasturtium

Parsley

Pot marigolds

Sage

Tarragon

Thyme

Plants That Might Require Tubs Rather Than Pots, As They Tend to Grow into Small Bushes

Bay

English lavender

Rosemary

Try grouping your herbs in large pots for color and aromatic effect. Planting distances shown on the back of seed packets or labels from the nursery aren't indicative for pot planting. You can begin with small plants or seeds and move the plants out when they grow too large, just as you would with any potted plant. To keep your potted arrangements looking beautiful and healthy, replace larger plants with small specimens of the same herbs. Many of the herbs listed here can grow extremely large and will become pot-bound, choking out other herbs in decorative arrangements. You can either re-pot them in a larger pot when they get too big, give them to friends, or transfer them to the garden in the spring after danger of frost is over.

Organic Garden Bug Killers

In HedgeWitchery, we try to be as safely organic as possible! This is good for you as well as the environment. To minimize predators in your magickal garden (and therefore extending into your life), try the following tips:

Build a toad habitat: This is extremely easy to do. I took an old bird bath without the stand and placed it in the corner of the garden that had the most shade. Then break up several large clay pots and arrange the pieces in and around the bird bath. Fill the bird bath with water. That's it. You have your very own toad habitat. Keep the bird bath filled with water to encourage your toads to stay. I also decorated my toad habitat with toad statues and magickal gems, then planted chamomile nearby. Toads bring prosperity to any garden and eat a lot of nasty bugs! The average toad consumes about 15,000 bugs in a single year, and they love slugs!

Erect a bat house: You can find these at garden supply stores. Each night, a bat can eat approximately 600 pests per hour, with prime targets being mosquitoes, cutworms, cabbageworms, and beetles. Hang your bat house in a tree or on a pole at least 15 feet above ground. You can even decorate the outside of the house with magickal symbols.

Hang a hummingbird feeder: Hummingbirds love red tubular flowers (trumpet vines draw them big time!). If you can't use a natural floral feeder, you can purchase one from your garden supply store along with the nectar mix. Hummingbirds eat tons of nasty insects. Some of their favorite flowers are lilies, snapdragons, and fuchsias.

Plant hot peppers, radishes, and marigolds in your garden: Even if you don't eat hot peppers, the plants are natural deterrents to insects and garden predators. You can also use the juice from the hot peppers in a safe plant wash (given on opposite page).

Plants that attract good bugs: Asters, black-eyed susans, dill, lavender, mints, morning glories, sunflowers, and yarrow. Good bugs eat bad bugs and help to keep your garden healthy. You can pick up a list of good bugs for your planting zone at most reputable home and garden stores.

Last year, I incorporated all five of these natural ideas into my garden and backyard plans. As a result, I had little difficulty with bugs, even though it was a bad year for Japanese beetles and whiteflies. To remove the Japanese beetles, I erected a large bamboo broom twenty feet away from my garden and hung a Japanese beetle trap there, along with magickal runes for banishment. To remove the whiteflies/aphids, I used the following natural formula:

Formula One (for Aphids)

I used this for my marigolds. Water plant before application. First, make garlic oil: mince one whole garlic bulb in a cup of vegetable oil. Put in jar and cap tightly. Set in refrigerator for two to three days. Then, mix together in a spray bottle:

> 1 tablespoon garlic oil
>
> 3 drops liquid dish soap
>
> 1 quart water
>
> ½ teaspoon lavender essential oil

Test formula on one plant. Wait 24 hours. If no damage, spray plants liberally.

Formula Two (for Japanese Beetles)

I used this for my garden. Water plant before application.

½ cup dried cayenne peppers

½ cup dried jalapeño peppers

1 gallon water

Optional: substitute 1 cup of dried habana peppers
for jalapeño and cayenne

Boil water, add peppers, and simmer for thirty minutes. Keep the pot covered while simmering, as the steam is highly potent! Cool. Strain. Pour into spray bottle. Test formula on one plant. Wait 24 hours. If no damage, spray plants after every rain or once a week during the height of Japanese beetle season in your area.

Formula Three

This is a general bug killer—I used this on my hostas. Water plant before application.

3 hot peppers

3 cloves garlic

1 small onion

1 tablespoon liquid dish soap

2 tablespoons peppermint essential oil

3 cups water

Purée peppers, garlic, and onion in blender. Add dish soap and water. Let stand for 24 hours. Strain. Pour in mister bottle. Test formula on one plant. Wait 24 hours. If no damage, spray plants.

Organic Sprays
(To Keep Plants Happy!)

Essential oils can keep your plants happy and healthy—just add formula to one gallon of water. Water plant well before applying solution. Shake bottle vigorously and spray your floral friends. Spray plants lightly every thirty days. If you don't wish to make your own sprays, buy organic soap sprays at your local nursery.

Bee Sweet Formula

> 10 drops peppermint essential oil
>
> 5 drops cinnamon essential oil
>
> 1 gallon water

Moon Wish Formula

> 5 drops lavender essential oil
>
> 5 drops sweet bay essential oil
>
> 5 drops clove essential oil
>
> 1 gallon water

Herbal Garden Gifts

Gifts from your magickal garden can bring great joy and healing into the lives of others. Here are a few ideas that share the fruits of your enchanted labor!

Magickal Vinegar

If you've raised plenty of herbs and have lots left over, why not make your own herbal vinegar? Not only will your vinegar make amazing hostess gifts during the fall and winter seasons for salads and cooking, you can use the vinegars in a variety of banishing spells! The use of vinegar in magick, cooking, healing, and even housework dates back over 10,000 years.

All you need is:

8 to 10 fresh herb sprigs

1 quart good-quality white vinegar

1 quart-sized glass canning jar with lid

Plastic wrap

Gift jars or small bottles

Ribbon

Wash and dry your herbs and place in quart canning jar. Add warm vinegar. Place plastic wrap over glass lip (metal lids will react with vinegar). Screw on lid. Put in warm, dark place for two to four weeks. Strain. Place vinegar in designer jars or bottles with plastic lids or cork tops. Add a sprig of the fresh herb inside the bottle. Decorate with fancy ribbon around neck of bottle or lid of jar. Feel free to mix and match your garden herbs for truly designer vinegars!

Here is a list of herbs that combine well in vinegar:

Basil

Bay leaf

Borage flowers

Chile peppers

Chive flowers

Dill seeds and leaves

Fennel

Garlic

Ginger

Lavender

Mint

Nasturtium flowers

Rose petals

Rosemary

Savory

Tarragon

Thyme

Here are several combination ideas for you to try:

Come-to-Me Love: To make this lovely lavender-colored vinegar, use purple basil that will naturally turn the vinegar a light lavender color, and add a few rose petals and lavender buds.

Home-Blessing: Basil, rosemary, and sage

Long Life: Ginger, chives, and savory

Healing: Chive flowers with lemon balm

Happiness: Parsley, thyme, and basil in red wine vinegar

Family Harmony: White distilled vinegar, purple ruffled basil, African basil, oregano, and rosemary

The nice thing about making your own vinegar is that you can also try using red vinegars, wine, or cider to come up with recipes that are truly your own. You can put in 8 to 10 springs as I indicated, or you can pack the jar with herbs if you like! If you don't want to mess with jars, just buy a plastic gallon jug of your favorite vinegar and pack with chosen herbals. Purchase small designer bottles and sterilize. Allow to cool, then transfer your aged vinegar from the gallon jug into the smaller bottles. Add a fresh sprig or two of one of the ingredients, seal, and decorate bottle with ribbon or raffia.

The length of time that herbs and flavors steep in vinegar depends upon taste. Some folks steep only for a week; others, like myself, steep for a month, strain the vinegar, add fresh herbs, and steep again. Vinegars are best kept steeping in a dark place at room temperature. Shake or stir contents at least twice a week. Make sure that the herbs are completely covered by the vinegar so they do not mold and turn into a health hazard! Be sure you sterilize decorative glass bottles before adding your brew, and strain all herbs and flavorings out of the vinegar. Be sure to date the bottles and keep them out of sunlight. Fruit vinegars tend to last as few as three months; herbal vinegars, about six months after opening. Always keep vinegar bottles capped tightly. As the grocery-store base vinegars in these recipes have at least a 5 percent acidity for safety, you shouldn't have a food-poisoning problem. Homemade vinegars, wherein you use apple cider or some other base, can be attacked by airborne bacteria, which is why such recipes are not offered here. Should you love making vinegars and purchase books on the subject, you will find that instructions, flavorings, and recipes vary widely. For additional instructions and an array of recipes, information, and tips, try the book *Herbal Vinegar* by Maggie Oster through Storey Books Publishing.

Herbal Bouquets for Cooking and Magick

Fresh or dried, herbal bouquets are great for both magick and cooking! In magick, hang the bouquets over the altar or place in a conjuring bag, or dip in spring water to asperge an area, candle, or other item. For cooking, just drop in the boiling water or frying pan for a great taste and easy cleanup!

To make the bouquet, simply gather the herbs together and tie with clean string, leaving a long tail (so you can easily pull the bouquet out of the cooking pot and toss away).

Happy home: basil, marjoram, and chives (for red meat or chicken)

Harmony: parsley, rosemary, thyme, and savory (for red meat or flavoring for beans)

Uncrossing: marjoram, thyme, sage, parsley, and bay (for red meat, pork, or chicken)

Love: dill, tarragon, parsley, basil, and lovage (flavoring for beans or fish)

Good fortune: savory, sage, celery tops, and chives (flavoring for beans, chicken, or red meat)

Growth and success: tarragon, chives, oregano, and parsley (for eggs and sauces)

Healing: sage, basil, onion tops, and bay (for red meat)

Banishing and cleansing: parsley, lemon verbena, rosemary, and red pepper (for fish)

Herbal Butters

Herb butters make wonderful gifts and will have your family amazed at the variety of new flavors they can experience on their breakfast breads, dinner rolls, vegetables, pasta, rice, and grilled meats. To make an herbal butter, wash herbs and pat dry. Chop finely. Add a few drops of lemon juice (for preservation) and mix into soft, room-temperature butter. Butter can be whipped until frothy, or you can form the butter by filling silicone novelty molds (used to make cupcakes or soaps) and refrigerate. Herb butters can also be frozen for a few months. Here are some great combinations:

Good fortune: parsley, marjoram, thyme, sage, basil, and a hint of garlic

Happy lunch: chives and dill

Prosperous bean butter: rosemary or winter savory, or a combination of the two

Abundance: garlic, thyme, and marjoram (for basting red meats)

Rooster: fennel or tarragon with dill (add a touch of lemon verbena for fish)

Herbal Sugars

In magick, sugar is often used as an attraction vehicle. Adding herbs that can be used in hot brewed or iced tea makes them invaluable for magick as well as food consumption, and they are so easy to make! Pack fresh herb leaves in granulated white sugar in airtight containers, such as Mason jars or small, plastic containers. Stir each day to prevent lumps and clumping. When the sugar remains dry and loose, remove herbs. Herbs you may consider using for sugars include a variety of mints, lemon and orange peel, or rose petals. To make unusual magickal sugars, try packaging herbal tea bags such as chamomile in the sugar, or mixtures such as a berry tea or apple tea. Dried apple slices can also be placed in the sugar. Using tea bags leaves only a trace of aroma but may serve your magickal purposes well.

Herbal Salts

Salt has always been a primary magickal cleanser that can be made more powerful with herbs from your garden. An added bonus? It's edible! The salt dries the herbs and at the same time absorbs the essential oils. Use only the parts of the herbs that are edible—that way you can use the salt either in magick or on the dinner table!

Finely chop chosen herbs, layering ¼-inch at the bottom of a Mason jar. Sprinkle with a thin layer of salt. Put in another layer of herbs, followed by the salt. Continue this layering technique until the jar is almost full. Cover the top layer of herbs completely with salt, and seal the jar. Let set for about one week. Herbs should be dry. Dump into a clean bowl, and stir thoroughly. You can put your herb salt in smaller, airtight containers or pour it back into the original Mason jar. For recipes, try the combinations listed under herbal butters or herbal bouquets.

Herbal Salt Substitutes

Can't have salt in your diet? Try these recipes, which are especially powerful if you have grown the herbs yourself! Powder the dried herbs in a spice grinder, blender, or use your mortar and pestle.

Happy Home Salt Substitute

Great for stews, soups, eggs, beans, and meats. Excellent for bland and no-salt dietary restrictions.

    3   tablespoons dried basil

    3   tablespoons dried thyme

    3   tablespoons dried marjoram

    3   tablespoons dried sage

    3   tablespoons dried winter savory

    3   tablespoons powdered milk (to keep the mixture from clumping)

When mixed thoroughly, transfer to shaker if you will use immediately or an airtight container if you plan to keep it for a while. You can purchase shakers with airtight caps at places like Bed, Bath and Beyond, kitchen supply stores, etc., or you can wash and sterilize glass spice containers from the grocery store when you have used all the contents (soak off the label before sterilizing, and add your own label and cap when container is completely dry after sterilizing).

Abundant Life Salt Substitute

- 2 tablespoons dried parsley
- 2 tablespoons dried basil
- 2 tablespoons dried oregano
- 2 tablespoons dried sage
- 2 teaspoons dried rosemary
- 1 teaspoon dried garlic
- 1 teaspoon dried onion
- 1 teaspoon dried black pepper
- 3 tablespoons powdered milk (optional)

When mixed thoroughly, transfer to shaker. Excellent as a general seasoning. For succulent baked fish, add 1 teaspoon of paprika and ¼ cup dried Parmesan cheese. Store in airtight container.

No-Salt Substitute for Chicken

- 2 tablespoons dried rosemary
- 1 tablespoon dried thyme
- 1 tablespoon dried sage
- 1 tablespoon dried marjoram
- 1 tablespoon dried winter savory
- 1 tablespoon dried basil
- 1 tablespoon dried parsley
- ½ teaspoon white pepper

oregano

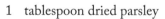
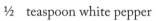

Berry Magickal Ink

Some practitioners believe that writing petitions in magickal ink (liquid that contains herbals, scented oils, and color that has been blessed and empowered before use) makes the attraction power of their work extremely powerful. Here's a natural recipe to juice up your spells!

You will need:

½ cup ripe berries (blueberries, raspberries, strawberries, blackberries, cherries, etc., or a mixture of various berries)

½ teaspoon vinegar (you can use your herbal vinegar— vinegar helps to hold the color)

½ teaspoon salt (to deter mold)

1 bowl

1 clean baby food jar

Strainer

Wooden spoon

Instructions:

Place berries in strainer. Hold strainer over bowl. With rounded back of wooden spoon, crush juice from berries and allow to drip into the bowl. Continue to add berries and crush until only pulp remains in strainer. Add salt and vinegar to the berry juice. Stir thoroughly. If your ink is too thick, add one tablespoon of distilled water. Store in baby food jar.

Note: Natural ink does not keep long. You can scent your mixture by adding a few drops of your favorite essential oil. Use this ink with a crow quill pen or feather pen you have made yourself. To make a feather pen, cut the tip of a large feather at an angle with a sharp craft knife, then carefully cut a slit in the angle. Dip pen in ink, dab on paper towel, then write! Repeat dipping the pen and dabbing on towel as needed.

Herbal Potpourri

Herb potpourris are extremely easy to make—you just need time for the mixture to age appropriately.

You will need:

A large glass jar with lid (or a huge airtight Rubbermaid container with lid)

Dried herbs, flowers, and spices

A fixative such as orris root or calamus root (1 tablespoon of fixative per 1 quart of flowers, herbs, and spices)

Your choice of essential oil for added fragrance

Instructions:

Mix dried herbs, spices, and flowers in large bowl. Add fixative. Toss like salad. Add your essential oil five drops at a time until you reach the aromatic level you desire. Toss again. Place in airtight container. Let sit for about thirty days, checking each week and tossing to ensure you are reaching the desired aroma. Add more essential oil if necessary. Once the mixture has cured, you can use the potpourri in sachets, around candles, in decorator bowls on the fireplace mantle, etc.

Fixatives can add their own aroma.
Here's a quick list:
Frankincense
Myrrh
Orris root
Gum benzoin
Calamus root
Storax
*Avoid powders—try to use chunks instead.

Harvest Home Bonfire/Cauldron Fire

Winter's not far off, and it is time to harvest those lovely herbs you've been growing all year. Time to thank Mother Nature and cut those herbs the HedgeWitch way! Note that this rite uses only primal language.

Timing: Morning, just after the dew has left the plants

Supplies:

       Large cauldron (use candle), burn barrel, or fire pit

13   apples (for love and long life)

4   large pumpkins (for abundance and good fortune)

       Dried straw or hay (for food in the house throughout the winter)

       Fire supplies (to unite with Spirit)—Supplies depend on whether you are using a candle in a cauldron or a fire pit in your back yard. For the fire pit, you will need logs, lighter fluid or pre-soaked logs, and a long-handled lighter manufactured for grill and bonfire use. Follow the directions carefully to avoid accidents and serious burns. For the candle, a handheld lighter will do.

       Pumpkin spice powder (for luck)

2   cups of any no-salt recipe (for cleansing; see recipes on pages 256–257)

Pumpkin Spice Powder

5   tablespoons ground cinnamon

3   teaspoons ground ginger

2   teaspoons ground allspice

2   teaspoons ground cloves

2   teaspoons ground cinnamon

1   teaspoon powdered sweet chocolate

Place the pumpkins (each standing for a direction—north, east, south, west) around the burn barrel. Intersperse the shined apples (for the thirteen moons of the wheel of the year). If you are using a bonfire or burn barrel, place a little straw in the barrel. If you are using a cauldron, place bound straw near the cauldron but not in it. Sprinkle unlit logs or candle with the pumpkin spice.

Face the east, and intone this chant three times:

>*Eastwards I stand, for favors I pray*
>*From goddess divine and lord of the day*
>*Earth lends her power and breath sends the spell*
>*Day's end will reveal that all will be well!*
>*It always works. Always a blessing!*

Smile, and breathe deeply. Light the candle or bonfire. Turn and face your garden. In your own way, thank the plants and earth for the bounty you are about to receive. Sprinkle any tools you will use to harvest with a little of the pumpkin spice. After you have harvested your herbs and dug up the annuals, turn the earth in the garden three times, removing any weeds you may find. Sprinkle the perimeter of your garden with any of the no-salt recipes to cleanse the earth and prepare her for her deep sleep. Return to your fire or candle, and thank Spirit for your fruitful harvest. Allow your garden to sit for three days, then cover the garden with straw or a winter compost mixture. Clean and disinfect garden tools so that they will be ready for next year.

Drying Your Herbs

Harvest your herbs in the morning after the dew has dried. I usually sing or chant as I cut the plants, shake off dirt, and remove dead or unsightly leaves now, rather than having to go through the herbs later. While still in the garden, I use rubber bands to make one-inch-thick stalk bundles, then tie with long cotton cord, leaving plenty of length at both ends so that I can easily hang the bunches later. I loosely tie the bundles on the garden fence until I'm ready to bring them all in. This saves time and keeps the bundles out of the dirt. I also label the bundles with tags from the craft store, looping one end of the cord onto a tag while I am still in the garden. This way I can easily identify the herb bundles at any given time. Bring your bundles inside and lightly rinse them, being careful not to get the tags wet. If you have not used pesticides and do not live in a high-pollution area, you don't need to wash off the leaves. Some organic gardeners believe that washing the leaves destroys some of the oils in the plants.

You might wish to wash the herbs you will consume, but not the ones you will use in potpourris or gris-gris bags (such as patchouli, which isn't edible). Whether you wash your herbs or not is entirely up to you.

Hang bunches upside down in a warm, dark, dust-free area with good ventilation. When bunches are dry and brittle (about two to three weeks), take them down and carefully remove leaves. Store leaves in jars or plastic bags. Do not crush leaves until you are ready to use them in cooking or magick.

For short-stalk herbs such as thyme or needle-type herbs such as rosemary, I poke a small hole in the bottom of a paper bag, then insert the herb bundle in the bag with the cut stalks at the top of the bag and plenty of empty space in the bottom of the bag. Twist the top of the bag, secure with rubber band, tie cotton cord around bag, and hang. This will keep the small leaves from falling all over the floor and help to retain the flavor of the herb. These herbs can also be dried loose on a clean window screen placed on a few bricks (to allow air circulation under the screen). Flip herbs every few days until dry, then store as indicated above.

Pumpkin Seed Recipe

In magick, the pumpkin is a symbol of abundance and good fortune. Toasted pumpkin seeds are a great snack, and they can be ground (once toasted and flavored) and added to your favorite bean dish (also served to draw abundance and good fortune to the home). Being able to eat the seeds makes Halloween pumpkin carving even more magickal, especially if you have empowered your pumpkin for abundance and good fortune!

You will need: Pumpkin seeds; cooking oil, olive oil, or butter; garlic salt or other herbal flavorings such as onion powder, cayenne pepper, or one of the no-salt recipes given in this book; cookie sheet; paper towels.

Instructions: Wash and pat dry pumpkin seeds. Lay out seeds on paper towels and allow to dry for 24 hours. In bowl, toss pumpkin seeds in oil, then add your herbal flavoring. Preheat oven to 250 degrees and bake for one hour, tossing every 15 minutes until golden brown. Cool thoroughly. Store in airtight container. Lasts about three months at room temperature.

Yule Hostess Good Fortune Gift

A lovely basket of your herbal delights will be most welcome at Yule! Add this recipe and a bottle of wine for a truly heart-warming gift.

Long Life Mulled Cider Spice

1½	cups smashed cinnamon chips
1½	cups dried, chopped orange peel
1	cup whole allspice berries
½	cup whole cloves
1	tablespoon dried nutmeg (smashed, not powdered)
½	teaspoon star anise (smashed)
4	small pieces of dried ginger root (add one root to each bag)
4	small cotton bags
	Plastic wrap
4	glass mugs
	Ribbon or pine or holly sprigs, optional

Mix ingredients thoroughly and pack in cotton bags. Wrap in plastic. Place one bag in each glass mug. Add ribbon and sprigs of pine or holly as decoration.

Include bottle of wine
OR
sweet cider in basket.
(Recipe can be used
in warm wine or sweet cider.)

star anise

Summary

In keeping with the flow of the seasons and Spirit in Nature,
I began this HedgeWitchery course in the spring of the
year, right before the first thaw. Now, as autumn leads to
winter and my magickal garden lies sleeping,
it is time to celebrate the harvest!
I do hope that the rites, tips, techniques, and formulas provided
in this book have brought you hours of fulfillment and months of
pure joy. Remember: changing your life is as simple as a choice.
Believe!

Sincerely,

Silver RavenWolf

Recommended Reading

If you liked this book, or would enjoy more information on various topics, you may wish to read those listed below:

Witchcraft

Solitary Witch by Silver RavenWolf (Llewellyn)—a full-bodied reference on modern Witchcraft/Wicca.

The Witches' Sabbats by Mike Nichols (Acorn Guild Press)—an excellent reference on Wiccan holidays.

Herb Gardening and Herbal References

A Heritage of Herbs: History, Early Gardening and Old Recipes by Bertha P. Reppert (Early American Society Publishing)

Beginner's Guide to Herb Gardening by Yvonne Cuthbertson (Guild of Master Craftsman Publications)

Brother Cadfael's Herb Garden by Rob Talbot and Robin Whiteman (Little, Brown and Co.)

Cunningham's Encyclopedia of Magical Herbs by Scott Cunningham (Llewellyn)

Gardening on a Shoestring by Rob Proctor (Johnson Books)

Giant Book of Garden Solutions: 1,954 Natural Remedies to Handle Your Toughest Garden Problems by Jerry Baker (American Master Products)

Herb Mixtures and Spicy Blends, Introduction by Maggie Oster (Storey Publishing)

Herbs and Spices: The Cook's Reference by Jill Norman (DK Publications)

Herbs for Health and Healing: A Drug-Free Guide to Prevention and Cure by Kathi Keville (Rodale Publishing)

Rodale's Illustrated Encyclopedia of Herbs by Claire Kowalchik and William H. Hylton, editors (Rodale Publications)

Spiritual Gardening: Creating Sacred Space Outdoors by Peg Streep (Inner Ocean Publications)

The Complete Book of Essential Oils and Aromatherapy by Valerie Anne Worwood (New World Library)

The Gardener's A–Z Guide to Growing Organic Food by Tanya L. K. Denckla (Storey Publishing)

The Herb Gardener: A Guide for All Seasons by Susan McClure (Storey Books)

The Organic Garden Book by Geoff Hamilton (DK Publishing)

Soap Making

300 Handcrafted Soaps by Marie Browning (Sterling)

Making Transparent Soap: The Art of Crafting, Molding, Scenting & Coloring by Catherine Failor (Storey Publishing)

Melt & Mold Soap Crafting by C. Kaila Westerman (Storey Books)

Melt & Pour Soapmaking by Marie Browning (Sterling)

The Soapmaker by Janita Morris (Watson-Guptill Publications)

Feng Shui Techniques

Feng Shui Life Planner by Lillian Too (Hamlyn Publishing)

Lillian Too's Easy-to-Use Feng Shui: 168 Ways to Success (Sterling)

Practical Feng Shui by Simon Brown (Cassell Publishing)

Total Feng Shui: Bring Health, Wealth and Happiness Into Your Life by Lillian Too (Chronicle Books)

Candle Making

Great Candles by Stewart D'Arcy Hyder (Sterling)

Appendix 1
Your Garden Journal

One summer I ordered some beautiful rubber stamps from the Stampington company, many of them focusing on artistic herbal themes. About a month or so after I received my box of goodies, a package came in the mail. Someone at the company took a composition book and covered it with interesting paper designs and stamped artwork, with the finishing touch of a brad and a bow. I knew immediately that this surprise gift would become my gardening journal.

This journal grew into a combination of the business of gardening (what I bought, where, when, and why) to small entries on what I'd accomplished over the growing season. When the moon turned to new in April 2008, I dug out the journal and reviewed what I'd written last year in preparation for the gardening year to come. I was amazed at how invaluable the information I'd written proved to be. Use some of your April days to create your own truly magickal gardening journal. To give you some ideas, here's how I originally set up my entries:

Plants purchased: By the end of 2007, I had three pages filled with plants purchased, noting where I bought them (a note that proved invaluable as a shopping guide for the following year). I also recorded the number of plants purchased. For example, one entry read: "3 Rosemary—Country Market." Another: "8 White Sage—poor condition—Blinkers—6 survived." The "6 survived" means that six of these plants survived through that growing season.

Supplies and tools purchased: Again, another three pages here by the time the season was done. Under this category, I wrote down everything from mulch and tools to garden goodies (statues, fountains, supplies for my toad house, etc.). Here, too, I wrote down where I purchased what. For example, I bought twenty garden stepping stones with a Celtic knot design from a large retailer. When spring 2008 rolled around, I found seven of these stepping stones either completely disintegrated or broken in half, so I updated the entry to show they were a poor long-term buy. Granted, I should have collected the stones in the fall and brought them in, but they added a bit of mental light to the autumn and winter gloom, and so I left them. If I choose to replace them this year, I'm now more informed on maintenance, but to save myself money and lugging, I think I'll just stick with the colored flagstone and be done with it. So, a note to self on this one: choose wisely when purchasing concrete manmade items for the garden.

Purchased fertilizer and repellants: When I first began my HedgeWitch project, I decided that I would go totally organic unless something drastic should occur (which it didn't). I read every label thoroughly before I bought the product to ensure that if I said the plant was raised organically, it really was! I also learned a few inexpensive tricks along the way, like using three doses of white vinegar to kill dandelions, strong sea salt water for getting rid of weeds around the patio stones (just don't put it where you want something to grow), soap spray for getting rid of aphids, and fox/wolf urine (yup) on the stones of the raised beds to keep the bunnies, groundhogs, and cats away. For these entries, I added how many bottles or bags of the product I bought and whether, over the season, it worked or not.

Planting hints: On these pages, I kept a record of plant compatibility. For example, put chives with roses to keep black spots off your fragrant blooms. Basil goes with tomatoes (both need a lot of water). Add hot peppers to all your garden beds to discourage bug pests, and plenty of marigolds to ward off the vicious, long-fanged bunnies! This page helped me to choose what and how many plants of this type to buy and grow in my next year's crop.

Plant-buying guide: To all things there is a season and timing, and each locality will be different, and each year will vary based on the weather. Last year, due to my granddaughter's birth, my growing season started late. On top of that, we had a cold spell in early July, and nothing wanted to ripen. When I first put in my herbs last year, by the time I got to the greenhouses and began choosing what I wanted to raise, many of the plants I needed were sold out. This year, I recorded in my journal which plants were available when. For example, it is April yet, and although it's a warm one, the greenhouses follow the traditional timing for this area: don't plant much outside before May Day due to fear of a late frost. Even so, every flat of green peppers was sold out of the local greenhouses by the end of the second week in April. This led me to believe that many folks buy early and then place the plants in a protected area, most likely in the home, until they can plant outside. That way they get the healthiest, earliest choices.

My entries look something like this: "2008 Seeds—available in March; 2008 Seed Starters—available in March; Replacement Garden Tools—available in March; Most Herbs—available mid-April; Most peppers and tomatoes—available late April" (and so on). "Ferns—available in April, but wait for more lush varieties in May."

Following the rules of the moon (plant above-ground crops new to full, below-ground full to new), I started most of my own seed plants (moonflowers, broccoli, beans, sugar peas, snapdragons, foxglove, and morning glory) between the new and full moons in April so that they would be ready to go into the ground in May. I placed the compact mini greenhouses in an upstairs room with the most light. They are doing great! My daughter, however, started her seeds two weeks before mine, during the waning moon. She reported that her seeds did absolutely nothing until the moon turned to new and began growing, yet my seeds sprouted in just three days and literally blew off the greenhouse covers with their accelerated growth! Here is an excellent example of moon garden timing!

My plant-buying guide page also has best-price information as well as notations for garden-related trips. For example, the local greenhouses this year are charging $2.49 for a single herb or tomato/pepper plant. Before we shopped at the greenhouses, we decided to visit a few other places. For the first time this year, our family went to the Herb Fest at the York Fair Grounds in mid-April. Here, about a hundred (or so, didn't really count) vendors plied their 2008 seasonal wares. As we'd never been there, we didn't know what to expect, but we decided no matter what we thought of it, a day out with our grown daughters and a great lunch would be a lot of fun. The show focused mostly on herbs and herb-related products (which was great, because that's what I grow), but only a handful of vendors actually sold live herbs. The remainder carried herb-related products—such as soaps, oils, teas, crafty thingamabobs, and such. Like many magickal gardeners, I've learned to make these things on my own over the years and therefore put my buying dollars in other areas. For the plants, however, prices here ranged either a bit below market or, more usually, at market price. If, however, you bought in bulk, some herb vendors gave a discount. At the Herb Fest, we found what I call local exotics (stuff you can't really find at the greenhouses or, if you do, there's only a plant or two), such as patchouli, valerian, vervain, etc., making the trip worthwhile as far as stocking my garden with some unusual varieties. Too, the show was well organized and aesthetically pleasing—overall a worthwhile trip for us. My journal notes that we should visit again next year.

The following week, our shopping agenda stop was the flea market at Williams Grove. Here, local farmers and small growers bring their plants and produce (along with all the other expected flea market regalia). Price range here was below market—from $1.00 to $1.69 a plant. Although everything looked great and healthy, the herb selection was somewhat limited—rosemary, globe basil, tomatoes, peppers—nothing too exotic, but if you were in the market for a nice azalea or other garden trimmings, this was definitely the place to shop, and absolutely the choice in pricing for those regular garden-variety herbs. So, I made a note in my journal to be sure and check out the flea market first next year before purchasing elsewhere. Perhaps there is a flea market or open market near you that will carry bargains like I found.

Items removed: This category lists all the things I removed from the garden and property area, regardless of whether they directly affected the gardening process. I kept a record of this effort because sometimes you simply don't see the rewards in cleaning and organizing. I also listed whether or not this process cost me any money. For example, I had three trees and several bushes removed last year by a local boy. I listed how much I paid him for this service. This year, if I have him remove something else, I'll know how much I gave him last year and increase it. My personal motto is never insult hard labor; help him make his time valuable to both of you.

Gifts received: When people know you are totally into gardening, they will purchase gifts for you that revolve around that interest. I kept track of all the gifts I received that related to my gardening, and then, in the fall when harvesting (and throughout the growing season when possible), I made sure that these individuals enjoyed the proceeds of their gifts, which ties into the next category…

Gifts given: This can be separate or go along with the Gifts Received page. Not everyone likes everything you produce. For example, I make great herbal vinegars, but not a lot of my family members use herbal vinegars—yet they love herbal butters. I also make soap, and like other products, everyone has a particular soap they adore and those types of soaps they hate. On this page, I have listed who likes what, and what it is I gave them, so that during the 2008 growing season I can pay special attention to what is appreciated where. That way, no one is disappointed and the right energy goes to the right person.

Fertilizer chart: Most plants should be fertilized about every two weeks or so. When I fertilized, I would write down the date and what plants received the fertilizer. I think I'm the only person in my area that fertilizes at midnight, but as the old moon lore goes, it certainly works, and it is kinda cool to be tromping around out there in the dead of night encouraging your babies to grow! I also till in the dark for optimum weed control. This page of the journal also lists how much fertilizer I use, so that I know next year how much of what to buy to last me through the season.

Watering chart: Different plants require different amounts of water. I kept a list of which plants needed the most water and which needed the least so that I wouldn't overlook anybody, and next year I will plant accordingly.

Winter survivors/losses: This is a new category I designed for spring 2008. Many herbs, such as basil, are annuals, so you know they aren't going to survive through the winter—dig out the roots when the season is done. There are those, however, like rosemary, hyssop, tarragon, and savory that can make it through at least one or two winters if the weather hasn't been too blustering. In early April, I began walking the garden, looking to see who would wake up and who had bitten the big one and gone on to garden summerland. At first, I thought nothing survived, but as the days grew warmer, I was pleasantly surprised at which plants had made it through my first bumbling attempts at winterizing. My list this year looked like this:

Winter survivors: 1 rosemary bush, 2 oregano plants, summer savory, winter savory, tarragon, hyssop, 2 Berggarten sage, 2 golden thyme (just barely); 1 crawling thyme; chives.

Winter losses: All the lavender (this I attributed to really lousy soil in that area); both bay trees (started too late and the root system just wasn't strong enough); 2 rosemary bushes (this surprised me); parsley (this was also a surprise, as usually my parsley makes it through anything); all white sage (this was a disappointment); lemon verbena (caught a blight).

By keeping this list, I knew what I had to replace this growing season, which helped to save me money when shopping for 2008, which brings us to the last list…

2008 garden universal shopping list: Here, in the spring, I write down everything I want. This doesn't necessarily mean I will buy everything on this list, so really it is a combination wish list and purchase list. I don't write "wish" because often people believe that many wishes don't come true. The word "wish" isn't a nice, sturdy, I'm-a-gonna-git-it wording. I find that if I write what I want in black and white (or green and white), many times I will be gifted with something I really wanted on this list (even though I didn't specifically ask anyone for it). That's why I call it a universal shopping list. The universe *loves* to give you a bargain, you just have to want to receive it! As the season progresses, I check off everything I've purchased or received and add new items as I think of them to the bottom of the list. For example, this year I knew I had to replace the fire pit, but like every other American family, we are minding our budget because of the horrendous gas prices. I didn't need the fire pit for gardening per se, I needed the pit for ritual and magick, so I figured I'd get the garden together first and then see what was left over for the pit. However, I still wrote down exactly what I wanted in regard to the fire pit. Here's a sample of this year's list and a note or two of what I generally use the items for (just in case you were wondering—also, this isn't everything in my gardens, simply what I want to buy or replace for the 2008 season):

Rosemary (food, ritual, magick, and for soap)

White sage (food, ritual, magick, and for soap)

African basil (food)

Golden thyme (food and soap)

Eucalyptus (for cleansing rituals, winter decoration, and soap)

Horehound (for cleansing rituals)

Valerian (for ritual)

Vervain (for ritual and magick)

Patchouli (for money rituals and soap)

Red wagon (for hauling)

Globe basil (food)

Peppers (red and green)

Tomatoes

Lettuce

Beans (seeds)

Moonflowers (seeds; ritual)

Four o'clocks (seeds; ritual and magick)

Morning glory (seeds; ritual and magick)

Cucumbers (seeds)

Marigolds (seeds; magick and garden protection, soap)

Sugar peas (seeds)

Parsley

Larkspur (seeds; ghost protection)

Sunflower (seeds; success magick)

Variegated sage (food)

Berggarten sage (food)

Purple basil (food and lavender-colored vinegars)

Lemongrass (cleansing rituals, dream pillows)

Chamomile (success and cleansing rituals, dream pillows, soap)

Trellises (need at least 10)

Gardening pots (large, need at least 8, 10 better for growing different varieties of mint)

Mulch (11 bags to start)

Lavender (cleansing rituals, dream pillows)

Electronic owl

Bird bath

Starter garden panels for seeds (8)

Selection of mints (for magick, teas, ritual, soaps)

1 load of topsoil for new flower garden area

1 load of organic soil for herb garden area

Shovel, red

Rake, red

Fire pit, moon and stars design with cover and grate

Bunny fence

Fish fertilizer

I wrote this list the first week of April. As of today, approximately two and a half weeks later, I have purchased or received everything on this list except for one item, the organic topsoil for the herb garden stash, and that is on the way—just stalled in transit due to inclement weather. It pays to write your list! Many of the items on this list were gifts from the universe (meaning I didn't have to spend any money to get them—like my new fire pit!). Get out your pen and start listing what you want!

Notes for next year: These are just quickies, and for me they have a lot to do with timing. For example: "Put herbs in earlier next year—June was too late. Start moonflowers and other seeds beginning of April. Front bed receives too much shade, move tomatoes and peppers to middle or back bed. Cold snap in July split tomatoes. Front area needs better soil next year" (and so forth).

Journal entries: These are by date, and I simply wrote down what I did on that day, or sometimes, what I had accomplished that week if the time of the season was slow. Last year's entries for April and May were minimal. We were waiting for our granddaughter to be born, and I knew I would be away for at least a week when the happy event occurred. I spent these two months cleaning, weeding, and designing. I began with a single spade (as I had no garden tools of my own, I'd always borrowed my father's tools) and did all the work by hand on my knees down in the dirt. As the season progressed, I purchased more tools to make the work easier. I'm glad I did it this way, because I learned what I really needed, and more importantly, what type of tools I liked to work with. I also learned which tools were not worth their cost. For example, I bought this weed grabber thing, thinking how much work it would save. It isn't worth the metal it was made of. I gave it away, thinking maybe I wasn't using it right, and told the person so. They couldn't make it work, either. Sometimes my journal entries would be only a line or two, and other times I would go on for a page or so. Just depended on my mood and how much I accomplished. Many of my entries contained the ingredients I used when designing a soap, butter, food recipe, or vinegar using the proceeds from my garden (many of these formulas can be found in this book). Here are some entries from my 2007 journal, to give you an example:

July 14: Most of my moonflowers started at the end of May became potbound, so I had to prepare a bed (been meaning to do it) of their own. I transplanted several along the back porch (11 plants) and 7 plants along the garden fence row. The soil there isn't the best, but I have to put them somewhere. Moonflowers are climbers, and I had a heck of a time finding them something to climb on. Began clearing the weeds between the beds this week. My daughter's rose bloomed! Added 6 bags of organic Black Forest soil to herb beds. Could use 2 more. Cleansing ritual for Arnold. Made empowered herb water. Note to self: Buy more trellises next year.

July 15: Another rose today!!! Began tearing up the pathways between beds. What a terrible job. Several years ago, Dad put down old carpet because some gardening book told him to do it. What an unbelievable mess. I'd like to call that author out here and have them clean up this mess. The trash collector is going to hate me this week. I'm covered head to foot with black soot. Yuck. Six done, one to go. I have decided to go with red tan bark. Maybe 7 bags will do. Healing ritual for Heather. Created a healing soap for her to use.

July 16: Finished clearing out all the pathways. Super high humidity. Picked my first beefsteak tomato. Grilled ham with an herb bundle of sage, thyme, and basil. Added savory and tarragon to the asparagus with a nice sauce. Baked potatoes in foil with fresh sage and rosemary. Excellent!

July 20: I can't believe it: the dogs mowed down the rose bush. Broke to bits. Such a shame! It took 11 bags of tan bark for the pathways. Built my toad habitat! The garden looks super! Made another batch of gardening soap. Prosperity ritual for Joanne. Poured a prosperity candle for her.

August 10: Finally, the moonflowers bloomed! Moonflowers have been my signature plant for years, and I have always been able to grow them. I thought they would never flower this year. I know I put them in too late and moved them around too much. I'm so glad that they finally took off. Several super hot days and three whopper thunderstorms. I made nine bottles of thunder water for magick and ritual during those storms. Peppers finally getting big, but the tomatoes split because of all the rain. Mints all died from some sort of blight. Too much sun, I think. Next year I'll plant them in container pots so I can control their environment better. My ferns are so beautiful on the back porch! Grandma, you would be proud!

…and so forth.

Recipes and formulas: This section holds my tried-and-true formulas, from organic bug spray to ingredients I use for family-favorite soaps, vinegars, teas, room sprays, and more.

Although the description of my journal pages may seem like a lot of work, it really didn't take much time at all to put the book together. Once I had the categories the way I wanted them, I often spent only a few minutes jotting things down when the opportunity arose. Near the end of the growing year, I added pictures of the fruits of my labors. I used the journal many times over the growing season, then read it at the end of harvest and then once more in April when I was preparing for the new season. Not only did my little book become an invaluable record for the business of growing my own garden, it also became a written testament of how I spent my time throughout the planting and harvest year. These days with everything computerized and the threat of losing your data in a heartbeat, or of systems changing so fast your electronic diary of ten years ago can no longer be read, having a good, old-fashioned journal with a cover you can run your fingers over and pages you can lovingly turn isn't a bad idea after all. Even if you are not a full or part-time gardener, perhaps you have a friend or family member that would love to receive a garden journal as a gift like I did. You never know how inspiring your creative efforts can be!

Appendix 2
How to Make Florida Water

Florida water can be made with or without alcohol, and can be made with raw herbs or with essential oils. The shelf life of waters made with alcohol is longer. Raw herb water should be refrigerated.

Do not ingest either of these waters! And as with all formulas, if you have sensitive skin, take care with any herbal recipe.

Florida Water with Alcohol and Oils

½ gallon 90-proof alcohol

1 ounce lavender essential oil

1 dram lemon essential oil

1 dram citrus (such as tangerine or bergamot) essential oil

1 dram lime essential oil

½ dram clove essential oil

HedgeWitch Florida Water with Water and Raw Herbs

Fill a one-quart Mason jar with the following:

Spring water

2 slices orange

2 slices lemon

2 slices lime

Fresh mint from the garden

Fresh lemon balm from the garden

Fresh hyssop from the garden

1 fresh rosemary sprig

1 fresh basil sprig

Pack jar with the herbs as full as you like. Boil spring water (enough to fill the jar). Pour into Mason jar (note: please use a canning jar or Pyrex brand glass container as these can withstand the boiling water). Make sure the jar is warm before pouring in the boiling water. Allow mixture to cool completely. Strain. Pour liquid into a sterlilized jar or bottle. Keep in refrigerator. Potent for three days.

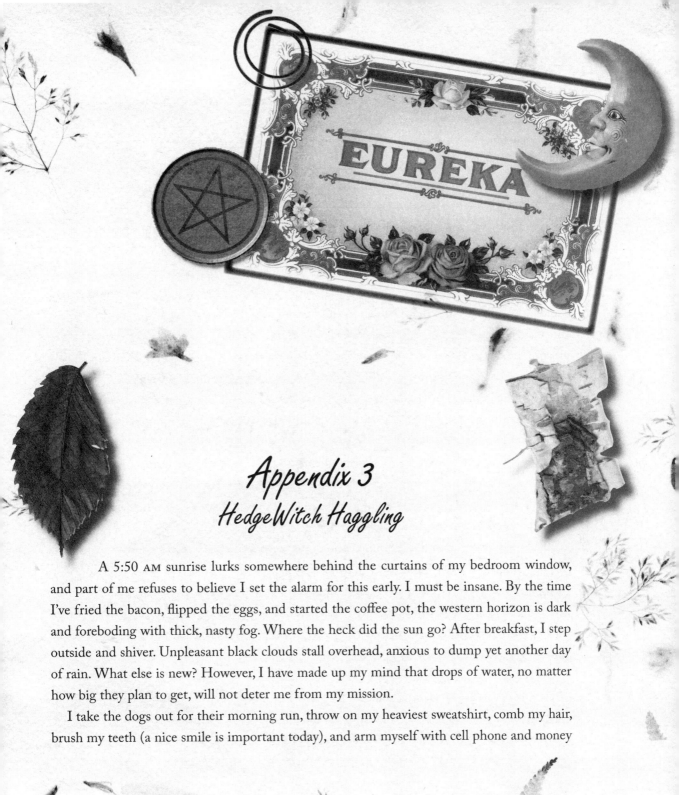

Appendix 3
HedgeWitch Haggling

A 5:50 AM sunrise lurks somewhere behind the curtains of my bedroom window, and part of me refuses to believe I set the alarm for this early. I must be insane. By the time I've fried the bacon, flipped the eggs, and started the coffee pot, the western horizon is dark and foreboding with thick, nasty fog. Where the heck did the sun go? After breakfast, I step outside and shiver. Unpleasant black clouds stall overhead, anxious to dump yet another day of rain. What else is new? However, I have made up my mind that drops of water, no matter how big they plan to get, will not deter me from my mission.

I take the dogs out for their morning run, throw on my heaviest sweatshirt, comb my hair, brush my teeth (a nice smile is important today), and arm myself with cell phone and money pouch securely attached to my blue jean belt loops hidden under that oversized hoodie. Beats carrying a purse.

The sky looks really evil, but the clouds hold as I motor into the parking area. I'm surprised at the amount of people here, given the potential weather. Obviously, I am not the only determined soul out for a bargain at 8:00 AM on a gloomy Sunday morning—but I will bet you that I'm one of the few people here with a magick formula for bargaining in my mythical back pocket! Today I have a special job to do: I am testing my HedgeWitch haggling secrets at the flea market.

I'm pretty excited as I huff my way up the hill and into the vendor area. I've never haggled for anything before. At least, not consciously. Up until now, I was one of the hundreds of thousands of Americans that listened to the rules of middle-class society in my youth: to ask the price, or to dicker over the amount of any object, was…well…uncouth, disrespectful, and greedy. The fact that just about every other culture on the face of the planet exercises the art and science of haggling somehow didn't make it into my educational curriculum.

As children, many Americans are taught that the other side of bargaining—auctions—are good. Attempting to lower the price of anything else (other than coupons dictated by the seller) is considered rude. I believed this myth of misinformation up until last month when two things occurred—I wrote an article on belief and our economy went into the toilet. Now gas prices are high, and like everyone else, I have bills to pay—I need food and clothing, not to mention paying utilities and the mortgage. Let's not forget house insurance, laundry detergent…you get the picture, because you're right here with me.

Like you, I'm not into cheating anyone—I just want a fair price, and since I can't get it at the gas pump, I've got to look for it in other venues. After watching the news the other day, I found myself insulted that many large companies involved in the making and selling of creature-comfort items (soda, makeup, toys) don't plan to lower their prices, feeling that Americans will continue to spend top dollar on their products to relieve themselves of the stress of higher prices they are experiencing elsewhere.

Oh yeah?

See ya soda, hello to making my own iced tea from my garden all summer long! Toys? I'm pretty darned crafty, so guess what my granddaughter will be getting for her first birthday? Cool handmade stuff. And cosmetics? Hrumph! A little sunshine for blush (if we ever get any sunshine), a splash of lip gloss, and a dash of eyeliner, and I'm good to go. If large corporations think they are gonna predict my behavior...well, we'll just see about that!

Too, after writing on the subject of belief, I realized that some of my conscious and subconscious beliefs about the energy exchange of my buying behavior was only making other people richer and me poorer. Time to align my brain on that one! Today is my experiment of taking charge of my financial buying power.

The wind blows, and I can smell the impending rain. Undaunted, I adjust my hoodie. People around me walk either silently or exchange words in soft, low chatter. It's either the weather, the time of day, or both, gently subduing the atmosphere. Not unpleasant, just slightly ghostie. I sort of wish I'd brought someone along, but my experiment this time requires I work solo.

Today will be my first official experience in haggling, but not at HedgeWitch shopping. For the past three weeks, I've been using a technique that helps me find exactly what I want, employing the primordial language you read about here. To date, this has been incredibly successful for me. Now, after researching how to haggle on the Net, and understanding this is an acceptable and even desirable social process for both buyer and vendor, I'm ready to combine my primordial language technique with the art of bargaining.

For me, step one in the science of shopping has always been to go with a plan. As my footsteps crunch on the gravel, I review in my mind what I want to find at the flea market today:

Item Number One: A good-condition, portable, sturdy, wire shopping cart that rolls well on any surface and collapses easily to go in the trunk of my car when I'm not using it. This is my highest priority.

Item Number Two: A new, plain sweatshirt for gardening. I plan to add embroidery to spice it up. I'm not into name-brand products unless the brand name is known for high quality.

Item Number Three: A handcrafted photo book for my granddaughter. I'd seen one last week that really caught my eye, but I thought the price a bit high. Yes, I could make my own, but her birthday is right around the corner, so time is a consideration here.

Armed with my new knowledge that it is okay to haggle, I'm ready to rock 'n' roll! I particularly look for personal creativity when flea-market shopping. Seeing the creative, hard work of others always brings me joy, even if I don't buy the item. As I round the first bend of the pathway, I remind myself of haggling rule number one: believe you will get a deal.

I've made a few "be prepared" alterations in my plan for today. I broke all the twenties I was carrying with me in my little money bag into ones, fives, and tens at the convenience store outside of the market. I put the money in various jean pockets: tens in the right upper pocket, ones in the left, fives in the lower right. Haggling for a few bucks, winning, and then handing the vendor a twenty seemed a bit on the gauche side. Plus, having exact change and knowing precisely where it was located on my person would save transaction time should I strike a fair bargain. This splitting the cash into denominations actually served me well by accident, as you will see.

I also know a bit of information that will be helpful today. This is my fourth week at this large flea market. I have a pretty good idea of who the regulars are and of who might be just passing through. I even look at license plates to see where the vendor is from. Stickers, decals, business addresses, and school slogans all give you a general point of origin if you are observant. Although I treat all vendors with respect, I remind myself to be extra nice to the regulars should I wish to visit them again. They might, or might not, remember me. I want to leave them with a good impression regardless of any deals.

Down the path I march, deciding to begin at the far end of the site and work back toward the car. Three quarters of the way down, I spy the shopping cart I want. I have already done general haggling rule number one: research the market value of the item.

The retail value of the type of cart I want ranges from $80 to $40 brand-new (this information was from a fast Google search). The asking price if I were selling such an article used at a yard sale would be 2/3 to 1/3 of the price, depending upon condition. This means the highest a seller might ask could be $54 and the lowest $13. I now follow haggling rule number two: scope out the item from a distance, then make a closer inspection. It's best if the seller is busy with someone else at this time, as it gives you a nonstressful way to think about your opening bid…

Which allows you to now move into haggling rule number three: size up the seller, but don't make snap judgments on hair, clothing, etc. This is a flea market, after all. Look at the general window of prices the seller has marked on their items (if they are marked at all). Remember, numbers are magickally powerful and can tell you something about the seller without him or her knowing it. For example, if he or she uses a lot of fives, they desire immediate change in their life. Number eight? Self-mastery and confidence on the physical plane has been reached in many areas. Lots of twos? They like socialization and partnership. They will compromise on most sales. Fours? They desire stability and may have a firm asking price or need a little extra coaxing. Of course, this rule fluctuates, but it is an interesting one to keep in mind. And if the seller is well coiffed, sports designer clothes, or is dripping with accoutrements of gold in a flea market environment, you've got a barracuda or a shyster on your hands—tread carefully (or not at all).

General haggling rule number four: once you have sized up your vendor and carefully observed your target item, set the price in your mind that you are willing to pay. Before you even begin, agree with yourself that you will not go over this price and that you will walk away if a satisfactory deal cannot be had. Now cut this number in half; this is your opening bid.

Haggling rule number five: clear your mind and focus. Before approaching the seller, remove all extraneous numbers from your mind and repeat your low-bid number nine times silently in your head. End with the HedgeWitch affirmation: "Always a blessing. Thank you."

Okay. I'm ready. That shopping cart is calling to me. I now follow general haggling rule number six: do not haggle in front of other customers. Wait for a respite in sales. The vendor normally does not advertise that he or she is willing to make a deal.

I wait patiently, checking out a few other items, then circle back. I employ magickal haggling rule number seven: speak in a low, clear tone, and smile.

"Good morning," I say.

She smiles.

"I'm interested in the shopping cart out front. Will you take four for it?" Notice I didn't say, "I'll give you four bucks for that cart out there" or "Bet you can do better on that price you've got listed on that cart" or "Tell ya what: I've got four bucks here that says I can walk outta here with that cart." I've actually heard haggling like this. Here, the buyer is being a bully and tries to immediately, through language, remove the control from the vendor. Big mistake. "I'll give you…you can do better…I can walk outta here"—all these phrases suggest that the vendor is a subservient, helpless stooge, and even if they don't recognize the words, their inner selves will immediately bristle. This is definitely not the energy we want here. What we want is for the vendor to feel he or she is in control of the bargaining process. Back to the story…

She grins. "I paid more'n that for it. Nothin' wrong with it. Good tires. Even collapses. Eight."

Haggling rule number eight: speak as you are spoken to, succinctly and politely. This builds a light rapport with folks. If you launch into your best diction and lift your chin, you've just turned off 90 percent of the population. Empathy is the key. I learned this from signing thousands of books and giving hundreds of seminars. Divas have no place at the bargaining table.

This price, although incredibly reasonable, is over my agreed limit yet under the marked price on the cart. I find myself naturally hesitating, which is actually general haggling rule number nine: silence is your best friend when the vendor gives an offer you don't like.

"Seven!" she says, naturally filling the void of my silence.

I smile again. "Sold!"

I now follow haggling rule number ten: silently thank the universe. Which takes us into haggling rule number eleven: always work in cash. Give exact cash if possible. That way, the vendor feels satisfied with the deal and has no idea about that fifty bucks lurking in your shoe for emergencies. Never pull out wads of cash and flash your good fortune—it's bad for the vendor's impression of his or her own generosity, and bad for you if someone is watching how much money you are carrying. Which also leads us into the way you're dressed. Although it sounded like I slapped on clothes for simple utility this morning, that wasn't the case at all. If you are shopping for a bargain, don't overdress (and that includes jewelry and makeup). My sweatshirt color choice is black—a power choice, and clean. My jeans are in good condition. My walking shoes match the sweatshirt. I'm not carrying a purse. You can't see my cell or my money bag. My good watch is home in its box. I don't need it—I can always get the time off my cell if I have to. I have small pearls in my ears, and unless you're into jewelry, you won't know they are real, and yet I'm not walking around with unfilled punctures in my head. My religious necklace is tucked inside my sweatshirt; it holds more power there, anyway. Displaying your religious persuasion with gaudy jewelry tells some vendors you are insecure. I have a canvas shopping bag stuffed in the kangaroo pocket of my hoodie (and we'll get to why I'm carrying this in a moment).

Grinning from ear to ear at my first haggling success, I march over to the cart and whisk away my purchase, but not before I turn and thank the seller and mention that this will be such a handy item on this day. She is a regular, so I make sure to look appropriately pleased, which wasn't hard at all. As I trundle down the path, I am elated. I have completed my first successful haggle in less than ten minutes, saving myself top retail end $73, low retail end $33 by choosing a good-condition used item. I growl delightedly to myself—I am on a roll! The vendor initially wanted $23—a savings to me here at the flea market of $16. No matter how you slice it, I got a great deal! On top of that, a woman passes by with a cart much like mine.

She has taken a collapsible laundry bag and used it for a liner for her cart. What a cool idea! I'm so pleased I'm about to bust. I'll pick up my liner at the grocery store on the way home!

A little further down the path, a well-dressed woman stops me. "Where did you get that cart?" she demands. "Did you buy it here? Where? I've been looking all over for a cart like that since the market opened, and I can't find one."

Lucky me, I think, staring at her, because as yet I've not been able to get a word in edgewise. "I found it at one of the regular vendors," I finally sputter, motioning with my hand and pointing, "up the path. It was the only one there that I saw."

"I walked right by there ten minutes ago," she said, "and I didn't see any carts." She looks at me suspiciously and leans closer, her paper cup sloshing hot coffee on the ground with her eagerness. "Where? Where did you get it? Where, up there?"

I looked at her rather helplessly. How do you give directions at a flea market? Turn right at the vendor with hundreds of junk boxes? Like…there are *tons* of those. Turn left at the hot dog stand (one of twenty along the way)?

"Oh, never *mind*," she says, showing her exasperation at my bumbling brain by jerking her cup this way and that. Without warning, she spins on her heel and gallops off in the direction of my pointing finger, which I'd inappropriately not remembered to lower.

I shake my head, clutching my newly haggled cart protectively. Might not be a bad idea if she knocked off on that coffee. We see only what we choose to see, I muse to myself.

Now I'm doubly excited, because I'd found something that someone else wanted—she apparently walked right by it and missed it! I chide my victorious feelings on the matter. Gloating is base—not spiritual at all! Still, I nearly skip past the sweatshirts. I banter jauntily with the seller. With newfound confidence, I walk away with a sweatshirt for a buck. Current WalMart price for similar design and color? $16.22. Target? $9.99. Clearance Target, but only in limited colors? $4.00. Here, I could pick any color I wanted and still save money. Also, the drive to the market was much closer than that of the nearest Target, so I didn't have to expend any extra gas. I have also followed haggling rule number twelve: carry your own canvas shopping bag empowered with chamomile and calendula essentials to attract positive energy. This way, the vendor doesn't have to fiddle with stuffing your purchase in a nondisposable plastic bag, and you are being earth-friendly. Besides, it makes you smell nice.

Hot diggity, the dark clouds thicken overhead but I'm nearly dancing through the flea market. Two items purchased on my list, and so far I've spent only eight dollars. I make my way over to the vendor I saw last week that offered the handcrafted photo books. The Sunday before, she wanted $25. I didn't buy one, not because I thought the price was unfair, but because I'd already spent my dollars elsewhere. It just wasn't in the budget that week. As I walk up to the table, I see that she has only one left: the one I originally wanted! In perfect condition, marked for five dollars, beautifully handcrafted. No haggling here: *sold*. I sincerely thank her for her creativity and tuck the book in my canvas bag. Always a blessing!

I walk away from her table, smiling. I have now purchased all the items I wanted on my list for a grand total of $13, and for all intents and purposes, I am done shopping. However, I'm still working on my technique and haven't experienced a full variety of haggling scenarios. My research isn't finished. I pause, thinking about where I want to go next. It starts to drizzle.

My daughter calls me on my cell. Could I pick up something she had ordered from one of the inside vendors? She didn't want to bring my granddaughter out in the rain, and I didn't blame her. I enter the building and spy a table of rubber stamps (my secret passion). There is a huge selection. Some are priced and some are not. I decide to try general haggling rule number thirteen: if some items are marked, and some are not, and you like several items, make your selection that includes both priced and unpriced items, then offer half or a third of the market price of your total selection as your opening bid.

I observe that the stamps were brand-new. I've been buying stamps for several years and quickly calculate the retail price in my head, which would be thirty bucks without tax—more at a specialty shop. The vendor is an older woman with a weekly indoor stand, yet I'd never seen this large table of stamps before. "Good morning," I say, holding out my choices. "Would you be willing to take ten dollars for these?"

She smiled a greeting (much like the first woman) and then muttered to herself, counting up the prices in her head of the marked and unmarked stamps. "Heck," she said, "why not?"

I nearly fainted with my luck. I paid her the exact amount of cash, withdrawing only one ten from my pocket. I thanked her, made a comment about how much fun I would have using the stamps, and moved on to the next vendor to pick up my daughter's order. As this was a transaction already agreed upon by my daughter and this vendor, I didn't haggle. I paid the bill and walked over to pick up the item where she had it stored.

And fell in love with a basket. A very cool basket, just like the one I'd looked at in a department store a month ago and simply felt I couldn't afford. That basket retailed, new, at $65. I turned to the vendor, eyebrow raised. "Not mine," she said. "It belongs to that guy over there," and she motioned toward a gentleman that appeared to deal in Civil War memorabilia. Now, this wasn't something I'd researched, but as I like baskets, I have a general idea of their price range, what to look for condition-wise, etc. It was in perfect condition, exceptionally sturdy, and the lid fit securely. Okay, so it smelled a little musty. "Would you take ten dollars for this?" I asked, and fell, unaware, into haggling rule number fourteen: act dumb (except, of course, I was really being dumb).

"What's it marked?" he asked.

I blushed, I know I did. "I don't have my reading glasses on and I must have missed the price. I'm sorry." Which, in my case, was totally true. Forget fine print without the spectacles.

He grinned as I handed the basket over. "Yeah, we get older, but it sure would be nice if our peepers remained the same."

I agreed.

He flipped the basket around to check the small white sticker I'd missed, peered at me over his own glasses, and said, "Ten'll do."

I handed over the cash. One ten from the pocket of my jeans.

He pulled a pad over and began writing. "What d'ya think I should call that basket?" he asked.

I hefted the basket and turned it around, eyeing it carefully. "It looks like a cobra basket to me," I replied.

"Then that's what it'll be," he said, writing the words *cobra basket* on the pad. "Happy to make the sale," he said.

"Always a blessing," I replied, not realizing I'd said the words aloud.

"That it surely is."

I tucked the basket in my new shopping cart and headed out the door, glancing down at that little white sticker: $26. Being sincerely dumb, I just saved myself sixteen bucks.

Haggling rule number fifteen: affirm your good fortune. I used a HedgeWitch technique after I left the building (and well out of earshot of any vendor) and muttered with glee: "I always get a good deal." (*Always* being the primary word). Words have incredible power if we use them correctly. However (very important rule here), a word or phrase is only special and powerful if it is special and powerful to you.

I have now reached the far end of the flea market, and my cart is loaded. I decide to go back to the car, drop off my purchases, and return to finish my haggling experiment in the upper area. Halfway back it starts to rain a bit harder. I lift my hoodie and make a beeline for the parking lot. Having sold my books at open-air festivals, I know that bad weather truly hurts sales, even if you are prepared for it. From the seller's side, rain was always disheartening—but now I'm on the buyer's side of the bargaining fence, and I know that this rain will actually be of benefit to me. I also know I haven't much time: only the hardiest vendors will remain open. The rest will pack up quickly and get the heck out of the market. It is these vendors I will target.

Beep, beep squeals my car alarm as I lock up. The rain begins to pound the ground, and the upper area buzzes with vendors throwing items this way and that into their vehicles. Laughter, shouts, clanking, and the steady drum of rain on truck hoods and SUV roofs fills the air. I wrangle two pieces of furniture I can refinish myself and give as gifts later on in the year—one for a buck and one for five dollars. Both male sellers called these bargains "your lucky rainy day sale" as I struggled the furniture away.

It is here that haggling rule number sixteen came into play by accident: act like you ain't got no more money other than your lowest bid (or when you hit your cut-off bid number).

One of my favorite opening lines at flea markets when I want to make a purchase is: "Who's the boss?" This is a pleasant, empowering way to draw the vendor to you and makes him or her feel in charge. A smile from you is also very important—showing you're not being flip. Boss-man (once I figured out who he was) and I begin to haggle in the pouring rain over that last piece of furniture. My highest bid number was five bucks—this wasn't an antique, and I'd have to put some work into making it presentable. By now, the furniture was sopping wet and heavy as all get out, and he had a ton of stuff yet to load—all things in my favor. This being the case, I go real low. The sticker price is thirty-five bucks. "Five bucks," I say.

"Seven," he says.

I fall silent, look at the ground with consternation, rummage in my pockets. I have forgotten to say "Sold!" So far, I've been really successful in my haggling. Two bucks wasn't going to kill me, and he was being pleasant even though we both might be going swimming in the parking lot in a minute or two. I sigh, resigned to give him the seven dollars, and shove my hands in my pocket again, except my one's pocket is empty. I'm frustrated, and I know that expression showed on my face. I am sure I have more ones. I dig deeper, the rain is now slinging like spit from a boxer in the tenth round, and I truly am on the verge of saying, "No, thank you." I manage to whip out a crumpled five, but no one-dollar bills. I look up, ready to open my mouth to let the object go, and he says, "Five bucks it is, missy."

Sold.

Through the mud I slog, loading up the car, as yet unaware that the universe had decided I have one more lesson to learn. I head for the tented area, hoping to find a last-minute bargain. I'd seen a rack of dresses on my first trip down through the market. My husband and I are building a magickal scarecrow for my garden, and I wanted something unusual and inexpensive to dress my enchanted effigy. There are local magickal rules to creating a garden scarecrow, which is why I wanted something new, rather than clothing worn by someone I know. The vendors, a husband-and-wife team speaking Spanish, were packing up.

As I begin to haggle, I'm kicking my mental self for my incredibly weak knowledge of the language. I can speak nouns and verbs (thanks to Llewellyn author Ray Malbrough) but no pleasantries or modifiers. My broken non-skill makes for lousy rapport, and I'm silently wishing I'd dragged Ray along with me. Don't get me wrong, the wife spoke perfect English—but I knew that to enter her comfort zone, I should be able to communicate better on her terms. To me, it is my responsibility as a buyer to make the vendor feel at ease, not the other way around. If the vendor feels they shine on center stage, then I actually have the upper hand in the bargaining process. Not too friendly, mind you. You can overdo it if you're not careful.

And here is where I met my only failure of the day. First, she misunderstood why I wanted the dress. She was, naturally, assuming I wanted it to fit me. I could hardly tell her I desired a size obviously larger than me to hang on a magickal scarecrow, so I stuttered, searching for plausible words. Her main focus, at the moment, was to put me in a smaller dress. The price tags on both dresses said $20.

"Would you take $5 for this dress?" I asked, touching the larger dress.

She shook her head and pointed to the smaller dress. "Twenty dollar," she said, restating the price on the tag.

"Seven," I said and then remembered I didn't have any ones on me.

She rolled her eyes (bad sign), her gold earrings swinging wildly with the jerky, aggravated movement of her head. "Twenty dollar," she insisted. "New!" she exclaimed, pointing at the smaller dress.

"Ten." I withdrew a ten from my pocket, reaching for the dress. This is haggling rule number seventeen: when all else fails, with cash in hand, reach for the item. Don't take it. Just flash the money and reach for it. Leave the control decision with the vendor. He or she can hand over the item and make the sale, or not.

In this case, it was not. "Twenty dollar," she repeated, one hand positioned firmly on her hip, smaller dress dangling from the other, and I could tell she was getting angry—that scowl on her face and her body language were definite warning signs. Uh-oh. At this point, her husband is grumbling at her in Spanish, telling her she ought to let me have the dress and get on with it. They can't stay in this rain. They have to get moving, finish packing up, and go! (He said a few other things, too, but I'm not going to repeat them.)

It is a funny thing about me—I can't speak the language, but if they enunciate their words and don't rattle like a runaway freight train (which we are all apt to do when we are excited), I can ferret out those nouns and verbs just fine. And I could see this sale was not going to go my way, because now she was furious with her husband because he'd just insulted her, and I was second banana in her field of attention and a stubborn customer at that, trying to buy a dress that wouldn't fit correctly.

I smiled politely and bowed out, saying, "It certainly is a beautiful dress. Thank you, but no thank you." Which goes back to the fourth haggling rule: be prepared to walk away, no hard feelings.

Which goes hand in hand with haggling rule number eighteen: If the energy is bad or turns bad, or the seller has those bad vibes going, politely disengage and walk away. Speaking from an energetic point of view, the dress was now filled with negativity from our miscommunication and their argument. Who knows what other insults they hurled at each other that morning with the garment hanging right there to catch whatever? I could have cleansed the dress, but it simply wasn't worth it to me. Bad mojo? Let it go. Don't bring other people's pain and anger into your life. No physical item is worth the angst.

I could have walked away dejected at this haggling lesson, but I viewed it as a lesson in human interaction. I had actually thought of a more creative way to dress the scarecrow last night and had even gotten out of bed at 2:00 AM to draw up a diagram. The dress wasn't on my list, and indeed, my creative focus did not include a dress at all. I realized that part of my failure in this instance had to do with my previous plans that I'd already committed to paper. I hadn't released this plan in my mind (because I liked it) and so, without the release, there could be no attraction. This, my friends, is haggling rule number nineteen: attraction always requires some sort of release or alignment. It's like breathing. You pull the air into your lungs, use what you need, and expel what your body doesn't need. Attraction/release, or release/attraction, is a fundamental law of the universe. Without this process, you don't get stuff. Ignore the process? You'll find yourself unhappy and empty-handed.

As I avoided mud puddles back to the car, I reviewed what all I'd learned today and how my general haggling tips and magickal haggling ideas I'd worked on performed well in every instance but one, and how that experience in itself turned out to be the most valuable lesson of the day.

At home, I left my goodies on the back porch until I could cleanse them, took out the dogs, and then stepped into a luxurious hot shower. With that steaming water pounding away the morning chill, I thanked Spirit for my good fortune and released any negativity I'd collected along the way. It's good to be a haggling HedgeWitch with a plan, I thought. When you believe all great things are possible in the universe, nothing can stop you—not even the poor economy or clouds dumping buckets of rain on your personal parade.

Welcome to my world!

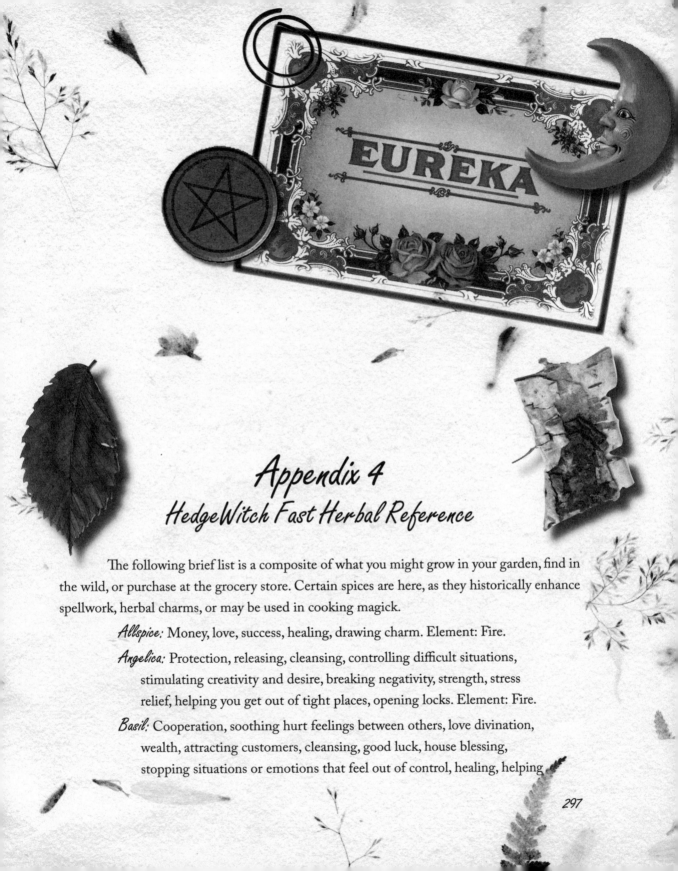

Appendix 4
HedgeWitch Fast Herbal Reference

The following brief list is a composite of what you might grow in your garden, find in the wild, or purchase at the grocery store. Certain spices are here, as they historically enhance spellwork, herbal charms, or may be used in cooking magick.

Allspice: Money, love, success, healing, drawing charm. Element: Fire.

Angelica: Protection, releasing, cleansing, controlling difficult situations, stimulating creativity and desire, breaking negativity, strength, stress relief, helping you get out of tight places, opening locks. Element: Fire.

Basil: Cooperation, soothing hurt feelings between others, love divination, wealth, attracting customers, cleansing, good luck, house blessing, stopping situations or emotions that feel out of control, healing, helping in studying, making people stop bugging you, clearing the head, dream magick, banishing lies. Element: Fire.

Bay (Sweet): Healing, strength, clearing the mind, wishes, sweet dreams, money. Element: Fire.

Beans: Money, luck, growth, abundance (especially of food), prayers to the dead, preventing quarreling, fertility magick, good fortune, strength. Element: Air.

Cabbage: Luck, good relationships, happy marriage, balance, stress relief, bountiful partnership in business. Element: Water.

Calendula (marigold): Abundance, riches, self-control, happiness, cleansing, dream magick, strength, admiration, fast and healthful closing of wounds after accident or surgery. Element: Fire.

Carrots: Lust, passion, fertility magick, opportunity, creative ideas. Element: Fire.

Celery: Mental acuity, love, passion, lust, divination, dieting magick, attracting desires. Element: Fire.

Chamomile: Good fortune, money, cleansing, releasing, attuning to higher self, aligning with Spirit, beauty, peaceful sleep, happiness, dieting, reducing problems that have gotten out of control, curbing a burning tongue (people that talk too much or people who talk trash), magick for eating disorders, prayers for children. Element: Water.

Chervil: Awakening creativity or the positive spirit within the self, bringing warmth to a cold atmosphere, increasing vitality, clear sight, dreaming magicks, blessings for women. Element: Fire.

Chili pepper (hot peppers): Speed, love, lust, fidelity in marriage or business, attracting desires and personal success, removing unwanted energies from your life. Element: Fire.

Chives: Promoting flow in any situation, cleansing, use in new ventures. Element: Fire.

Cinnamon: Longevity, strength, speed, good fortune, happiness, cleansing, success, love, passion. Element: Fire.

Clove: Love, money, cleansing, passion, protection, spirituality, attracting fame and fortune, removing stress, meditation, easier breathing in tough situations, easing the pain of heartache. Element: Fire.

Comfrey: Healing, travel safety, stability, anti-theft and property protection, rebuilding anything broken (healing, business, career, spirit), fertilizer, money spells. Element: Water.

Cucumber: Fertility, harmony, fidelity, friendships, healing. Element: Water.

Daisy: Love, lust, fame, popularity, joy, boosting energy, healing wounds, assisting in magick done during the day (especially at the noon hour). Element: Water.

Dandelion: Flowers for wishes and calling good spirits, making money and bringing golden opportunity with courage, expansion in business; use the leaves for protection (the word *dandelion* is French, meaning "lion's tooth" because of the shape of the leaves; mix dandelion and nettle leaves together, steep, and pour water around doorstep to keep evil people from your home). Element: Air.

Dill: Fast growth, help in starting a new venture, money, protection, lust, love, stopping gossip, prayers for children, abundance. Element: Fire.

Eucalyptus: Protection, cleansing, healing, harmony, longevity, family unity, joy, cooling down a hot situation, encouraging someone to cough up the truth, breaking fevers, purifying the sick room (rosemary boosts the power). Element: Water.

Fennel: Healing, protection, cleansing, remove evil spirits or energies. Element: Air.

Fern: Luck, protection, longevity, health, money-drawing, rain magick, good fortune, finding treasures within yourself, beauty. Element: Air.

Garlic: Protection for soldiers and emergency personnel, healing, anti-theft, cleansing, removing evil spirits, protection against foul weather or circumstances, protection against gossip, protection for travelers and vehicles, good luck, increasing personal strength and energy (mix with honey). Element: Fire.

Horehound: Healing, protection, petitions to the gods, mental acuity, quick thinking, studying, breaking evil spells, taking the hot air out of a bully, encouraging someone to face their fears and overcome them, overcoming sluggishness or feeling overwhelmed. Known as the master healer's herb. Element: Air.

Hyssop: Cleansing, removing evil spirits and ghosts, purifying an area. Element: Fire.

Ivy: Used in magick to find the truth of any matter. Protection, healing, fidelity, abundance even during hard times, better listening habits or encouraging someone to listen to what you are saying. Element: Water.

Lavender: Cleansing, happiness, joy, protection, sleep magick, longevity, harmony, attracting customers to a business, divination, beauty, stress relief, spells against depression. Element: Air.

Lemon balm (melissa): Uplifting feelings, joy, harmony, laughter, increasing longevity, use to eliminate all those little headaches of life. Element: Air.

Lemongrass: Divination, clear thinking, cleansing, removing evil people from your life, lust. Element: Air.

Lemon verbena: Love, attraction, cleansing, anti-nightmare, friendship, encouraging people to see your worth, finding riches in unusual places, reducing anxiety, harmonizing your spirit, aligning your beliefs. Add to other herbal mixtures to increase their strength. Element: Air.

Lettuce: Good fortune, protection, sleep magick, fidelity, love. Element: Water.

Lovage: Love, attraction, cleansing, friendship, help in meeting new people. Element: Fire.

Mint: Money, healing, travel, protection, love, lust, friendships, happiness, joy. Element: Air.

Apple mint: Love, friendship, passion, money.

Chocolate mint: Love, lust, money.

Mountain mint: Money and stability.

Orange mint: Cleansing, money, happiness.

Peppermint: Stress relief, help in better understanding a situation, reduce the feeling of being pulled in too many directions too fast.

Pineapple mint: Family happiness, good fortune, positive abundance in the home.

Spearmint: Mental acuity, studying, taking tests, stress relief.

Morning glory: Considered poisonous, but added here as the blue flowers in your garden promote peace and happiness on the property. Seeds used in sleep magick pillows, and root can be used as a substitute for High John. Element: Water.

Nettle: Breaking curses, sending back negative energy, healing, lust, busting ghosts, stopping fears, stopping danger, stopping a run of bad luck, building personal strength, guarding against disease. Used in fertility magick to guard against impotence. Element: Fire.

Onion: Breaking a cycle of sickness in the home, cleansing, healing, money, dreams, wish magick (onion skins), protection against stalkers and gossip. Element: Fire.

Oregano: Love, joy, happiness, relief from depression, money, health, shielding your garden against evil. Element: Fire.

Parsley: Cleansing, lust, fertility, speaking with a clear head, stopping misfortune. Element: Air.

Patchouli: Earth Mother magick, petitions to the dead, money, lust, prosperity, separating someone from you who does not really love or like you, beauty, stress relief, focus, erotic dreams, mental energizer, helps to keep feet on the ground. Element: Earth.

Peas: Good fortune in business, money magick, love-drawing, holding on to your savings, attraction (especially the flowers). Element: Earth.

Radish: Love and lust, banishing people who are bugging you. Element: Fire.

Rosemary: Love, lust, mental powers, cleansing, sleep magick, youthful outlook on life, protection, relief from nightmares, anti-theft, happy family, attracting good garden spirits, stimulating ideas or an old project, fertility, courage and fortitude, heats up any situations, prevents bride or groom from getting "cold feet," beauty aid. Element: Fire.

Rue: Offering to the Herb Mother, health, cleansing, love, recuperation from illness, mental acuity, breaking hexes, stopping gossip, banishing stalkers, house blessing, attracting money, circle casting. Element: Fire.

Sage: Expansion, wishes, wisdom, protection, longevity, abundance, money luck, toad guardian, cleansing. Element: Air.

Savory: Mental acuity, money (especially if added to dried beans), appreciating what you have (the thank-you herb), stimulating creativity, helping stop diarrhea of the mouth. Element: Air.

Sunflower: Strength, riches, fame, fortune, health, wisdom, wishes, guardian of the gardener. Element: Fire.

Thyme: Health, healing, sleep magick, divination, cleansing, courage, sports magick, intuition, increased energy, attracting good garden fairies, stopping panic attacks, cleansing the magickal area. Used against all poisons. Element: Water.

Tomato: Abundance in the home, prosperity, love, lust, home and garden protection. Element: Water.

Valerian: Sleep magick, love, cleansing, guarding against lightning and sudden strikes of misfortune, stopping quarrels, reducing worries, helping stop panic attacks, healing, balance during withdrawal symptoms. (Root smells awful.) Element: Water.

Vervain: Speeds up any spell. Love, cleansing, harmony, money magick, attaining the rank you desire, protection (particularly against the storms of life), healing, regaining stolen articles, acuity in speech. Element: Earth.

Woodruff: Protection, success, victory, attracting money, guarding the garden, often used dried in potpourri for money flowing into the home, keeping old ideas fresh, revitalizing a project, strength, breaking a stagnant situation, overcoming insomnia. Element: Fire.

Appendix 5
HedgeWitch Meditation for
Manifestation and Problem Solving

This is a very fast, very easy meditation that works best if done once in the morning and once at night for three days for a super big problem, and just one day for an itty-bitty difficulty. Do the meditation for seven days and seven nights to manifest large items, or three days and three nights for small items. Choose a signature fragrance that matches your intent. For example, mint is good for matters of the mind and money; lavender, chamomile, lemon, or orange work for healing. To manifest an object, like a new car, find something that smells like the object. (For a new car, they sell a "new car smell" at the automotive store as a spray freshener! Please be sensible in choosing your aroma. For example, inhaling gas fumes to bring gas for your car to you would be harmful; choose only safe scents and smells.)

Step One: Begin by taking three deep, even breaths. Close your eyes during this time, and imagine yourself surrounded by a circular hedge of your choice (ivy, flowers, bushes, etc.). This hedge is akin to a magick circle. Take three more deep, even breaths, this time inhaling your chosen aroma and visualizing your desire.

Step Two: Thank the gods, ancestors, or Spirit (whatever you believe in) for several good things that have recently happened to you. Remember to smile when finished with this part of the meditation, and repeat, "Always a blessing." Inhale the aroma three more times and repeat, "Always a blessing."

Step Three: Imagine that your right leg is guarded by a white snake and that your left leg is guarded by a green snake. In your mind, allow the snakes to grow in size, up to the trunk of your body. Let them intertwine like a caduceus.

> *Note:* The snakes are in line with the caduceus and DNA. If you have an aversion to snakes, you might try envisioning climbing vegetation like a moonflower or morning glory.

Step Four (for Problem Solving): In your mind, allow the two heads of the snakes to become one, and let this large snake head jut out from your third eye. Command the snake by saying, "I want _____," and be very specific. Repeat this desire three times, and remember to smile. Believe that you are more than capable of finding the solution you seek. Finish by saying, "Always a blessing," and allow the snakes to return to their original position—the white guarding the right leg, the green guarding the left leg. Let them coil into perfect circles, one on either side of you. Take one deep breath, and smile.

(for Manifestation): In your mind, allow the white snake to cross over to your left arm and run out of your left arm. Allow the green snake to cross over and run out your right arm. Imagine that the snakes are magnetized. Say out loud, "I want _____," and be very specific. Repeat this desire three times. In your mind, pull whatever it is that you desire toward you. Remember to smile. When the object reaches you, envision grabbing

the item and pulling it to your chest. Believe that you are more than capable of receiving this item. Finish by saying, "Always a blessing," and allow the snakes to return to their original position—the white guarding the right leg, the green guarding the left leg. Let them coil into perfect circles, one on either side of you. Take one deep breath, and smile.

Step Five: Take three deep, even breaths, again inhaling your chosen aroma. Say, "Thank you! Always a blessing. It always works," and smile. Visualize your circle hedge melting into the ground. Take one deep breath, open your eyes, and smile again.

Index

Llewellyn Ordering Information

Order Online:
Visit our website at www.llewellyn.com, select your books, and order them on our secure server.

Order by Phone:
- Call toll-free within the U.S. at 1-877-NEW-WRLD (1-877-639-9753). Call toll-free within Canada at 1-866-NEW-WRLD (1-866-639-9753)
- We accept VISA, MasterCard, and American Express

Order by Mail:
Send the full price of your order (MN residents add 6.5% sales tax) in U.S. funds, plus postage & handling to:

Llewellyn Worldwide
2143 Wooddale Drive, Dept. 978-0-7387-1423-3
Woodbury, MN 55125-2989

Postage & Handling:

Standard (U.S., Mexico & Canada). If your order is:
$24.99 and under, add $3.00
$25.00 and over, FREE STANDARD SHIPPING

AK, HI, PR: $15.00 for one book plus $1.00 for each additional book.

International Orders (airmail only):
$16.00 for one book plus $3.00 for each additional book

Orders are processed within 2 business days.
Please allow for normal shipping time. Postage and handling rates subject to change.

Always a blessing

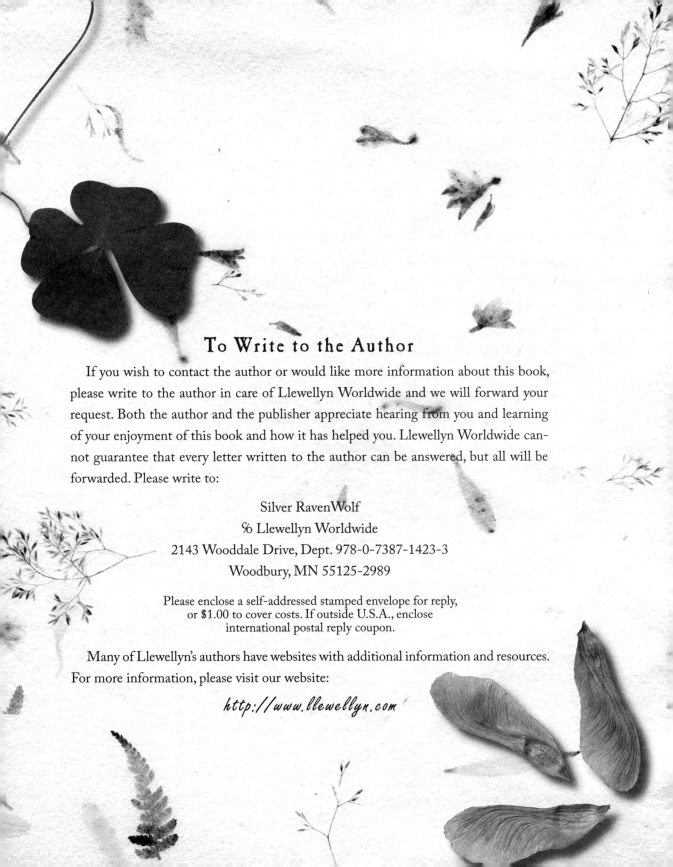

To Write to the Author

If you wish to contact the author or would like more information about this book, please write to the author in care of Llewellyn Worldwide and we will forward your request. Both the author and the publisher appreciate hearing from you and learning of your enjoyment of this book and how it has helped you. Llewellyn Worldwide cannot guarantee that every letter written to the author can be answered, but all will be forwarded. Please write to:

Silver RavenWolf
℅ Llewellyn Worldwide
2143 Wooddale Drive, Dept. 978-0-7387-1423-3
Woodbury, MN 55125-2989

Please enclose a self-addressed stamped envelope for reply,
or $1.00 to cover costs. If outside U.S.A., enclose
international postal reply coupon.

Many of Llewellyn's authors have websites with additional information and resources. For more information, please visit our website:

http://www.llewellyn.com